ULTIMATE

Skiing
Adventures

100 Epic Experiences
in the Snow

Alf Alderson

© Pascal Gertschen

A catalogue record for this book is available from the British Library
ISBN 9781912621224

Cover image © Pascal Gertschen

Designed by Daniel Stephen
Printed in Bulgaria by Multiprint

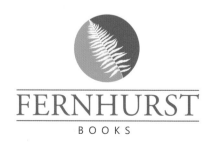

FERNHURST
BOOKS

INTRODUCTION

'Skiing' has never been as diverse as it is today – the term covers pootling down easy, manicured pistes in ski resorts, the wild freedom of backcountry freeriding, the rewarding if hard work of schlepping uphill on touring skis, cat- and heli-skiing for the fat of wallet and even, in a roundabout way, snowboarding.

Which means that one skier's 'amazing ski experience' may not be another's; if you're just getting into this marvellous sport then your first blue run (see, for example, Les Arcs, page 34) will probably and quite rightly be an amazing experience, whereas if you've been at it for decades it may require a helicopter drop on some remote Kamchatkan volcano (see page 182) for you to describe your ski experience as 'amazing'.

What you'll find amongst these pages are ski experiences to suit just about everyone who enjoys clipping into a pair of bindings. I've been fortunate enough to visit the majority of the destinations featured here whilst working as a ski journalist for the last couple of decades, and I've tried to include a good global spread, although obviously the well-established ski resorts of the European Alps and North American Rockies get the bulk of the coverage; and I have to admit to a tiny amount of favouritism – those regions where I've skied most, such as France and British Columbia, probably get more than their fair share of coverage, but then again, they both have world-class ski resorts by the bucketful.

That said, the book also features plenty of ski experiences in lesser-known mountain ranges, from the un-named peaks of Iceland's north coast to the spectacular volcanoes of Kamchatka.

Hopefully a few of them will inspire you to dust down your skis and hit the slopes, because when all is said and done, reading about skiing is one thing, but doing it – well, that's amazing.

Alf Alderson

Les Arcs, French Alps
Autumn 2020

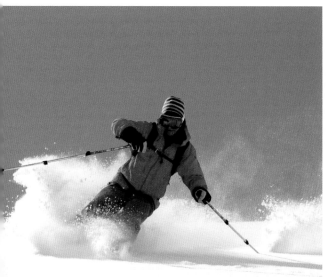
The author skiing at Les Arcs

Mountain Stats

Note that mountain stats are given in imperial measures for USA and South American resorts, a mix of imperial and metric for Canada depending on the resort and metric in Europe and elsewhere.

Also bear in mind that the piste grading system in North America is different to that of Europe, as follows:

EUROPE
Green = Beginner
Blue = Intermediate
Red = Advanced
Black = Expert

USA
Green = Beginner
Blue = Intermediate
Black Diamond = Advanced
Double Black and/or Triple Black Diamond = Expert

CONTENTS

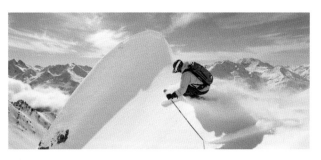

Western Europe

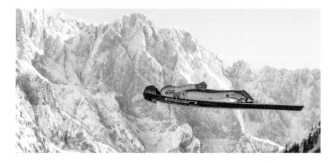

Eastern Europe

Scandinavia

North America

Rest Of The World

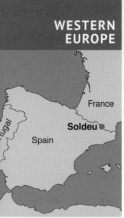

France
Soldeu ●
Spain
ortugal

Access
Nearest airport:
Toulouse Innsbruck
(175km)
Train station in
L'Hospitalet-Près-
L'Andorre (20km)

Ability Level
Beginner – expert

Season
Nov/Dec – Apr

Other Local Activities
Heli-skiing,
snowshoeing,
cross-country skiing,
snowmobiling, dog-
sledding

Resort Stats
Top: 2,560m
Bottom: 1,710m
Vertical: 850m
Lifts: 64
Pistes: 210km

www.grandvalira.com

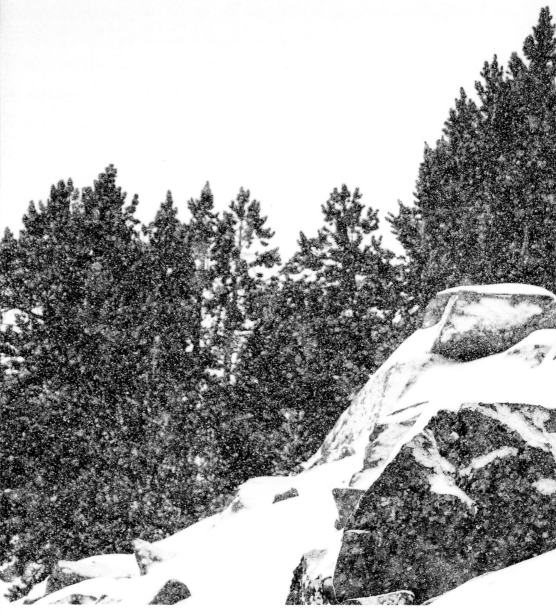

SOLDEU, ANDORRA
Skiing with the Sun God

The wisdom of calling a ski resort 'Sun God' is questionable (surely 'Snow God' would work far better in promotional terms?) but despite the name, Soldeu actually has pretty reliable snow, which along with generally north-facing slopes, good grooming and extensive snowmaking means the sun for which the resort is also renowned isn't necessarily going to put a dampener on the skiing.

And said skiing is pretty good, particularly since the Grandvalira ski pass that's required to ski here covers the entire 210km network of slopes that make up Soldeu and neighbouring linked resorts such as Pas de la Casa and El Tarter, along with access to Ordino-Arcalis at no additional cost (but you need transport to get there), and you may even score discounts if you book in advance online.

Soldeu is best-known for its novice and early intermediate terrain, with lots of fun blue and red pistes spread across the entire ski area, whilst the ski school – which is made up primarily of native English-speaking instructors – is renowned throughout the ski world for the quality of its teaching,

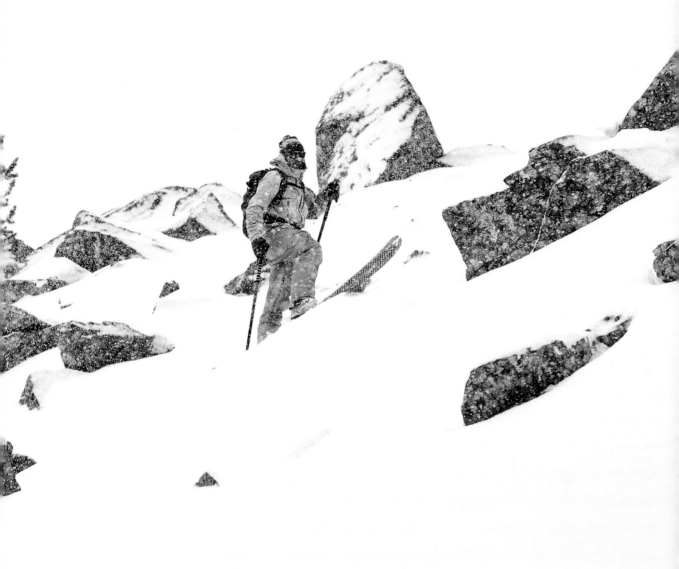

and not just for beginners but for any level of ability. Freeride and freestyle lessons are also available for more advanced skiers, and there are three terrain parks, with a 'park only' pass available and one of them, Snowpark Xavi, is dedicated specifically to beginners and intermediates.

Whilst the resort (and Andorra in general) has long been a favourite with intermediate and beginner skiers looking for a fun week on the slopes, this can prove to be of benefit to those skiers in search of something a little more challenging, since it means that the off-piste terrain gets tracked out far less quickly than in those ski areas which are renowned for their freeriding. There's even a snowcat tow to the lift-free bowl between Riba Escorxada and El Forn, whilst these two areas also have ski itineraries that are marked on the piste map; in recent years Soldeu has featured on the Freeride World Tour, which says much about the quality of the off-piste terrain.

Of course, it's not all perfect – no one would describe Soldeu as a particularly attractive settlement, spread out as it is in a ribbon development along a busy road, and the mountain scenery is pleasant enough but not as dramatic as many other ski areas, but as they say in Yorkshire, "You don't look at the mantelpiece when you're poking the fire" – and if you're just here to ski, whether to improve your technique or check out some of the underrated off-piste terrain, the Sun God may well provide you with what you're after.

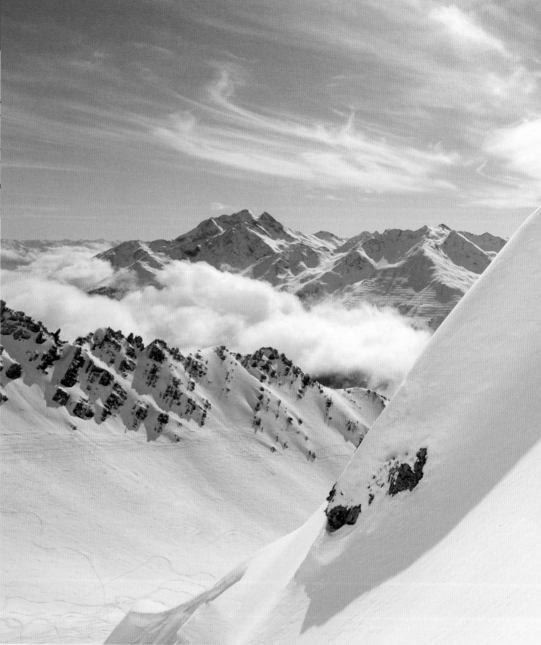

Germany
Poland

Austria
St Anton
Hungary

Italy

Ser

Access
Nearest airports:
Innsbruck (95km),
Friedrichshafen
(130km)
Train station in resort

Ability Level
Beginner – expert

Season
Nov/Dec – Apr

Other Local Activities
Snowshoeing,
cross-country skiing,
tobogganing, outdoor
pool, ice skating,
sleigh rides, hiking

Resort Stats
Top: 2,650m
Bottom: 1,305m
Vertical: 1,345m
Lifts: 38
Pistes: 160km
(includes itineraires)

www.
stantonamarlberg.
com

ST ANTON, AUSTRIA
Burning the candle at both ends

If you ski – which presumably you do since you're reading this book – it's highly likely that you owe a debt of gratitude to St Anton, even if you've never been there. For it is here in the resort that calls itself the 'Cradle of Alpine Skiing' that the 'Arlberg technique' of ski teaching was developed by local instructor Hannes Schneider in the 1920s, and whilst it has obviously been updated and largely superseded over the intervening hundred years, elements of it still feature in some ski lessons, and the older you are the more likely it is you'll have learnt to ski using some derivative of the Arlberg technique.

And good technique is a useful thing to have if you take on some of the more serious slopes of this quintessential Austrian ski resort. St Anton is one of the world's prime destinations for experienced skiers looking for deep snow, steep slopes and challenging off-piste terrain.

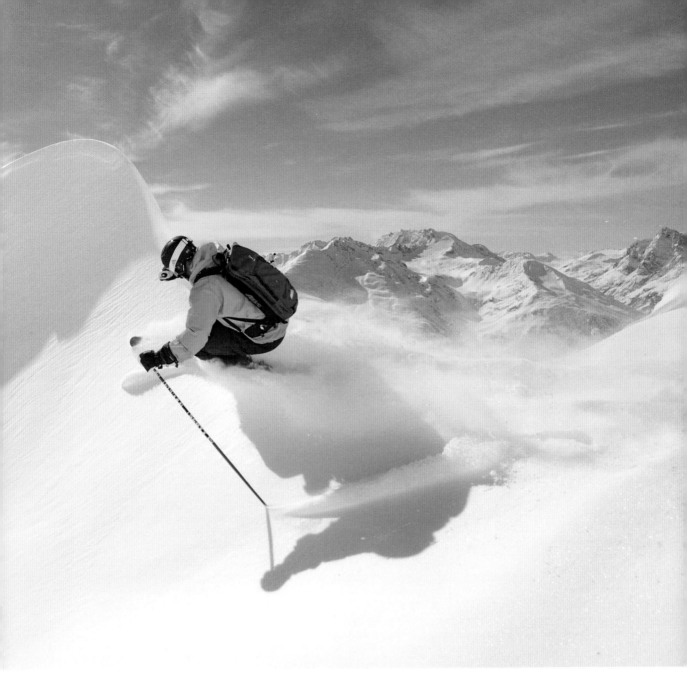

Famed backcountry runs include the North Face, accessed from the Gampberg chair, the spectacular tree-skiing of the Langen Forest and the vertiginous Valhalla Couloir, which is accessed by rope and offers 1,200 metres of thrilling 'vert'.

Not all the fun is away from the lifts by any means, however. St Anton has some tremendous bump fields if that's your kind of thing, and because of its size, there is a huge selection of red and blue runs that will appeal to strong intermediate skiers (be warned, however, that many of these reds and blues are steeper than they would be in most other resorts).

The St Anton ski pass also covers Lech, Zürs (see page 10) and the Sonnenkopf area above nearby Klösterle, so there's more skiing here than you can go at in a season, let alone a week or two.

Like many of the world's classic ski resorts St Anton isn't just about skiing. The attractive, bustling ski town is famed for its nightlife, with many visitors coming here to party just as hard as they ski – from the infamous Moosewirt and its oompah-based action to the raucous Krazy Kanguruh and Underground on the Piste on the resort's lower slopes and the likes of 'Bar Cuba' in town, where the action will continue until long after midnight, this is a ski resort where burning the candle at both ends is a way of life for many.

Modern-day take on the 'Arlberg technique'
© Hermann-Meier.de /
Tourist Association St
Anton am Arlberg

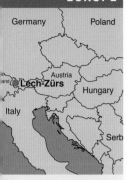

Germany
Poland
Austria
and Lech-Zürs
Hungary
Italy
Serb

Access
Nearest airports:
Innsbruck (115km),
Friedrichshafen
(130km)

Ability Level
Beginner – expert

Season
Nov/Dec – Apr

Other Local Activities
Snowshoeing,
cross-country
skiing, tobogganing,
paragliding, ice
skating, sleigh rides,
hiking

Resort Stats
Top: 2,450m
Bottom: 1,450m
Vertical: 1,000m
Lifts: 47
Pistes: 180km
(includes 'ski routes')

www.lechzuers.com

LECH-ZÜRS AM ARLBERG, AUSTRIA
Something for everyone – and plenty of it

Lech and Zürs occasionally have a problem that most other ski resorts would welcome, and most skiers would consider not to be a problem at all – the snowfall here can be so heavy at times that both of the villages can be cut off from the outside world.

Lech averages 8 metres of snowfall per winter, Zürs even more, and the linked resort of Warth boasts a massive 11 metres. Of course such heavy snowfall may put many of the slopes out of bounds for some time due to avalanche danger – the more so since most of the slopes are above the treeline – but the chances are that there will still be some decent skiing to be had somewhere even when it's dumping, and when the weather and snow conditions settle down you'll find masses more skiing to go at (it's also worth noting that the Lech-Zürs ski pass also allows you to ski in St Anton (page 8) although you have to get there on the free ski bus or the paid-for post bus).

Lech-Zürs is a ski area that is big enough and varied enough to appeal to all levels of skier. Warth, which was only linked in to the ski area a few years ago, has predominantly north-facing slopes which can hold excellent powder.

Zürs is one of the most historic ski areas in Austria, with the country's first 'proper' ski lift being built here in 1937, and Lech gets lots of sunshine (not always a good thing, of course).

For more advanced skiers the mix of off-piste terrain such as that from the top of the Steinmähder chair is excellent, and there are several exciting 'ski routes', which are essentially marked, avalanche controlled routes which are neither groomed nor patrolled.

Lech-Zürs is also the only place in Austria to offer heli-skiing – experienced skiers are dropped on the summit of Mehlsack for their powder experience whilst first-timers can give it a go on the Schneetäli-Orgelscharte where conditions are less challenging.

And any visiting skier of intermediate level and above will almost certainly want to take on the famed 'White Ring', a ski circuit of 5,500 vertical metres and 22km that harks back to the origins of the ski area in the 1930s and 40s. If you're not too bothered about trying to beat records for completing the circuit it's well worth taking time out to enjoy a picnic at one of the two viewing platforms at Rüfikopf and Madloch – the panoramas are sensational.

Fast, modern lifts – several with heated seats – allow you to access the terrain quickly and easily, and whether you want to blast the pow, cruise the reds, practise technique on the blues or simply learn on the nursery slopes there's plenty of everything for everyone here in what is one of Austria's most historic ski regions.

Last blast of the day © Sepp Mallaun / Lech Zurs Tourismus

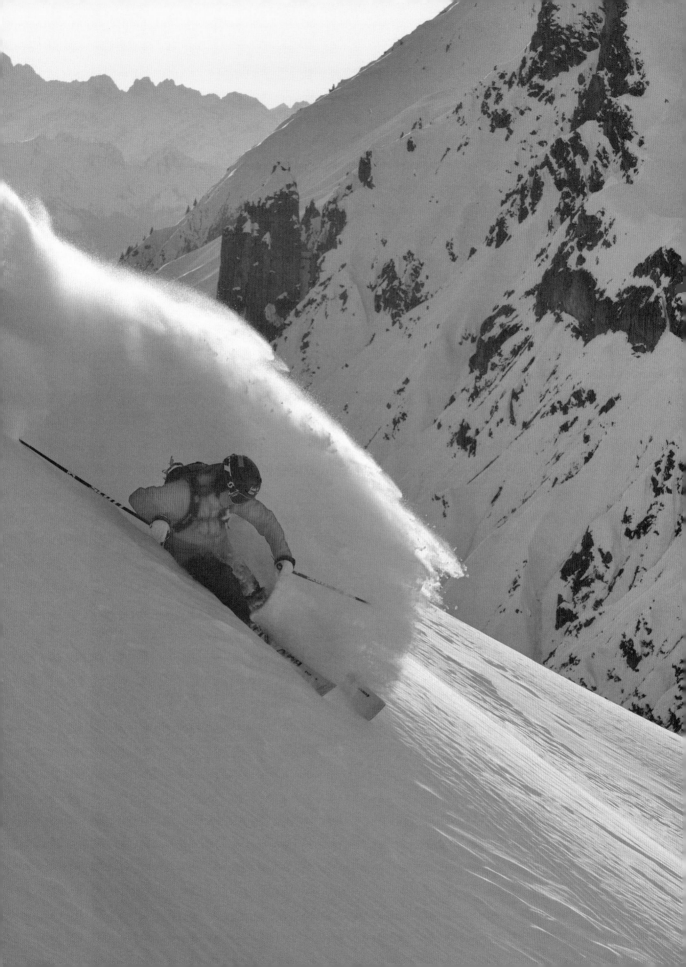

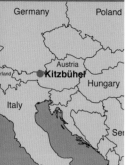

Access
Nearest airports:
Salzburg (75km),
Innsbruck (95km)
Mainline railway
station in resort

Ability Level
Beginner – expert

Season
Dec – Apr

Other Local Activities
Snowshoeing,
cross-country
skiing, tobogganing,
paragliding, ice
skating, hiking

Resort Stats
Top: 2,000m
Bottom: 760m
Vertical: 1,240m
Lifts: 57
Pistes: 230km
(includes 'ski routes')

www.kitzbuehel.com

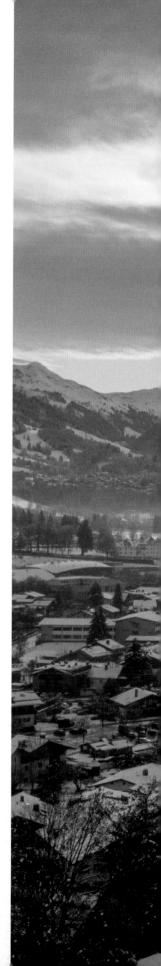

KITZBÜHEL, AUSTRIA
The tolling of the bell

Skiing is Austria's national sport, and perhaps nowhere is this more apparent than every January when the infamous Hahnenkamm Downhill ski race comes to Kitzbühel. It seems like every ski racing fan in the country – as well as a good number from further afield – have descended on this beautiful old medieval town to bang away at cow bells as they watch the fastest men and women in the world hurl themselves down the hideously steep 'Streif' at speeds well in excess of 100kph.

The Hahnenkamm (German: 'rooster's comb') is actually the name of a mountain above Kitzbühel, which hosts Super-G, Downhill and Slalom races over a long weekend in mid- to late-January, with the 'Streif' ('streak' or 'stripe') being the route of the downhill race, generally regarded as the most demanding on the World Cup circuit.

The course features highly technical, 'fall-away' turns and is often plagued with bad light, snow or rain and limited visibility – so much so that in the last twenty years around half of the races have had to be shortened or even cancelled due to weather conditions, and at the time of writing the course record dates back as far as 1997 (Austrian Fritz Strobl in 1:51:58).

You'll be pleased to know you can actually tackle the 3.3km Streif (which featured in the vintage 1969 ski movie *Downhill Racer*) yourself when the races are over – if you decide to do so expect to encounter slopes as steep as 85 percent, with an average gradient of 27 percent.

If, on the other hand, you'd prefer not to compare yourself with the world's best ski racers (something that rarely works in your favour...), Kitzbühel offers plenty of alternatives. Over 80 percent of the ski area's 230km of slopes are graded red or blue, making it a perfect destination for intermediate skiers, whilst more advanced skiers will find plenty of challenging terrain – for instance, check out the steep Direttissima and the long 'ski routes' from the top of 1,935-metre Pengelstein towards Jochberg and Hechenmoos over a thousand metres below. There are also some very acceptable off-piste options.

Add to all this a great system of fast lifts (with a glass floor in one of the '3S' gondolas which connect Wurzhöhe and Pengelstein, the two main ski areas), a banging nightlife even if you're not here for the Hahnenkamm weekend and bucket-loads of Austrian alpine charm and it's easy to see why Kitzbühel has become synonymous with skiing.

Cold air inversion at dawn in Kitzbuhel
© lightsandsquares / shutterstock.com

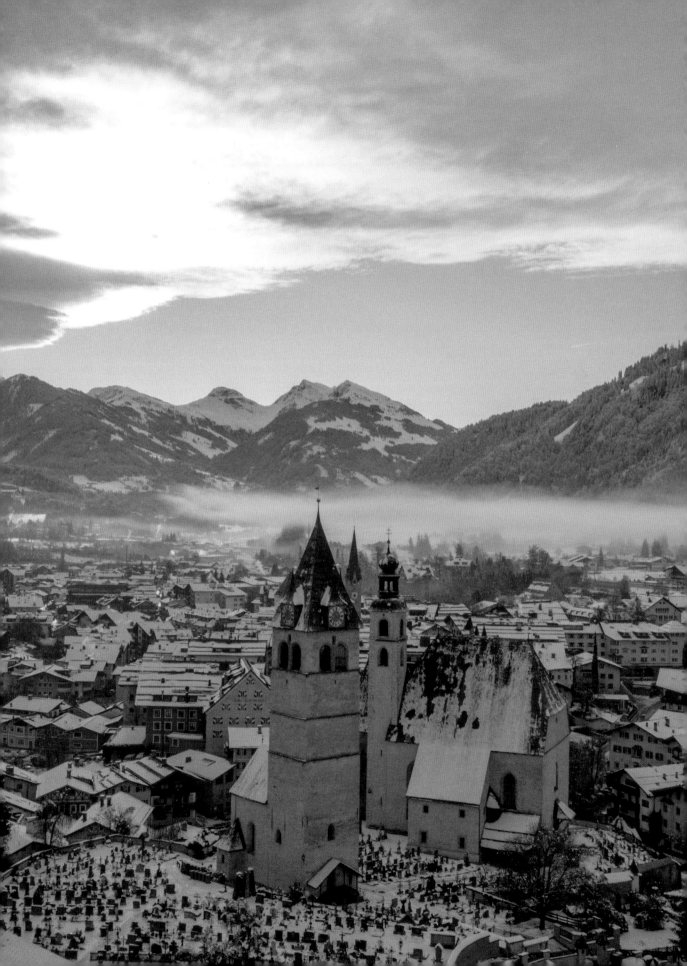

Germany
Poland

Austria
●Saalbach
Hungary

Italy

Ser

Access
Nearest airports:
Salzburg (85km),
Innsbruck (150km)

Ability Level
Beginner – expert

Season
Nov/Dec – Apr

Other Local Activities
Snowshoeing,
cross-country skiing,
tobogganing, hiking

Resort Stats
Top: 2,095m
Bottom: 830m
Vertical: 1,265m
Lifts: 70
Pistes: 270km

www.saalbach.com

SAALBACH-HINTERGLEMM, AUSTRIA
Laying down a challenge

No one could say that the ski area of Saalbach-Hinterglemm doesn't like to lay down a challenge. Marketing yourself as 'the coolest ski resort of the Alps', describing your area as a 'ski circus' and offering the biggest ski area in Austria along with the biggest ski circuit in the Alps are not the actions of a shy and retiring ski resort.

And whilst it's probably best left for others to judge just how 'cool' the place is since proclaiming yourself as such isn't really all that cool at all, the other claims made by the area's marketing bods are pretty indisputable; and that's without even mentioning that around 95 percent of Saalbach-Hinterglemm's ski lifts are 'fast' chairs and gondolas – the highest proportion of any major ski area in the world.

It's largely thanks to this latter fact that you can whizz around the resorts with ease – if you're the kind of skier who loves getting in the mileage you'll be in ski heaven and may even decide to take on the challenge of the area's 'ski circuit'.

This involves 65km of pistes, 32 ski lifts, 12,400 metres of vertical and, according to the resort's website, should be do-able in around seven hours by 'ambitious skiers'. The piste map has the route marked on it, which can be started at any ski lift along the way.

Skiers who complete the circuit can log their route and times online, with some fancy prizes (ski holidays, for example – in Saalbach-Hinterglemm, of course) for the fastest and there are badges and small prizes for everyone who successfully completes the route.

The downside to all this hooning around at maximum velocity is that you don't really get to see the attractive, broad shouldered, forested mountains that make up the ski area in great detail – but you can save that for another day.

Those forests can come in handy on bad weather days, of course, whilst another feature that more chilled out skiers will enjoy is the region's plethora of rustic mountain huts – all marked on the piste map – where you can stop for coffee or lunch. Excellent, friendly service is a feature of pretty much all of them, and stand-outs include the Ellmaualm for its great views and the two huts above Leogang – the Alte Schmeide which has live music and the AsitzBräu, which for good measure is also Europe's highest brewing museum.

Back down in the valley at day's end, don't expect to sit back and relax – another boast of Saalbach-Hinterglemm is that it has the best après-ski in the Alps, and there's no doubt that the place goes mad once everyone has unclipped from their bindings for the day. Spots such as the Hinterhag Alm in Saalbach and the Goasstall in Hinterglemm are classic Austrian après-ski venues where the music is loud, the beer flows freely and the table tops are the place to dance – in your ski boots of course.

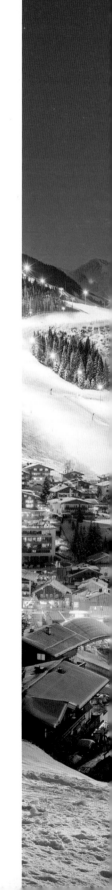

The coolest ski resort in the Alps? © YuriKo / shutterstock.com

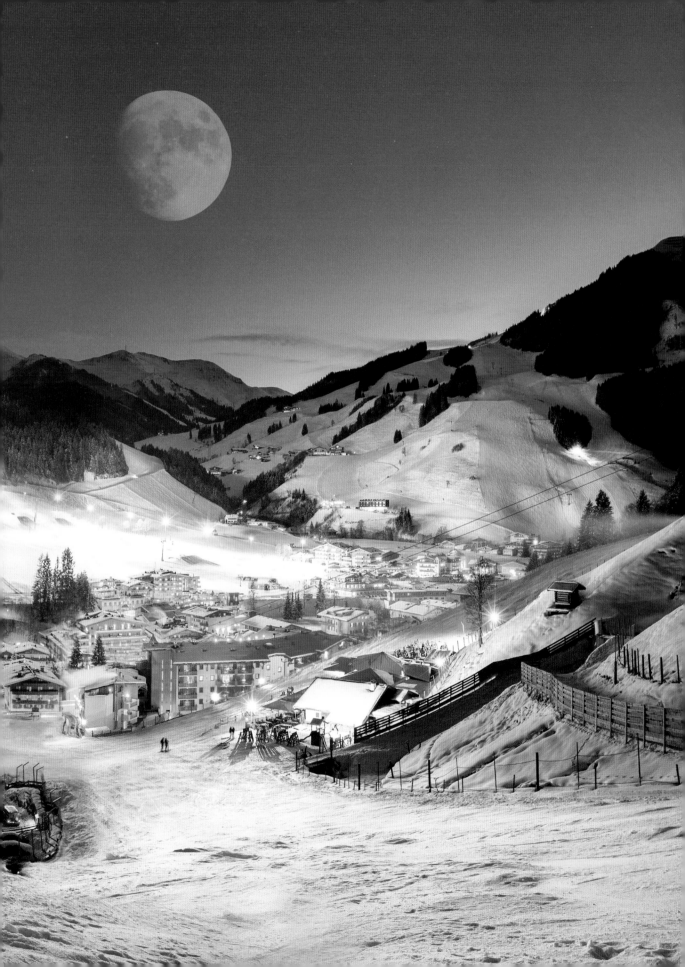

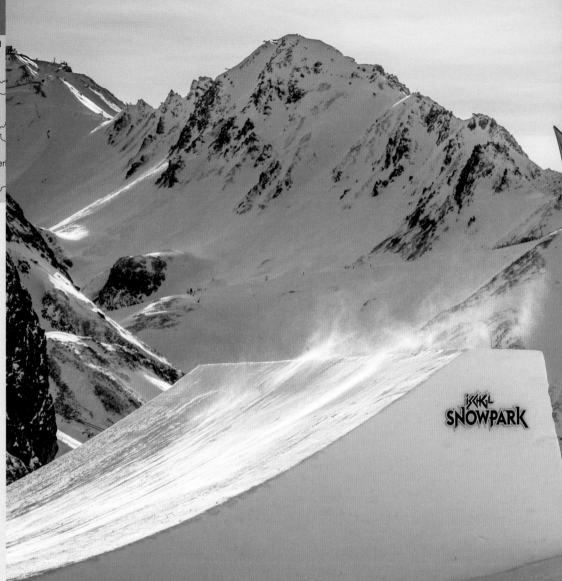

Germany Poland

Austria

Ischgl

Hungary

Italy

Ser

Access
Nearest airport:
Innsbruck (100km)

Ability Level
Beginner – expert

Season
Nov – May

Other Local Activities
Snowshoeing,
cross-country skiing,
tobogganing, ice
skating, hiking

Resort Stats
Top: 2,870m
Bottom: 1,377m
Vertical: 1,497m
Lifts: 45
Pistes: 253km
(includes 'ski routes')

www.ischgl.com

ISCHGL, AUSTRIA
Time to party

Many resorts tout themselves as party capital of the Alps, and it has to be said that Ischgl has a big claim to be top of that list. However, this presents a serious problem for any visitor – the après-ski is so vibrant that it's virtually impossible to avoid overdoing it in the bars and clubs every night. Combine that with a week of skiing and it takes some stamina to make the most of all that's on offer.

For full-on party animals the opening and closing weekends of the season are the time to visit, when Ischgl throws on free concerts which have in the past included the likes of Lenny Kravitz, The Killers, Sir Elton John, Robbie Williams, Tina Turner, etc., etc.

The opening party is in the town and the closing event upon the slopes, and when a top-rated band ain't belting it out for free Ischgl can offer the likes of the manic, booming Trofana Alm, the Hotel Elisabeth with its dirndl-clad dancing girls grinding it out atop the tables and the legendary Nikis's Stadl to "… entertain you" as Mr Williams might croon...

There are few better ways to shift any hangover you may inadvertently contract than swooshing down Ischgl's wide, user-friendly pistes the morning after the night before – and you can even organise

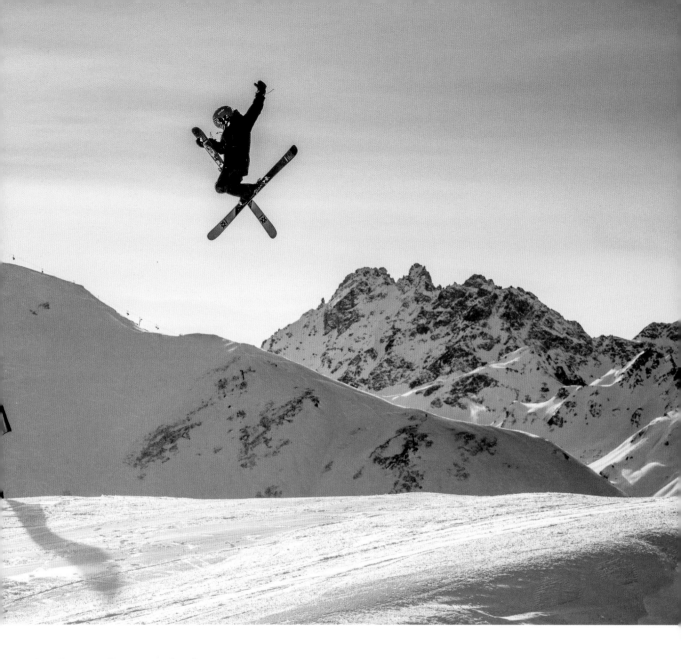

your late afternoon skiing around a little 'light entertainment' should you be in need of a bit of hair of the dog.

As the day draws down take a drink at the Pardorama restaurant high on the mountain above Ischgl town – it's the best place to watch the sun going down. Then take the Number 4 black run home – it's not a tricky black, just pleasantly steepish and sweeping, with fabulous views. And it will be virtually deserted for you at that time of day. Magic.

The Paznauner Thaya restaurant on the opposite side of the ski area is also a great spot on a sunny afternoon – but not for peacefully watching the sun set, more for raucous on-the-slopes après-ski with a rocking open-air disco. The atmosphere is great – but if you've had a drink or two, it's maybe sensible just to take the easy run down to the Silvrettabahn middle station and then hop aboard the gondola back to the village.

Or, if you're up for a more adrenaline-fuelled end to the day rather than one that's alcohol-fuelled, try to time things so you take a ride to the summit of 2,872-metre Greitspitze, Ischgl's highest point, on the Lange Wandbahn lift just before it closes, then take run Number 13 home. Going down via Idalp you have a fabulous 11-kilometre descent, and by taking the last lift up you'll avoid the worst of the crowds and enjoy the sun setting across the mountains with just your mates in tow.

Then you can pop into the Trofana Alms for a quick one – just the one mind, there's skiing to be done tomorrow. Yeah, yeah...

Germany

Poland

Austria
Mayrhofen

Hungary

Italy

Serl

Access
Nearest airports:
Innsbruck (70km),
Salzburg (170km),
Munich (195km)

Ability Level
Beginner – expert

Season
Dec – Apr

Other Local Activities
Snowshoeing,
cross-country skiing,
paragliding, hiking

Resort Stats
Top: 2,500m
Bottom: 630m
Vertical: 1,870m
Lifts: 58
Pistes: 142km

www.mayrhofen.at

MAYRHOFEN, AUSTRIA
Are you ready for Austria's steepest piste?

So, do you possess 'Physical fitness and perfect body control; skiing skills that are above average; excellent, sophisticated skiing technique'? If so, you may be ready to tackle Mayrhofen's infamous 'Harakiri' according to the resort website.

Touted as the steepest pisted run in Austria, the Harakiri is said to have an average gradient of 78 percent (38 degrees), so depending on the level of your 'sophisticated skiing technique' it will be either challenging or exciting, and possibly both.

Also known somewhat more prosaically as 'Piste 34', the run opened in the 2003-04 season and is, understandably, a draw for most competent skiers visiting Mayrhofen. The entire run is some 2km in length with the steepest section being around 400 metres long and conveniently located within view of the Knorren Chairlift for the amusement of those passing overhead.

The Harakiri is made more difficult by the fact that it's often very icy – this is not necessarily due to poor snow cover (in fact Mayrhofen is relatively snow-sure) but because grooming the slope is difficult due to its gradient, with any artificial snow that's added tending to simply slide down the slope (as a matter of passing interest grooming is only possible with a winch and a special snow groomer that has a 430-horsepower engine, a weight of nine tons, and a pulling force of four tons).

If the idea of skiing the Harakiri fills you with trepidation, you could try hitting Piste 12, aka the 'Devil's Run'. It isn't as steep as the Harakiri, but the most vertiginous section, at the end of the run, is known as the 'Harakiri Test', with locals reckoning that if you can handle this, you're ready to take on its big brother.

Of course, there's a lot more to Mayrhofen than the Harakiri. The town itself is attractive and has a pleasant bustle about it, whilst the rest of the slopes offer some great piste skiing for stronger intermediates (steepness seems to be a theme of much of the skiing here), and plenty of decent off-piste for those looking for more of a challenge, whilst free buses and trains link several neighbouring resorts as well as allowing access to the nearby Hintertux Glacier.

This has year-round snow cover, of course, as well as extensive and interesting skiing for everyone from expert to relative novice, and as such it's well worth taking a day away from Mayrhofen to explore what is some of Europe's finest glacier skiing.

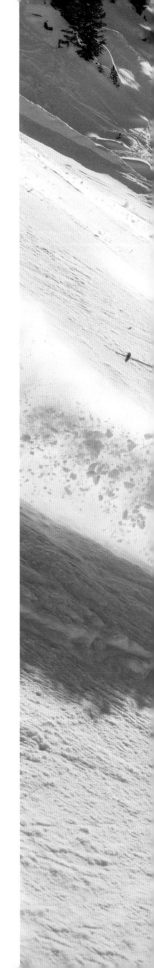

You want steep, you've got it at Mayrhofen's legendary Harakiri
© mayrhofen.at

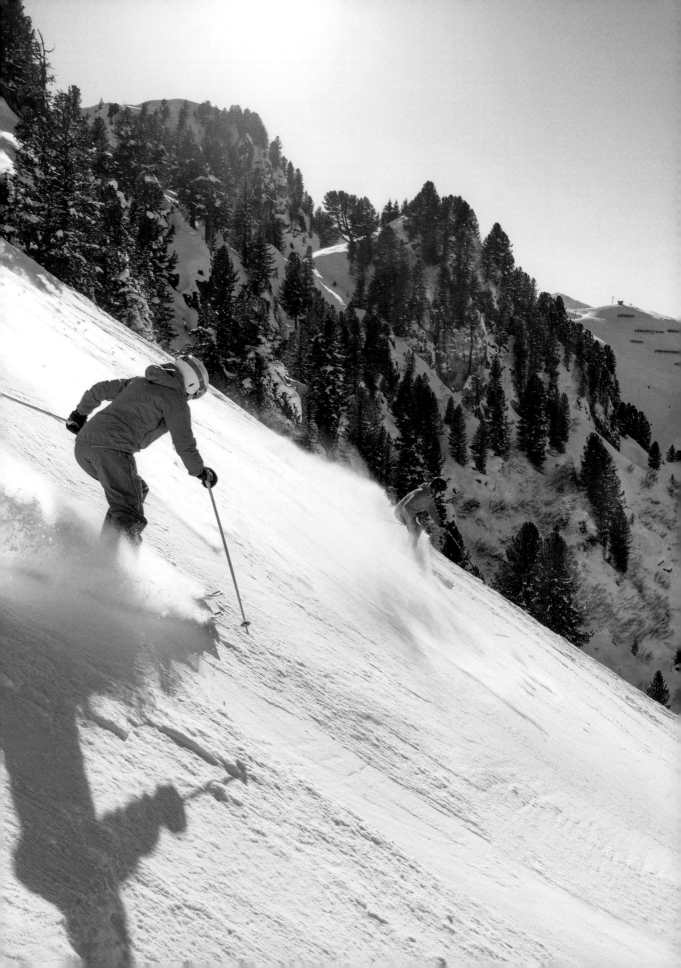

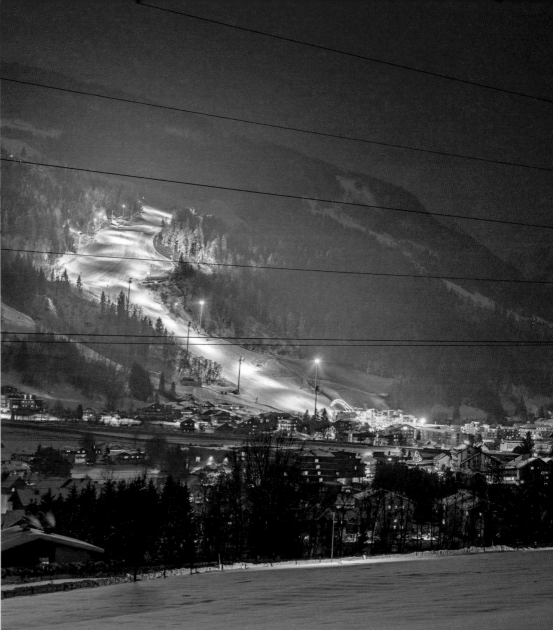

Germany   Poland

Austria
●Schladming
Hungary

Italy

Serb

Access
Nearest airports:
Salzburg (90km),
Munich (260km)
Mainline station in
resort

Ability Level
Beginner – expert

Season
Nov/Dec – Apr

Other Local Activities
Snowshoeing, cross-
country skiing, fat
biking, ice skating,
paragliding, hiking,
sleigh rides, ski yoga

Resort Stats
Top: 2,015m
Bottom: 745m
Vertical: 1,270m
Lifts: 44
Pistes: 123km

www.schladming-
dachstein.at

SCHLADMING, AUSTRIA
All things in moderation – almost

Whilst many ski areas promote the 'extreme' nature of their terrain in a bid to attract visitors, Schladming has a more practical and, you might argue, a more sensible approach; it doesn't bang on about how you can risk life and limb taking on its challenging slopes, it simply offers an excellent array of mainly intermediate terrain that will appeal to – well, intermediate skiers, which let's face it are the majority (this doesn't mean you should shy away if you regard yourself above this standard though – read on).

The welcoming town of Schladming lies beneath Planai, one of four linked mountains that provide keen intermediate skiers with a real sense of covering the ground as they flit from one peak to the other. If you manage to ski all four in four days or less, you'll be entitled to a small 'prize' from the tourist information office at the foot of Planai.

The scenery is never less than delightful as you zoom around, with all four mountains (Hauser Kaibling, Planai, Hochwurzen and Reiteralm) having forests almost all the way to their summits; the

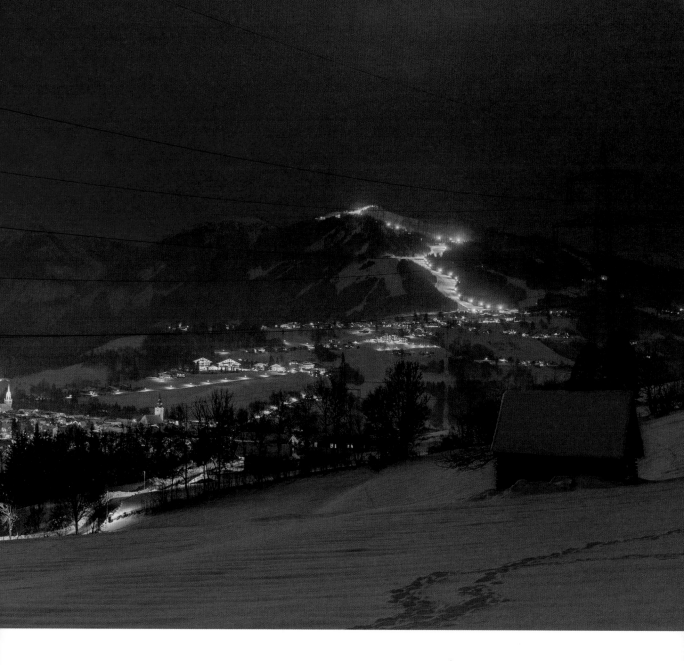

Schladming all lit up for the night races
© Tomasz Koryl / shutterstock.com

pistes run between them, of course, and because most are north-facing they tend to hold the snow well and remain skiable in bad weather. From the various summits you can enjoy lovely views down the Ennstal valley and of the spectacular Dachstein mountains.

The town itself also has a strong connection with ski racing, hosting the spectacular Schladming Night Race every winter as well as having been the venue for the 2013 World Championships, and skiers looking to emulate their heroes can clock their speed for free on the GUL speed run on Reiteralm.

But if you want to experience the real thing, make sure you're here for the annual World Cup Night Race in January, when a crowd of around 50,000 fans line the slalom course on Planai as the best skiers in the world hurtle between the gates.

The atmosphere is a cross between the FA Cup Final and Ben Hur; crowds roar, cowbells dong, national flags flutter, flares flare and the whole mad shebang is lit up by floodlights which glare off the snow more brightly than the sun; British competitor Dave Ryding has described approaching the start gate as "… like walking out at Anfield" (he is a Liverpool fan, mind).

Most of us will never see the slopes at Schladming from the same perspective as the likes of Ryding or Austria's own local ski hero Marcel Hirscher, of course, but we can always hit the GUL speed run and scare ourselves at high speed – or simply dream of ski superstardom as we cruise around Schladming's welcoming pistes.

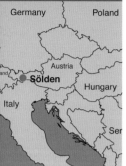

Germany   Poland

land   Austria
● Sölden
                Hungary
Italy
                    Ser

Access
Nearest airport:
Innsbruck (85km)

Ability Level
Beginner – expert

Season
Oct – May

Other Local Activities
Snowshoeing,
cross-country skiing,
tobogganing, ice
skating, hiking

Resort Stats
Top: 3,250m
Bottom: 1,380m
Vertical: 1,870m
Lifts: 31
Pistes: 144km

www.soelden.com

SÖLDEN, AUSTRIA
Welcome, Mr Bond

You've got to love a ski resort that features the best movie soundtrack ever on its website – I refer, of course, to the James Bond theme tune (and as proof that not everything related to James Bond comes dripping with gold, the guitarist who played the song's instantly recognisable riff, one Vic Flick, received a one-off fee of £6 for his labours in 1962).

The reason that Sölden's website features the tune is that much of the 24th James Bond movie *Spectre* was shot hereabouts. The resort's mountain-top Ice Q Restaurant became the 'Hoffler Klinik', a private medical clinic in the mountains, and the spectacular alpine chase scene was filmed on Sölden's 'Glacier Road'.

So, what has all this got to do with skiing? Well, not a lot to be honest, but whilst you're hooning around on your planks you may wish to take a break and pop into the '007 ELEMENTS' cinematic installation on the summit of 3,060-metre Gaislachkogl, one of Sölden's high points (although not the highest – that would be 3,250 metres on the Rettenbach Glacier).

The installation, which opened in 2018, covers some 1,300 square metres, mostly underground, and takes you on a high-tech journey through various galleries featuring video installations, sound effects, interactive stations and original gadgets and gizmos from the Bond movies. Oh, and there are also some fantastic views of the Ötztal mountain scenery when you get back outside.

As for the skiing, a fast and efficient lift system accesses a good range of terrain which varies from long reds and blues (the 'vert' here is almost 2,000 metres) to accessible blacks and fine off-piste terrain such as the various descents to the Rettenbachtal valley.

The real feather in Sölden's cap is that there are two high level glaciers here, the Tiefenbach and the Rettenbach, which more or less guarantee good snow conditions as well as providing runs of up to 15km in length.

Add to all this a predominantly easterly aspect to the slopes and extensive snowmaking and you're pretty sure of scoring decent snow during Sölden's very long ski season – October to May.

And when the skiing is over there's a very lively 'après' scene, starting on the slopes and then migrating down to Sölden's main street, where you'll find everything from live music and banging discos to table dancing; the Kuhstall Dancing Bar stays open until 5-6am, giving you time to throw back your last drink, throw down a quick breakfast and get out on the slopes without ever going to bed.

James Bond would approve...

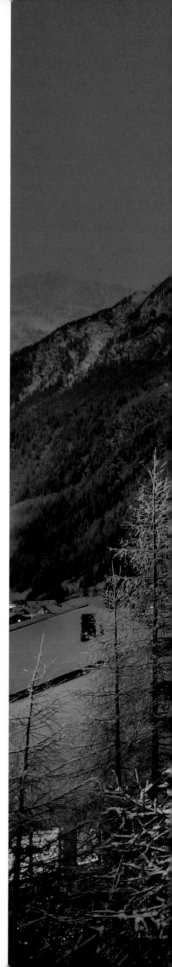

The sight when you leave the Kuhstall Dancing Bar at 6am?
© ansharphoto / shutterstock.com

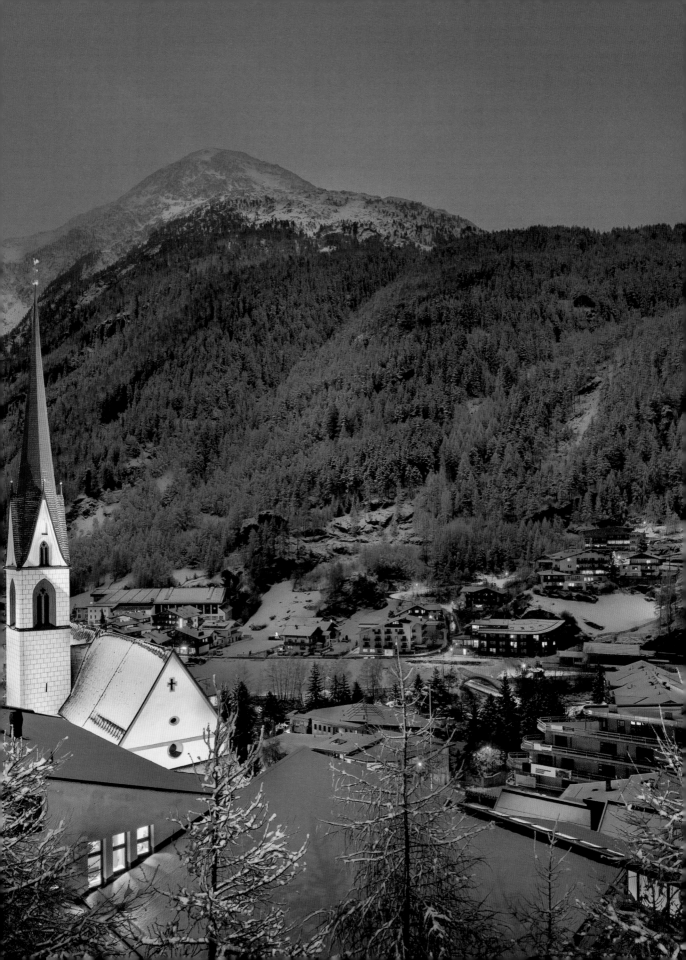

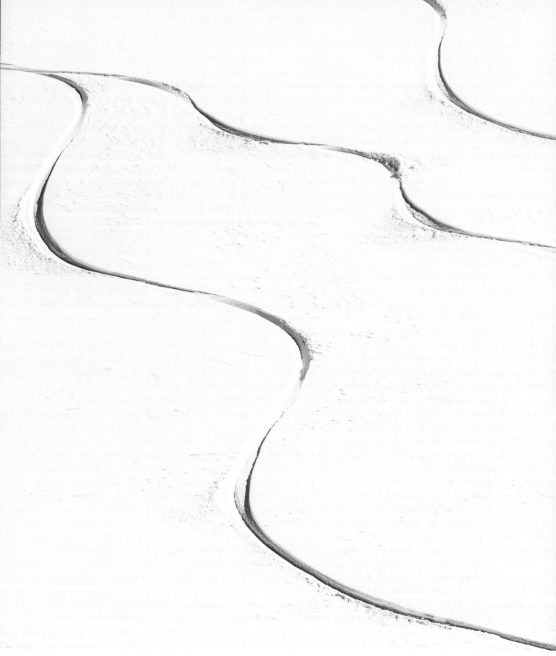

Germany   Poland

Austria
Stubai Valley

Hungary

Italy

Ser

Access
Nearest airport:
Innsbruck (45km)

Ability Level
Beginner – expert

Season
Oct – Jun

Other Local Activities
Snowshoeing,
cross-country skiing,
tobogganing, ice
skating, hiking

Resort Stats
Top: 3,210m
Bottom: 1,750m
Vertical: 1,460m
Lifts: 26
Pistes: 104km
(including 'ski routes')

www.stubaier-
gletscher.com

STUBAI VALLEY, AUSTRIA
'Welcome to the Powder Department'

As you drive along the 30km-long Stubai Valley to the south of Innsbruck, the Stubaier Gletscher beckons from the head of the valley – high, gleaming white and snow-sure, it offers some of the best glacier skiing and one of the longest seasons in the Alps.

Rising to well over 3,000 metres in height it's also more visually interesting than the majority of glaciers upon which you can ski, since it is pierced by rocky peaks, which add to the drama of the landscape.

The skiing is impressively varied for a glacier – there's a fine range of long, cruisy blue and red intermediate slopes along with a couple of exciting, steep blacks – the 'Daunhill' reaches as much as 31 degrees in places and the 4km-long 'Fernau-Mauer' at the far eastern end of the glacier is also challenging – don't be fooled by its easy upper slopes, things become much tougher as you descend.

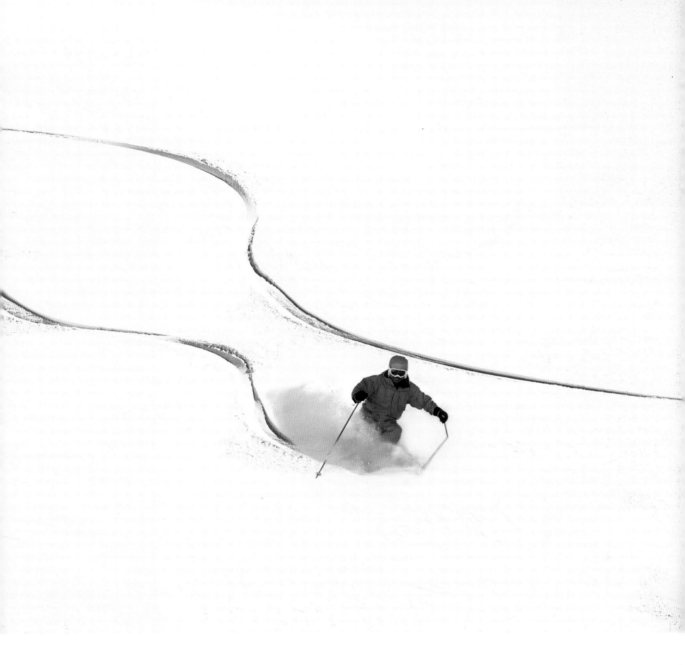

There's also a selection of 'ski routes' for more experienced skiers, of which the best is perhaps the 10km 'Wilde Grub'n' which offers 1,450 metres of vertical, and whilst you could argue that you're already 'off-piste' on a 'ski route' there's also an additional 13 freeride runs for which there's a separate 'Powder Department Off-Piste Map' – the routes can also be accessed as GPS tracks on your phone.

But this isn't all the Stubai Valley has to offer, for whilst the high, powdery slopes of the glacier will always be the main attraction for most skiers there are also three distinct ski areas lower down the valley too – Schlick 2000, above the village of Fulpmes, Elfer above the village of Neustift, and lower down the valley again, Serles.

The skiing in these lower resorts is neither as extensive nor as high as that on the glacier, but should the weather turn bad higher up, there's the option of skiing amongst the trees here.

And the options for keeping you entertained only get bigger if you buy the 'Ski Plus City Pass' when you ski the Stubai Valley. This gives you access to a total of 13 ski areas including the Stubai Glacier, of course, along with access to a heap of Innsbruck's visitor attractions, from museums to the Bergisel ski jump arena, free use of local buses and free admission to three different leisure/swimming centres.

Which effectively means the Stubai Valley offers something for everyone, whatever the weather.

Germany   Poland

Austria
Obergurgl   Hungary

Italy   Ser

Access
Nearest airport:
Innsbruck (95km)

Ability Level
Beginner – expert

Season
Nov – Apr/May

Other Local Activities
Snowshoeing,
cross-country skiing,
tobogganing, hiking

Resort Stats
Top: 3,080m
Bottom: 1,795m
Vertical: 1,285m
Lifts: 22
Pistes: 112km

www.obergurgl.com

OBERGURGL, AUSTRIA
Diamond geezers

If you're looking for one ski resort that captures the essence of Austrian skiing, Obergurgl has got to be a front-runner. It's one of the most snow-sure, non-glaciated resorts in the Alps.

It has traditional alpine charm, lovely landscapes, a decent range of skiing for all abilities and a handful of other local resorts can be skied for free if you buy a lift pass of three-days or more. If you like to concentrate on your skiing rather than your après-ski, the village is nice and quiet of a night time – as is linked Hochgurgl a little higher up the valley.

Given all this it's perhaps understandable why Obergurgl, the highest parish in Austria, calls itself the 'Diamond of the Alps', and if you catch it on a bluebird powder day you'll be in full agreement.

The area's two high points are just over 3,000 metres in altitude, and the slopes beneath, which are invariably very well groomed, offer some lovely intermediate terrain with spectacular mountain views which stretch as far as the Dolomites. Hochgurgl, which is linked to Obergurgl by a mid-mountain gondola, has the biggest array of flattering blues along with a few reds. Obergurgl has one of the area's best runs, a long descent beneath the gondola which is perfect for a mixed ability group of skiers since it has red, black and 'ski route' variants. It offers over 1,000 metres of vertical and, if you make it the last run of the day, it brings you back into town for what is usually a lively early evening après-ski scene (things are generally pretty quiet later in the evening).

Obergurgl also makes a fine option for family ski holidays thanks to its highly rated ski schools and good mix of terrain and the resort has a burgeoning freeride scene for more adventurous skiers.

Hochgurgl has some impressively steep freeride slopes higher up – these ease off in the middle of the mountain before becoming steeper again in the lower, more wooded, areas which provide a refuge from bad weather. With the recent opening of the second section of the Kirchenkar gondola the freeride potential has been extended even further.

Narrow gullies and steep slopes dominate the rocky terrain close to the summits, making them ideal for experienced freeriders, whilst those with less experience will find wider and more open powder fields lower down, and lower down still wooded terrain once more prevails.

Much of this freeride terrain can be accessed directly from the lifts, so no tedious hiking is required, and it doesn't always get tracked out by mid-morning, a rare thing in the powder-feeding frenzy of modern-day skiing.

Going for a diamond run – not common in Europe
© andreas ehrensberger / shutterstock.com

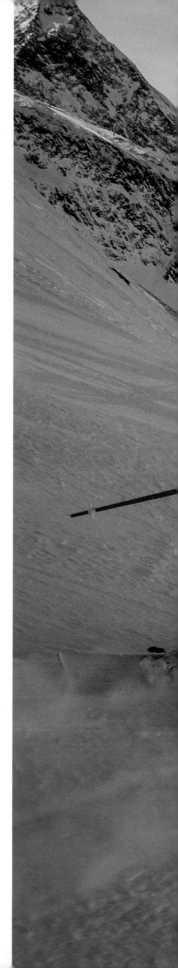

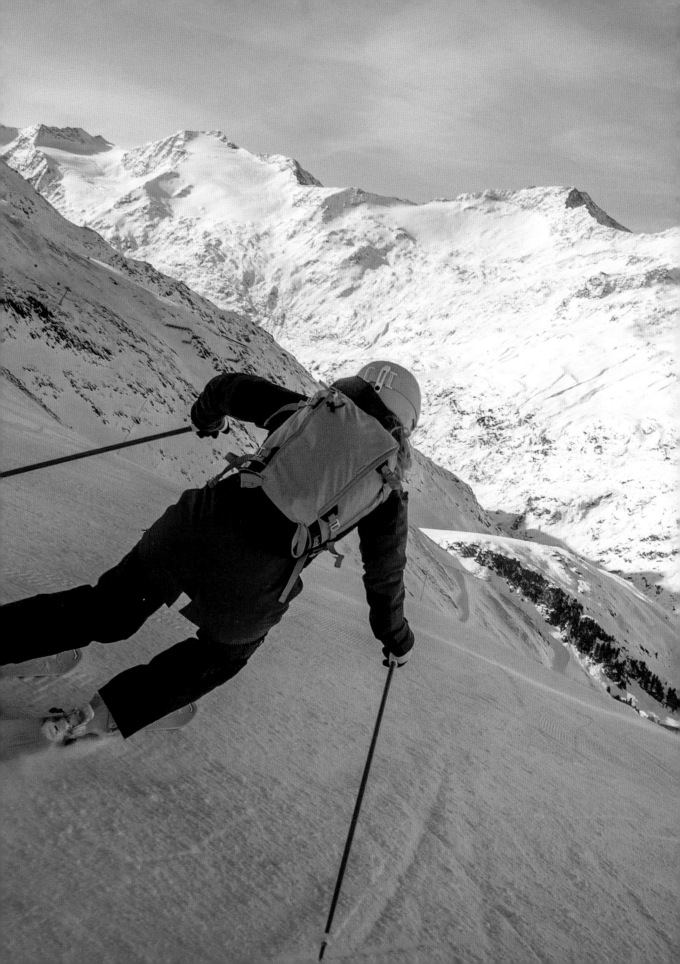

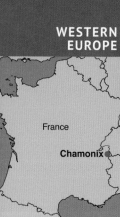

France

Chamonix

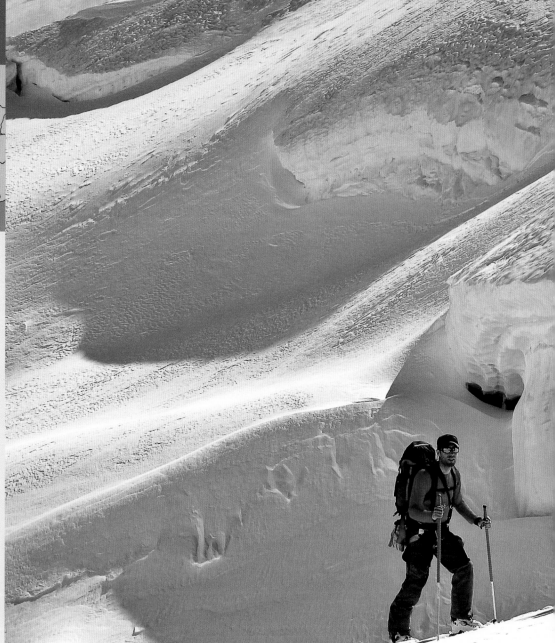

Access
Nearest airport:
Geneva (90km)
Mainline station in
town

Ability Level
Beginner – expert

Season
April although high
level ski touring is
possible for most of
the year

Other Local Activities
Mountaineering, ice
climbing, cross-
country skiing,
paragliding

Resort Stats
Top: 3,840m
Bottom: 1,035m
Vertical: 2,805m
Lifts: 42
Pistes: 115km

www.chamonix.com

CHAMONIX, FRANCE
Living for the moment

Chamonix is such a peculiar mix – the height of urbanisation and easy living in the town, the height of the Mont Blanc massif above the town, and the surreal combination of the two providing all the thrills any man or woman could want in an average lifetime.

There are few places in the world where you can be sipping a breakfast coffee in a swanky ski chalet at 8am, and traversing a knife-edge ridge with death drops either side at 9am. Depending on your take on these things, the description 'Death Sports Capital of Europe' may appeal or may have you running as fast as (safely) possible in the opposite direction.

The above is how well-known American climber Mark Twight once described Chamonix, and whilst it may be typically American overkill, Chamonix is undoubtedly one of the most spectacularly located mountain towns on the planet, a magnet for adrenaline junkies from freeriders to paragliders and downhill mountain bikers, and as such attracts the kind of individuals who consider leaping off a cliff

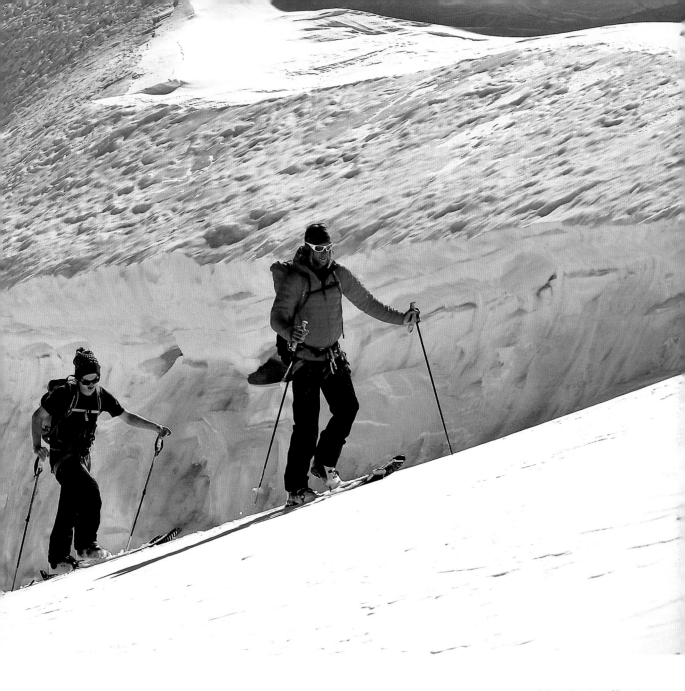

Ski touring above 'Cham'
© Alf Alderson

with or without a means of flight to be all in a day's fun.

The location alone is enough to cause a shiver of excitement in the most jaded of travellers. Mountains so jagged and pointy they're named after teeth, needles or fingers soar above the town, with the vast bulk of Mont Blanc standing proud above it all.

Fortunately, you don't need to be able to ski down slopes as steep as a wall to enjoy a visit to Chamonix. Five different ski areas are accessible from the town, albeit with varying levels of convenience since only two, Brevent and Flégère, are linked (free buses access all of them, mind).

On offer is everything from sheltered trees for when bad weather rolls in (Les Houches) to high, rolling cruiser pistes (La Tour) or, at Grand Montets above the pretty village of Argentiere, lofty and awe-inspiring ski terrain which takes in glaciers, frozen waterfalls and huge crags, as does the infamous Vallée Blanche, one of the world's longest off-piste descents.

When the skiing is over 'Cham' does something else it's also good at – it parties. Whether you want bustling craft ale bars, banging night clubs or glitzy casinos, they're all here. The danger is, of course, that too long in any of these will leave you light of wallet and heavy of head for the following day's skiing, but worrying about tomorrow isn't the way things are done in Chamonix – it's all about living for the moment, especially when you're on skis.

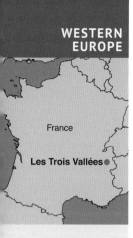

France

Les Trois Vallées●

Access
Nearest airports:
Chambery (100km),
Geneva (140km),
Grenoble (170km),
Lyon (180km)
Nearest train station:
Moûtiers (18km)
All distances given
are from Méribel

Ability Level
Beginner – expert

Season
Oct – Jun

Other Local Activities
Zip wires (including
highest in Europe),
tobogganing (longest
run in Europe) ice
driving, paragliding,
dog-sledding,
snowshoeing,
cross-country skiing,
paragliding

Resort Stats
Top: 3,230m
Bottom: 600m
Vertical: 2,630m
Lifts: 183
Pistes: 600km

www.les3vallees.com

LES TROIS VALLÉES, FRANCE
As big as it gets

There are – perhaps surprisingly – some skiers for whom
Les Trois Vallées (aka the Three Valleys) holds no appeal,
perhaps because of the overtly commercial nature of the
skiing that's on offer, but you'd have to be some special kind
of curmudgeon not to be able to enjoy some epic skiing
here, especially when conditions are good.

It is, after all, the world's biggest ski area and as such
the options are endless, whether you're a novice looking
for snow-sure beginner slopes (try Les Menuires), an expert
looking for high-altitude powder (check out Val Thorens, the
highest resort in the Alps, topping out at 3,230 metres) or
the kind of skier for whom five-star luxury is essential (book
into Courchevel, one of the most chi-chi resorts in France).
And there are actually more than 'Three Valleys' – a fourth
valley, the Maurienne, is also accessible from Val Thorens.

You can buy a lift pass for the whole area, but with so
much terrain to explore you need to seriously consider
whether you can make do with the cheaper option of a
single resort pass; most of the area's resorts are the same
size as any 'regular' ski resort, especially Val Thorens,
Méribel-Mottaret and Courchevel, and for anyone other
than intermediate cruisers looking to cover as many miles
as possible on their skis there will be enough within the
individual resort to keep you satisfied for a week or more.

Interestingly, there was once a plan to link the Three
Valleys with the nearby ski areas of Paradiski and the former
'Espace Killy' (now known simply as Val d'Isère and Tignes)
in the neighbouring Tarentaise Valley; this would have
created a truly enormous ski area bigger – literally – than
some small countries. However, the creation of the Vanoise
National Park in 1963 put paid to this plan, probably quite
fortunately since it has ensured that backcountry skiers and
ski tourers still have some magnificent, unspoilt terrain that
they can access from the Three Valleys.

The six resorts that make up the Three Valleys each have
enough individual character that most skiers will find a base
that's ideal for their needs, and to be honest, if you don't
enjoy skiing in the Three Valleys it's maybe time you hung
up your skis and took up baking or something...

*Former FWT competitor Jérémy Prevost doing his thing in
Méribel © Sylvian Aymoz / Meribel Tourisme*

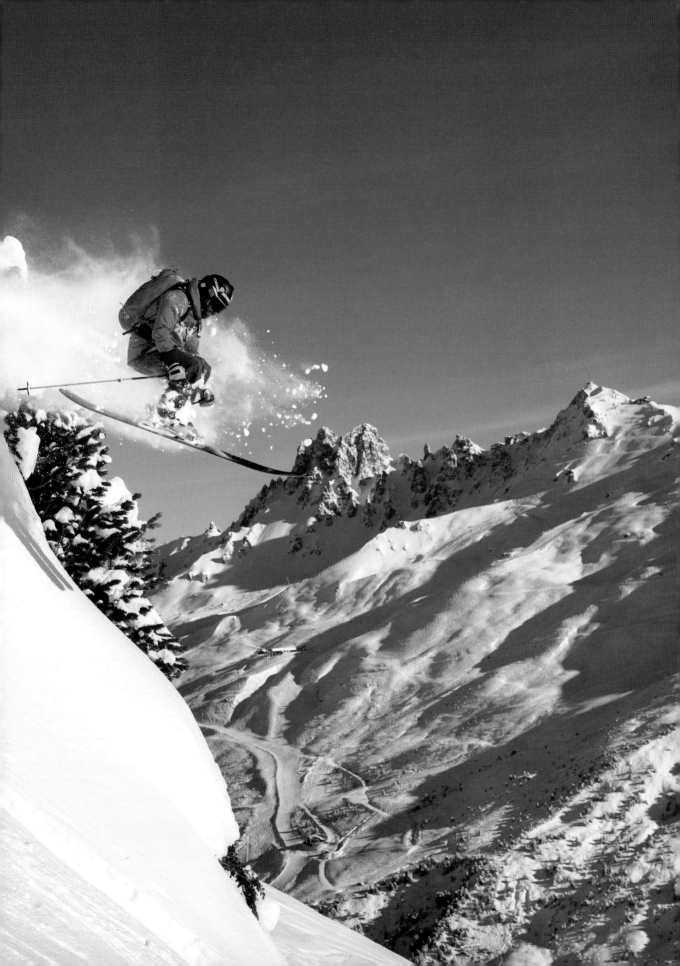

France

Val d'Isère

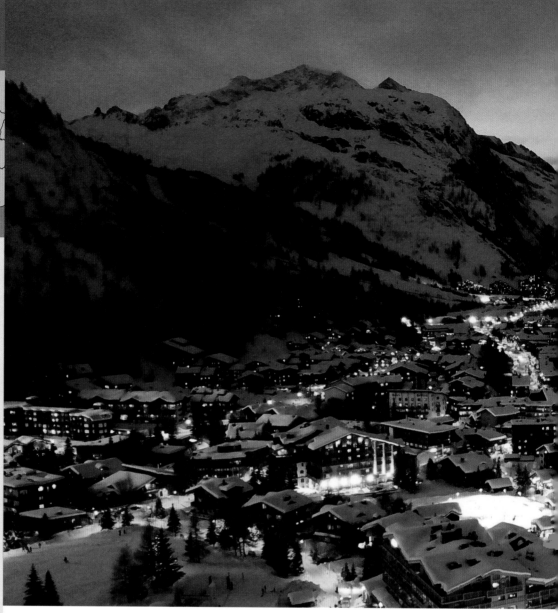

Access
Nearest airports:
Chambery (145km),
Geneva (225km),
Grenoble (210km),
Lyon (220km)
Nearest train station:
Bourg St
Maurice (30km)

Ability Level
Beginner – expert

Season
Nov – May; summer
skiing Jun – Jul

Other Local Activities
Ice skating, cross-
country skiing,
snowmobiling,
snowshoeing, dog-
sledding, paragliding,
ice climbing

Resort Stats
Top: 3,455m
Bottom: 1,850m
Vertical: 1,605m
Lifts: 88
Pistes: 300km

www.valdisere.com

VAL D'ISÈRE, FRANCE
Snow-sure 'Val' is a quirk of geography

Val d'Isère is one of the best-known ski resorts in the world, and for good reason – it is, quite simply, one of the biggest and best, especially when you factor in the easy access to neighbouring Tignes which easily places the area in the world's top ten in terms of size.

But size isn't everything (although more than 2,000 metres of lift-served vertical and 300km of pistes do help…). Val d'Isère also offers some of the most exciting and steep piste skiing around (check out the Olympic black on the Bellevarde face) and, when the weather gods smile on you, some truly mind-blowing lift-served off-piste terrain.

It also has an impressive back story for a purpose-built ski area; although the first drag lift was installed here in the 1930s it wasn't until the sixties onwards that the resort really developed, aided by the success of local ski racers Christine Goitschel, Marielle Goitschel and Jean-Claude Killy (the ski area was until recently known as 'Espace Killy'). The 1992 Albertville Winter Olympics saw 'Val' hosting many of the ski events, the Alpine World Championships were held here in 2009 and every December the Criterium de la Premiere Neige attracts the world's top downhillers – and as a measure of how snow-sure the region is, in the past it's had to be postponed due to too much snow.

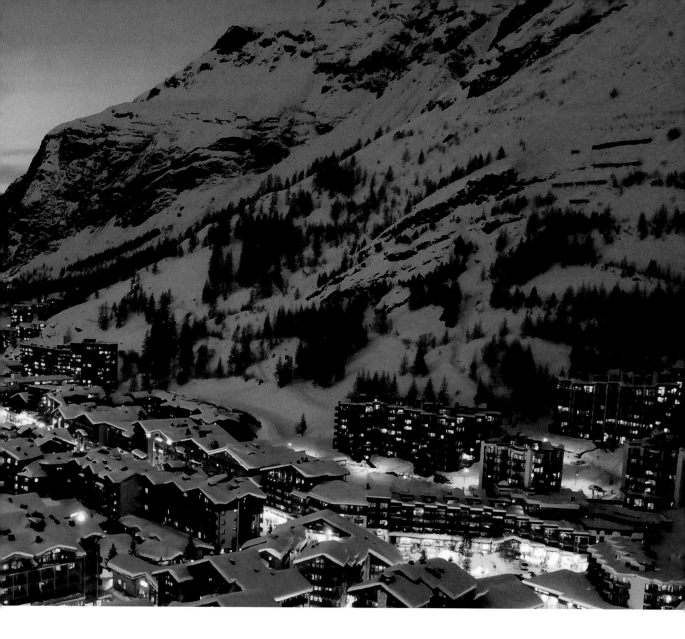

And although the resort has one of the longest ski seasons in the Alps (late Nov – early May) it ain't all over once the flowers start to bloom, since you can enjoy summer skiing above 3,000 metres in the mornings from June to mid-July on the Pissaillas glacier.

Due to Val d'Isère's altitude (the town sits at 1,850 metres and, unlike many modern French ski resorts, has been built in a rather attractive, traditional alpine style) temperatures on the mountain rarely rise much above freezing throughout the ski season, allowing the resort to offer a 'snow guarantee' to punters.

As Cédric Bonnevie, who is in charge of preparing the pistes, explains, this is thanks to a combination of altitude, a wide range of north-facing slopes and a quirk of mountain geography: "We don't just get our snowfall from the Atlantic. Our proximity to the Italian frontier allows us to benefit from some exceptionally heavy and highly localised snowfalls. This phenomenon, known as the 'retour d'est', occurs whenever precipitation comes up into Italy from the Mediterranean. It dumps copious quantities of snow on the French side of the alpine chain. Invariably, Val d'Isère is the only French resort that benefits from this effect."

It's worth keeping an eye on the weather charts for this phenomenon, because it can mean that while neighbouring resorts such as La Rosière (page 36) and Les Arcs (page 34) are basking in sunshine, 'Val' is being dumped on – if you like sunshine then that's no big deal, but if you call yourself a real skier you'll be making the short drive south to experience the best that 'Val' has to offer.

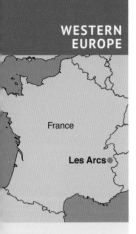

France

Les Arcs ●

Access
Nearest airports:
Chambery (130km),
Geneva (165km),
Grenoble (195km),
Lyon (205km)
Distances from Bourg
St Maurice
Arc 1600 accessible
by train/funicular
from Bourg St
Maurice

Ability Level
Beginner – expert

Season
Dec – Apr

Other Local Activities
Speed skiing,
bobsleigh (La Plagne),
tobogganing, ice
skating, hiking,
snowshoeing, dog-
sledding, paragliding

Resort Stats
Top: 3,250m
Bottom: 1,200m
Vertical: 2,050m
Lifts: 140+
Pistes: 425km

www.lesarcs.com
www.la-plagne.com

LES ARCS / LA PLAGNE (PARADISKI), FRANCE
Let the train take the strain

Les Arcs is one of the few ski areas in France where you can almost take the train right to the door; well, if you're staying in Arc 1600 you can. The SNCF train service to Bourg St Maurice can be reached direct from London and other European cities, from where an updated, glass-roofed funicular railway whisks you almost 800 metres up the mountain – hop out, clip in, ride up the Mont Blanc chair and one of the biggest ski areas on the planet awaits your pleasure...

For Les Arcs is a great deal more than simply Arc 1600; indeed, the resort consists of five separate but interlinked purpose-built ski villages not to mention the spectacular double-decker Vanoise Express cable car which takes you across a yawning void to La Plagne, where you'll find another rash of distinct ski villages that are also interlinked (and, like Les Arcs, also have a very modernist love-it-or-loathe-it architectural style).

The whole ski area of Les Arcs and La Plagne is known as 'Paradiski', and if you can't find enough skiing here to keep you satisfied there's not much hope for you. Indeed, it's debatable whether you even need to shell out the extra moolah for a Paradiski lift pass since the amount of skiing in the individual ski areas of Les Arcs and La Plagne, for each of which you can purchase a cheaper lift pass, is massive, as well as being varied enough to appeal to absolutely every type of skier.

Les Arcs is often regarded as a perfect intermediate resort thanks to its wide array of open, cruisy red and blue runs, and La Plagne has quite rightly developed a reputation as a family-friendly ski area, but there's a lot more to both than that; indeed, the Paradiski area in general offers some fantastic off-piste terrain for those willing to explore, with a huge amount of vertical that takes in everything from glaciers and high-altitude bowls to sheltered trees when the weather closes in.

The one thing you won't really find here is the kind of rustic charm that is common in Swiss and Austrian ski resorts – with the exception of villages such as sunny Champagny-en-Vanoise on the very edge of La Plagne and Villaroger on the southern edge of Les Arcs, the various settlements that make up most of the Paradiski area are very 'urban', in true 1970s French modernist alpine architectural style.

Sensitive souls may thus decide to forsake Paradiski's fantastic skiing for somewhere more 'chocolate boxy'; the rest of us, knowing better, will be heading upwards on one of the area's 140-odd ski lifts to rip it apart, since we're here to ski rather than appraise architectural styles...

Perfect skiing at Paradiski © Hugh Rhodes

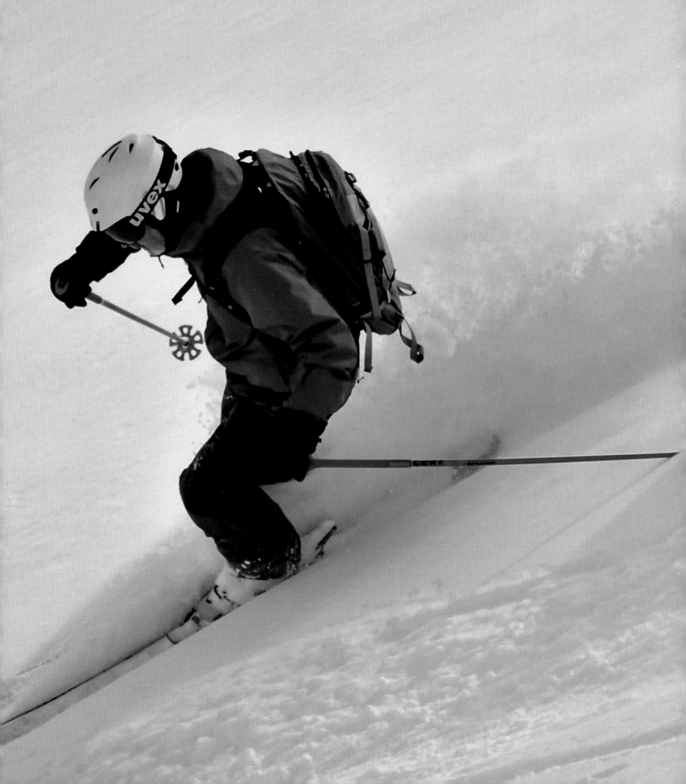

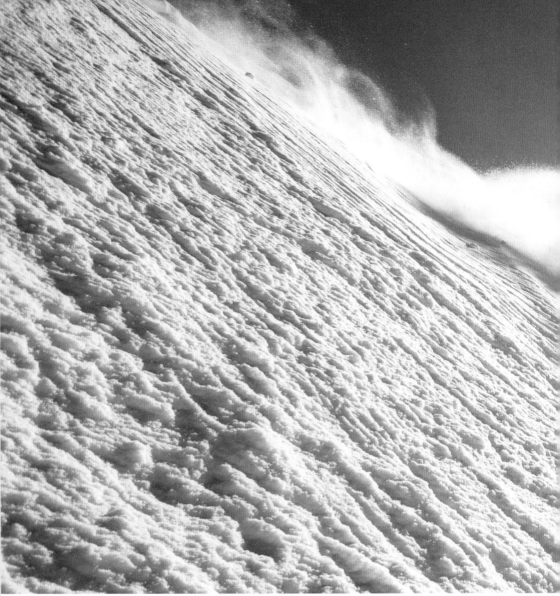

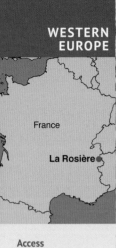

France

La Rosière

Access
Nearest airports:
Chambery (130km),
Geneva (165km),
Grenoble (195km),
Lyon (205km)
Distances from Bourg
St Maurice

Ability Level
Beginner – expert

Season
Dec – Apr

Other Local Activities
Heli-skiing, ice
skating, winter
hiking, snowshoeing,
paragliding

Resort Stats
Top: 2,800m
Bottom: 1,175m
Vertical: 1,625m
Lifts: 37
Pistes: 160km

www.larosiereski.com

LA ROSIÈRE, FRANCE
All change in border country

Until the last couple of years La Rosière was touted as the perfect family resort – its wide, gently angled slopes face predominantly south so catch the sun for much of the day, it has a good infrastructure and the panoramas from just about anywhere on the slopes are wonderful – the Mont Blanc Massif to one side, almost within touching distance, and the Tarentaise Valley to the other, with the mega-resorts of Les Arcs and Tignes readily visible in the distance along with dinky little St Foy just across the way.

And for more adventurous skiers there's the irresistible temptation of a day out in Italy at La Thuile, which is linked to La Rosière by a long, long drag lift. But more of that later…

Things changed in 2018/19 when a big new lift-accessible freeride area, Mont Valaisan, was opened, a combination of south-facing bowls and north facing steeps providing all the powdery challenge most skiers could ever want.

And so, in one fell swoop, La Rosière went from being a family ski resort to a resort for pretty much everyone. Sure, it doesn't have the area or altitude of many of its neighbours (the highest lift, the Mont Valaisan Chair, tops out at 2,800 metres) and the sun can do horrible things to the south facing slopes from February onwards, but let's not dwell on these small inconveniences.

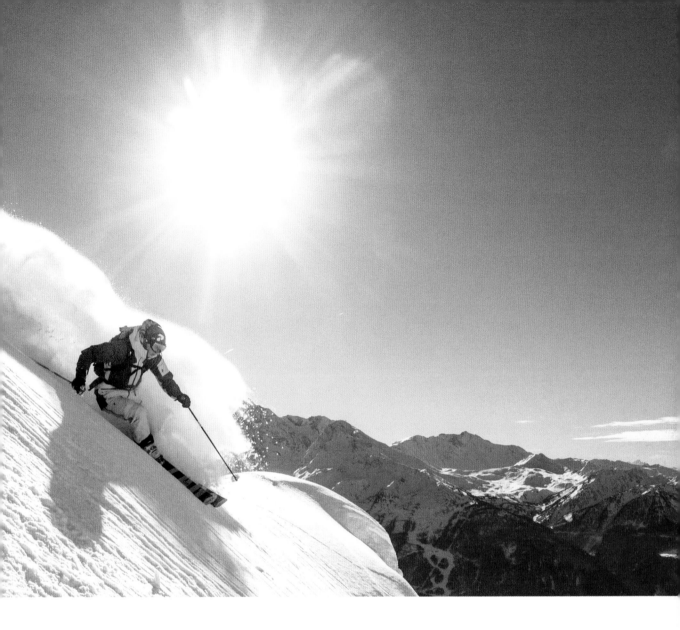

*'La Ros' on a bluebird day –
who needs a helicopter?*
© Julien Eustache

Indeed, 'La Ros' is the only ski resort in France where you can heli-ski. You actually get picked up by the helicopter just across the border in Italy since heli-skiing is illegal in France; you're then dropped on an Italian mountain top from where you can ski back into France.

Ironically, however, it's skiing in the opposite direction towards Italy which is one of the major attractions of La Rosiere, and you don't need a large bank account to enjoy it. The link to La Thuile, lying in the shadow of the mighty dome of Monte Bianco (Mont Blanc) adds a new and very enjoyable dimension to skiing here, and, in fact, the entire linked area is known as 'Espace San Bernardo', after the Col du Petit St Bernard which links the two; and yes, the eponymous big fluffy dogs can be found here too.

La Thuile's slopes tend to be north facing and steeper than those of La Rosière, so often offer a more exciting ski experience, and let's face it, a lunch break in an Italian restaurant is not only cheaper than dining in France but as a gastronomic experience it's also as good if not better than what you'll get across the border.

It's also surprising what a cultural difference a border can make; Italian skiers tend to be more garrulous than their French counterparts and everything from ski lifts to bars and restaurants are just a tad more rumbustious, which is no bad thing.

So, there's a good argument for saying that La Rosière now has it all; great family skiing, excellent freeride terrain and the opportunity for one or more days out in Italy. Who needs a helicopter with all that on offer?

France

Les Sybelles

Access
Nearest airports:
Chambery (86km),
Grenoble (115km),
Lyon (194km)

Ability Level
Beginner – expert

Season
Dec – Apr

Other Local Activities
Fat biking, cross-country skiing, dog-sledding, snowshoeing, paragliding

Resort Stats
Top: 2,620m
Bottom: 1,100m
Vertical: 1,520m
Lifts: 68
Pistes: 146km

www.sybelles.ski

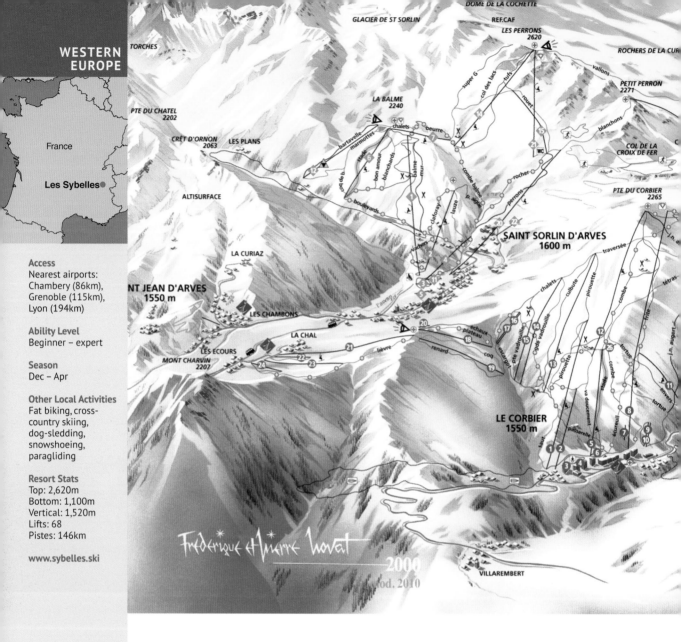

LES SYBELLES, FRANCE
The biggest ski area you've never heard of

France and skiing – think Three Valleys, Paradiski and any number of other huge, interlinked ski areas. Or maybe not...

Maybe think Les Sybelles instead. Heard of it? Not many skiers outside of France have, yet it's one of the biggest ski areas in a nation with some of the biggest ski resorts in the world.

Les Sybelles consists of six linked ski resorts in the Maurienne massif; St Jean d'Arves (1,550m), St Sorlin d'Arves (1,600m), Le Corbier (1,550m), La Toussuire (1,750m), St Colomban des Villards (1,100m) and Les Bottières (1,300m), with a claimed total of 260km of pistes (plus another 50km of Nordic trails), not to mention some very impressive and seemingly limitless freeride options.

All six resorts are small enough that you can explore them easily in a day or two, but you'll need a week or more to really get to know the whole ski area.

It lies in the shadow of the three mighty fangs of 3,514-metre Aiguilles d'Arves, with La Toussuire and Le Corbier featuring the kind of utilitarian 1970s architecture you either love or hate – both villages were developed some forty years ago in a no-frills style which would allow ordinary mortals to enjoy the skiing experience without dipping into their life savings.

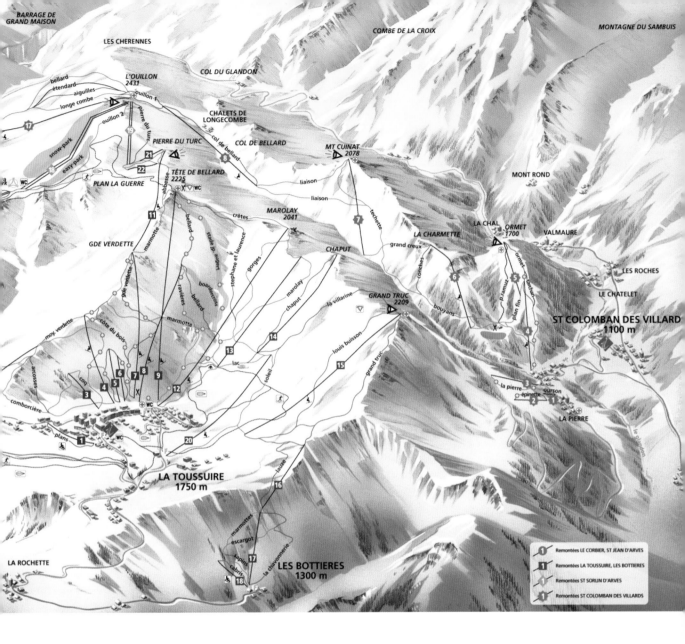

Les Sybelles' extensive piste map © www.sybelles.ski

And if you don't like the style – well you hardly see the resorts once you're up in the mountains, and Les Sybelles has also done a good job of situating its ski lifts such that they don't impinge on the scenery too much.

If you'd prefer a more rustic, alpine feel to your ski holiday, the other four villages that make up Les Sybelles offer this, so everyone is catered for – particularly when you consider that prices for everything from accommodation to ski hire tend to be noticeably lower than those in the nearby mega-resorts.

Local UIAGM guide Philippe Vincent (who has climbed the Aiguilles d'Arves well over a hundred times) explains that Les Sybelles aims to attract the family market, hence all the intermediate terrain – "But that's good for us, because it means the off-piste is never busy – and there is lots of it."

This is apparent from the resorts' various high points, from which Mont Blanc and the Tarentaise region are clearly visible to the north, along with heaps of expansive off-piste terrain closer to hand.

For skiers looking for something less testing, Les Sybelles has a lovely selection of easy blues and reds that will flatter any intermediate skier, and although some of the lifts are a bit slow (a matter being rectified over the next few years by the installation of several high-speed lifts) queues are a rarity. There are also some fine mountain restaurants such as L'Alpe above St Sorlin, where you won't spend the price of a new pair of skis on a salad and chips.

All in all, not bad for a ski area no one has heard of…

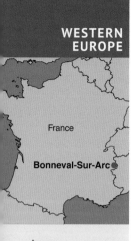

France

Bonneval-Sur-Arc

Access
Nearest airports:
Chambery (145km),
Grenoble (175km)

Ability Level
Beginner – expert

Season
Dec – Apr

Other Local Activities
Ice skating,
snowshoeing,
paragliding

Resort Stats
Top: 3,000m
Bottom: 1,800m
Vertical: 1,200m
Lifts: 7
Pistes: 25km

www.haute-
maurienne-vanoise.
com

BONNEVAL-SUR-ARC, FRANCE
Leaving the 21st century behind

Despite being one of the most snow-sure ski resorts in the French Alps, Bonneval is as low key as you can get. The village sits at an altitude of 1,800 metres in the Vanoise National Park and is a member of the group 'Les Plus Beaux Villages de France' which aims to preserve traditional architectural styles and cultural traditions.

Any building work has to remain true to the alpine vernacular style, telephone cables and street lighting is routed underground and shops and other businesses are not permitted to use large, garish signage.

The squat, stone-tiled houses and Baroque-style chapels have survived largely due to the village's high, remote location – when German forces razed many of the region's lower level, more accessible towns and villages on their retreat towards the end of World War II, Bonneval was left untouched.

Whilst tourism remains important to the local economy year-round, traditional transhumance agriculture and craft work are also still important – produce such as Bonneval blue cheese, Savoie tomme and cured ham and the work of local wood carvers is still very much a part of the local economy.

So, as a skier you may think that you'd stand out a tad in this traditional alpine setting. Not a bit of it. Bonneval has somehow managed to get the perfect balance of being a village that relies on skiing for much of its winter income but hasn't sold out to it.

And whilst the skiing infrastructure is all human-scale and basic, the resort's slow old chairlifts carry you up into a mountainscape that is far from human-scale and, for that matter, far from 'basic'.

'Spectacular' would be more the word of choice. The vast bulk of 3,638-metre Mont Albaron towers above the ski slopes, blue glaciers glinting on its steeper flanks, whilst its snowfields display the dark tracks of ski tourers heading for Italy, on the mountain's far side. This side of the massif faces north, and the '3,000' chairlift will allow you to access it.

Bonneval has only a modest 25km of groomed pistes and seven lifts, hence the resort's increasing popularity as a freeride destination, with the huge, cold, shadowy snow bowl directly beneath Mont Albaron's north face being the 'go to' area.

Take a break from the skiing at the low-key, friendly Restaurant Criou; the staff could be as diffident as they want since it's the only restaurant on the mountain, but there's an amiable atmosphere here as everyone from adrenaline-fuelled freeriders to family groups gather.

After heading back to search out more lines on the mountain as the afternoon sun sinks low in the sky, you'll eventually be forced back down into town. Why not stay the night in a traditional auberge and enjoy the luxuries of modern living whilst surrounded by the past?

'Bonne ski' at Bonneval © Daniel Durand / Fresh Influence

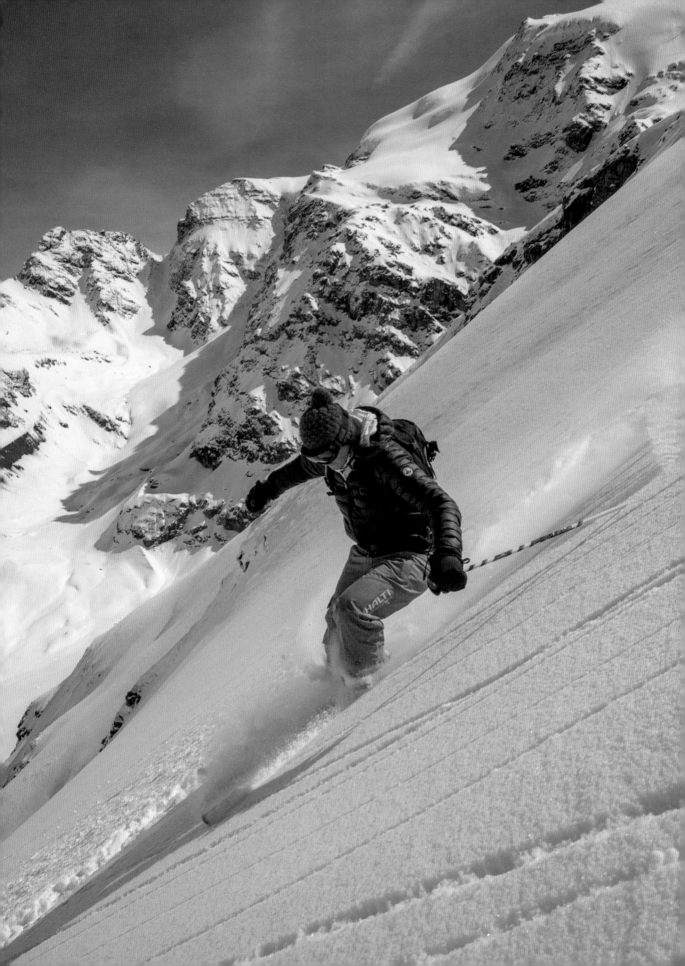

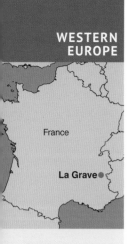

France

La Grave●

Access
Nearest airports:
Grenoble (77km),
Chambery (136km),
Turin (150km)

Ability Level
Intermediate & above

Season
Dec – Apr/May

Other Local Activities
Ice climbing, cross-country skiing

Resort Stats
Top: 3,550m
Bottom: 1,450m
Vertical: 2,100m
Lifts: 4
Pistes: 5km

www.lagrave-lameije.com

LA GRAVE, FRANCE
Two feet in La Grave

La Grave relies on an almost total lack of defined, patrolled or avalanche-protected pistes as its major attraction, with challenging steeps and hazardous couloirs like Les Trifides, Y Couloir and Le Pan de Rideau being the big attraction for those skiers capable of taking them on.

Even the drive to La Grave along the deep, dark defile of the Romanche Valley can be daunting, and as you roll into the medieval alpine village the daunting bulk of 3,983-metre La Meije can be glimpsed bearing down from the heights.

The mountain has its own weather systems, which can see it shrouded in cloud when other areas are clear and sunny, and hopping aboard La Grave's glacially slow 'pulse' lift to access the slopes is an experience in itself.

The lift takes you above snow-plastered firs and pines and then up into sunlit alpine scenery which would make a geography teacher weep; before and above you lie giant cliffs and crags, broken and splintered by aeons of frost and heat, with the folds and crevasses of glaciers tumbling beneath and, as you eventually exit the lift at a literally breathtaking altitude of 3,200 metres, you encounter La Meije in all her majesty.

You can go even higher on a couple of draglifts that give access to three easy blue runs and allow less accomplished skiers the chance to say they've skied La Grave, but these blues, despite the fact they take you past the spectacular Grotte de Glace – a hollow in the Girose glacier – aren't enough to keep you occupied for more than a morning, and are not the reason you come to ski La Grave.

Swedish ski guide Pelle Lang first skied here in the early 1980s following a tip-off from legendary French extreme skier Patrick Vallençant, who was famed for skiing unfeasibly steep terrain as well as for his motto "si tu tombes, tu meurs" ("if you fall, you die" – eventually he did), and, he says, La Grave "Already had a reputation for being very dangerous."

"I eventually moved here in 1989 and opened the Skier's Lodge and in the first few years there were never more than a handful of skiers, and every year we found new terrain to ski. It was all a big adventure and sometimes pretty scary, but skiing terrain like this it's pretty hard not to have the occasional close call."

Pelle goes on to recall how "... it was so quiet in those early days that sometimes the lift company would call us up in the morning asking how many clients we had in the lodge so they knew whether it was worth opening or not!"

Pelle reckons you don't need to be an expert to ski here, although it definitely helps. That said a descent such as the 'Chancel' is feasible for strong and adventurous intermediate skiers, and has the added advantage of taking you past the bustling and rustic Refuge Chancel, where you can grab a coffee (to steady the nerves perhaps) or lunch.

Yet even sitting in the sun enjoying your café au lait at the refuge can be a bit disconcerting. This isn't a chi-chi dining experience as in the mountain restaurants of Courchevel or St Moritz – the terrain almost growls at you, rising dramatically upwards to La Meije and the eponymous glacier clinging to its flanks, and dropping steeply away in what is the only way home. And diners at the refuge definitely won't be draped in furs and designer sunglasses – avalanche packs, sun-bleached ski jackets and beards are the norm.

La Grave's approach to skiing is to let people take responsibility for their own decisions, which is rather refreshing in our compensation-culture world – even so, it's worth bearing in mind the words of local ski patroller Pascal Guiboud, who advises: "This terrain demands respect."

Lift off at La Grave © Alf Alderson

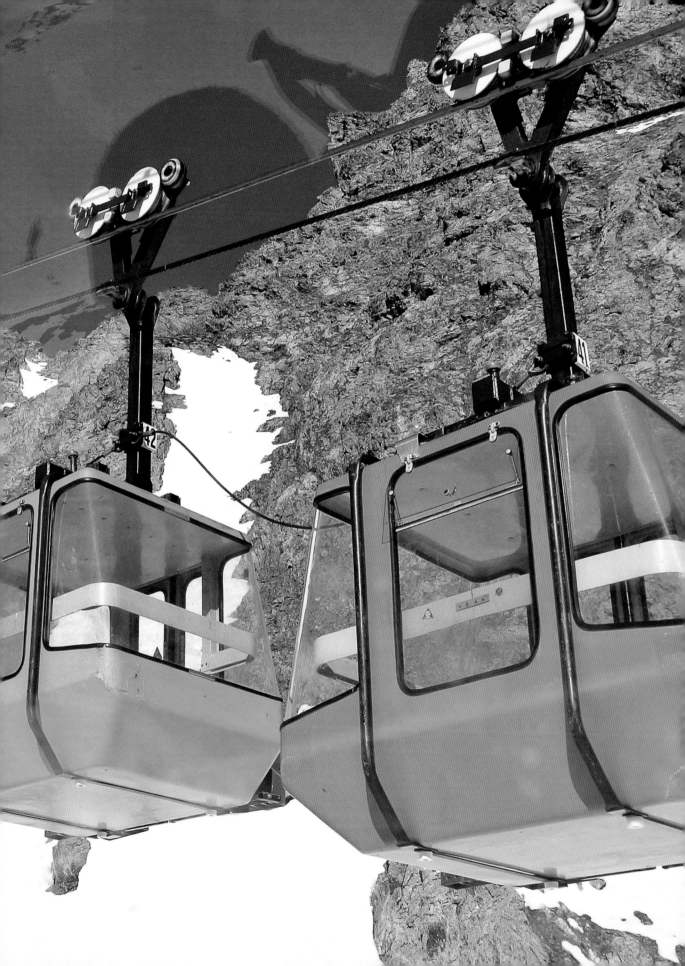

Germany

France

The Haute Route

Switzerland

Italy

ain

Access
Nearest airport to
Chamonix: Geneva
(90km)

Ability Level
Advanced – expert

Season
Late March – early
May

Distance
120km

Ascent / Descent
6,000m

THE HAUTE ROUTE, FRENCH – SWISS ALPS

The high-level alpine classic

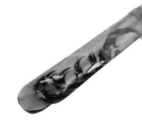

Probably the best-known ski touring adventure in the world, the Haute Route between Chamonix and Zermatt is also one of the best ski touring adventures, end of.

First undertaken in the mid-19th century as a summer mountaineering route by members of the British Alpine Club, it wasn't done on skis until 1911, when it gained the moniker 'The High Level Route', later translated to its current French name.

There are a variety of routes between the two iconic mountain towns, all of them taking in the most glorious alpine scenery and all requiring a high level of fitness, ability and commitment; and if the Haute Route itself isn't challenge enough for you (crampons, ropes and mountaineering gear will be required for some glaciated sections), it's possible to add ascents of various peaks along the way, including Mont Blanc, Pigne d'Arolla and the Breithorn – this will, of course, add extra days to what is usually a seven- or eight-day traverse.

You start in the shadow of one of the world's most famous mountains (Mont Blanc) and finish beneath one of the world's most beautiful mountains (the Matterhorn), staying overnight in high mountain huts, rising before sun up and working your way between some of the highest and most spectacular peaks in the French and Swiss Alps.

However fit you may be (the record time for the Haute Route, incidentally, is a staggering 18 hours 35 minutes by Lionel Claudespierre of Bourg St Maurice in April 2013) you'll be at the mercy of the elements and Lady Luck – bad weather, poor snow condition, accidents and equipment failure see only around half of the skiers who attempt the Haute Route succeed.

But if all goes well and you make a successful go of it you'll have the immense satisfaction of having completed one of the most legendary ski touring routes in the world.

Climbing on the Haute Route © R Scott / shutterstock.com

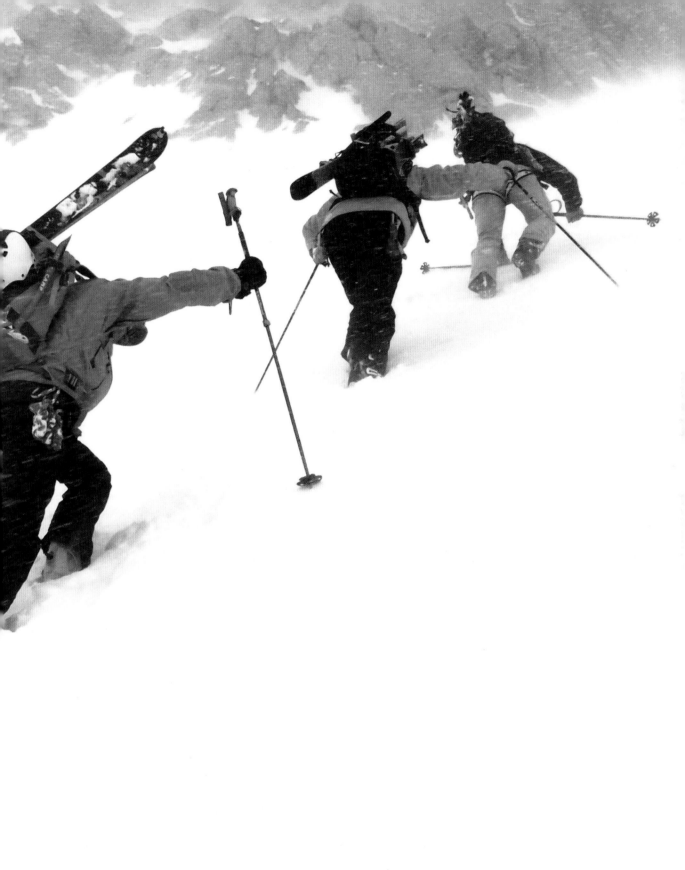

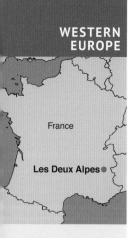

France

Les Deux Alpes●

Access
Nearest airports:
Grenoble (110km),
Chambery (130km),
Geneva (220km)

Ability Level
Beginner – expert

Season
Dec – Apr/May; high-
altitude glacier skiing
in summer

Other Local Activities
Snowshoeing,
paragliding, dog-
sledding, ice rink,
outdoor pool

Resort Stats
Top: 3,570m
Bottom: 1,300m
Vertical: 2,270m
Lifts: 47
Pistes: 200km

www.les2alpes.com

LES DEUX ALPES, FRANCE
It's a dog's life

I'm buried beneath a metre of snow above the ski resort of Les Deux Alpes in France in a cold, silent, friendless world – then suddenly there's a scuffling sound, followed by a pair of black paws frantically excavating the snow as Icare, the avalanche dog, bursts through to my rescue.

Fortunately, this is just an exercise – part of the annual two-week training programme in Les Deux Alpes for avalanche dogs and their handlers organised by ANENA, the French organisation for the study of snow and avalanches. But were it for real, Icare could very easily be the difference between life and death for an avalanche victim.

Avalanche deaths in the French Alps in recent years have remained steady at an average of around 30 per annum although scores more people are caught in avalanches and suffer injury each year; on average around 200 people get caught in avalanches annually, and each winter avalanche dogs rescue people buried in snow who are not wearing avalanche transceivers.

A trained avalanche dog can search one hectare of rough, snowbound terrain and/or avalanche debris in around 30 minutes – it would take twenty humans with avalanche probes around four hours to cover an equivalent area.

The speed with which an 'avy dog' may locate an avalanche victim is absolutely vital in a rescue, since around 90 percent of avalanche victims will survive if recovered in the first 15 minutes after burial, provided they haven't suffered fatal trauma. This drops to just 30 percent after half-an-hour and only 10 percent after two hours.

The dog is trained to search for 'pools' of human scent which are given off by buried victims – if still conscious the scent will be especially strong as the victim is highly likely to be panicking and may even be sweating despite the cold. The odour rises up through the snow pack before being carried away on the breeze, and when a rescue dog finds a potential human scent it will bury its snout and head into the snow to try to locate it more accurately.

If the scent intensifies the dog will start to dig and human rescuers will come along and assist with shovels; if the scent becomes weaker the dog will work outwards from the area to try to locate a stronger scent.

The dogs going through their paces at Les Deux Alpes are primarily Border Collies and Belgian and German Shepherds – along with Labradors and Golden Retrievers these are the main breeds used for the job.

Guy Anciaux, ANENA director, explains that after initial training at their local ski hills the dogs and their owners attend the two-week course in Les Deux Alpes. "But the dogs are not aware they're working," he points out. "For them it's all fun", and this is obvious by the barking, yelping and frantic tail wagging that precedes any exercise.

There's more to avalanche dog training than sniffing out buried journalists, of course – the dogs have to learn to ride on ski lifts and snowmobiles and in helicopters, for instance – but for the skiers looking on as the training continues there's a certain reassurance in knowing that those boundlessly energetic and enthusiastic mutts are there to learn how to be, quite literally, man and woman's best friend should the worst ever happen.

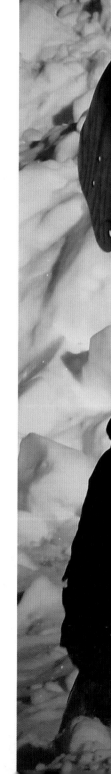

Man and avy dog in perfect harmony in Les Deux Alpes
© Jean Michel Morlot / ANENA

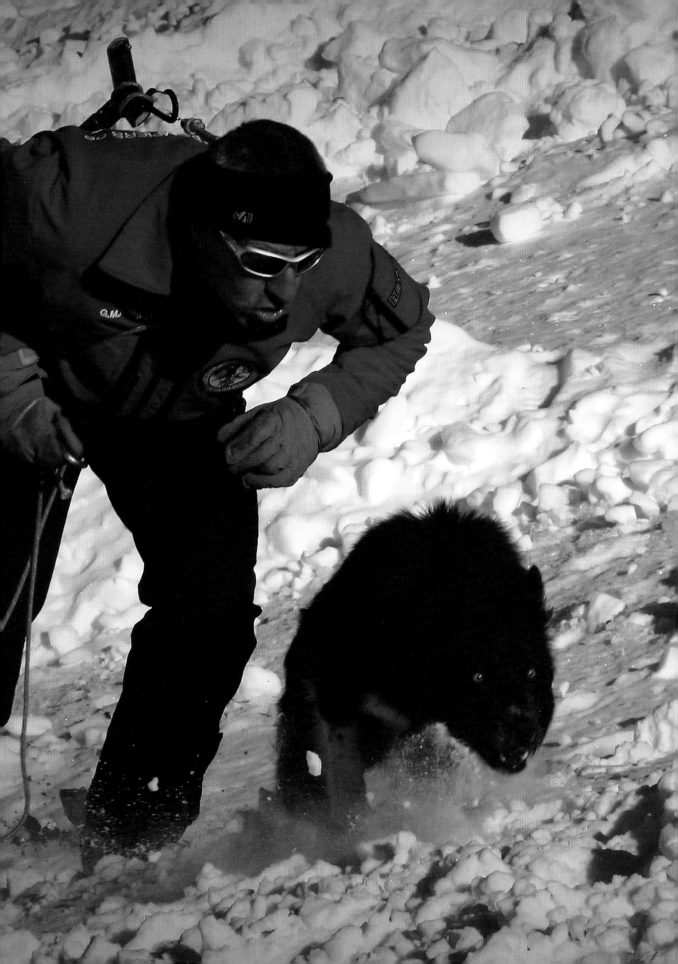

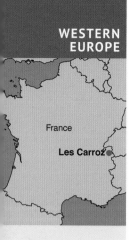

France

Les Carroz

Access
Nearest airport:
Geneva (80km)

Ability Level
Beginner – expert

Season
Dec – Apr

Other Local Activities
Snowshoeing, ice
skating, dog-sledding,
ice rink, skijoring,
hiking, outdoor pool

**Resort Stats (Grand
Massif Ski area)**
Top: 2,480m
Bottom: 700m
Vertical: 1,780m
Lifts: 69
Pistes: 265km

www.lescarroz.com

LES CARROZ, FRANCE
100 years old and still going strong

Les Carroz makes up part of the Grand Massif ski area – the fifth largest linked ski area in France – and is home to a classic of freeriding, the mighty Combe de Gers.

This huge, snow-choked bowl is the epitome of 'freeride' – slopes of different gradient and different aspect spread out over 800 metres of vertical, a few trees at the bottom to add interest, a hideously long and steep drag lift as the only means out and, three days after a snowfall, it's still possible to find untracked lines here.

It's also a neighbour of Flaine, and two more different ski resorts than Flaine and Les Carroz would be hard to imagine. Flaine is famous for its no-nonsense, utilitarian modern Brutalist architecture, whereas Les Carroz, which you pass on the way up to Flaine, is a much more traditional alpine village in a lovely balcony setting amongst trees.

One reason why Les Carroz is so much prettier than Flaine is that it recently turned 100 years of age, and as such is one of France's oldest, and therefore most traditional, ski resorts.

In short it's a pretty, bustling town in an attractive location and offers great skiing – not to mention being less than an hour from Geneva – what's not to like?

That's not to say Flaine isn't worth a visit, especially since it's so easy to access from Les Carroz. The austere apartments for which it is famed are what they are – and love them or loathe them they have, along with similar accommodation blocks in the likes of La Plagne, Les Arcs and Avoriaz, allowed skiers on a tight budget to enjoy the pleasure of the mountains and ensure that the sport has become far less elitist than it once was.

And if the 'urban' environment and hubbub of Flaine's lower slopes is all too much, just hop aboard the Grand Platières gondola, hop off again at what is the 2,480-metre high point of the Grand Massif and enjoy one of the best views in the French Alps. The entire Mont Blanc Massif is almost within touching distance, and you can see all the region's iconic peaks (Grandes Jorrases, Aiguille du Midi, Mont Blanc, Dome du Gouter, etc.).

From here skiers of pretty much any ability can enjoy the 14km Pistes de Cascades, a blue run which winds its way from the high alpine down through cool green forests to Sixt at 760 metres.

There's some fun off-piste to the sides of the run too, with the easily angled slopes and proximity to the piste making a great introduction to freeriding, the more so given the amazing views of truly wild alpine scenery along with the prospect of spotting wildlife such as bearded vultures, ibex and chamois.

There are no ski lifts in Sixt but a free bus to Samoëns village allows you to gradually return to Les Carroz via a mix of ski lifts, wide, open pistes and, if it appeals, a sneaky little run through woodland down a 'ski rando' trail, by the end of which you'll have done pretty much a full circuit of the Grand Massif.

That said, you'll have only scratched the surface of what's on offer – which makes the perfect excuse to spend a few more days in Les Carroz checking it all out.

Les Carroz – a traditional resort © www.lescarroz.com

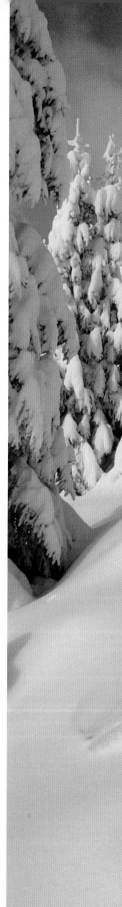

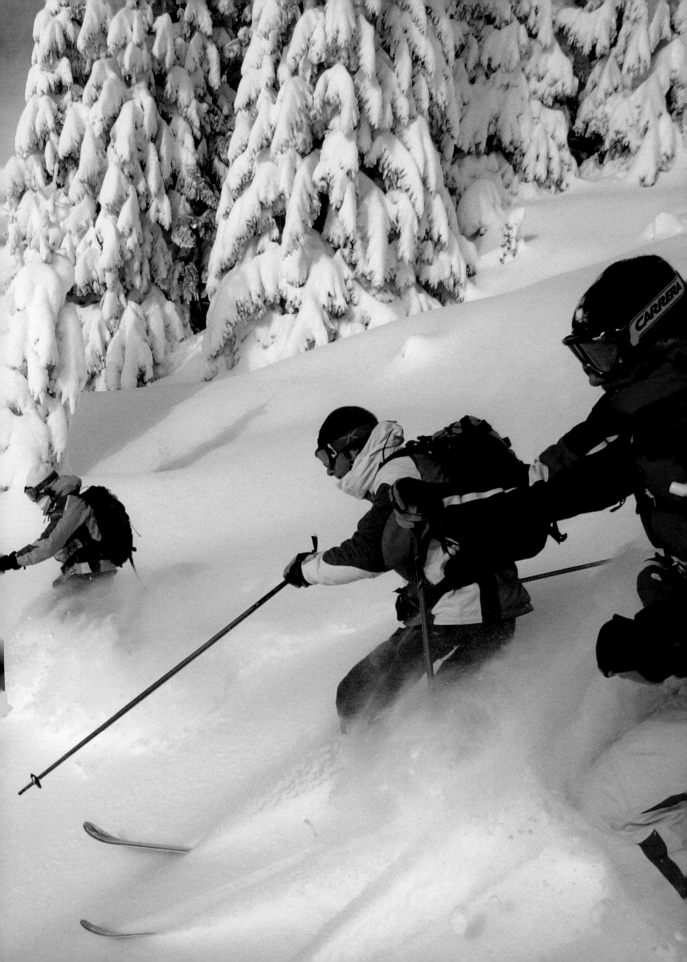

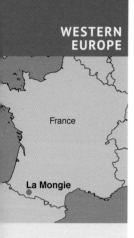

France

La Mongie

Access
Nearest airports:
Lourdes (48km),
Pau (116km)

Ability Level
Beginner – expert

Season
Dec – Apr

Other Local Activities
Snowshoeing, dog-
sledding, cross-
country skiing

Resort Stats
Top: 2,500m
Bottom: 1,400m
Vertical: 1,100m
Lifts: 34
Pistes: 100km

www.n-py.com

LA MONGIE, FRENCH PYRENEES
Back to the Seventies

At the centre of the Grand Tourmalet ski area in the French Pyrenees, the purpose-built resort of La Mongie is defiantly Seventies in style and appearance, which won't appeal to everyone; but this isn't really a problem as the village is lost in a huge snow bowl amongst the imposing peaks of the Midi-Pyrenees which soar above, culminating in the 2,872-metre Pic du Midi de Bigorre and its summit observatory which looks every bit the lair of a James Bond villain.

You can access the Pic du Midi by cable car from the centre of town, and from the summit there are various off-piste descents. For confident skiers this is likely to be one of the main reasons for visiting La Mongie.

All the descents of the Pic du Midi are steep and challenging however, so you may want to psyche yourself up by spending the night here first – the observatory offers overnight accommodation which includes dinner and a tour of the observatory, not to mention incredible sunsets (no Bond villain, though...).

Even if you have no desire to take on the steeps of the Pic du Midi it's worth the ride up to the observatory just for the panorama, which stretches from Catalonia to the Basque Country; and you can take the lift back down when you've had your fill and enjoy a good selection of red and blue runs above La Mongie.

Freeriders will love not just the Pic du Midi but also the surprisingly large array of side- and backcountry terrain. For intermediates there's an enticing selection of often sunny, uncrowded pistes (the long, blue-graded Bergers is a classic) along with attractive tree runs above Bareges, which as an authentic alpine village is considerably prettier than La Mongie.

The more than adequate selection of beginners' slopes are easily accessed as they're right in the centre of La Mongie; and the considerably lower cost of skiing here than in the Alps makes the resort a good option for first-timers.

In recent years the region has seen excellent snowfalls, and, since most of the accommodation in La Mongie is ski in / ski out, it has a lot going for it if you like to spend most of your ski holiday on skis (how else would you spend a ski holiday?).

Why not book into the Crete Blanche hotel in the middle of town but also right beside the pistes? It remains a classic of seventies' style, with all that's needed to complete the picture being Brigitte Bardot and Serge Gainsbourg sipping martinis in the bar whilst clad in tight ski pants and sucking on Gauloises cigarettes.

Not the classic chocolate box alpine hotel, perhaps, but still an authentic piece of French ski culture.

Descending from the Pic du Midi Observatory © Luis Pantoja

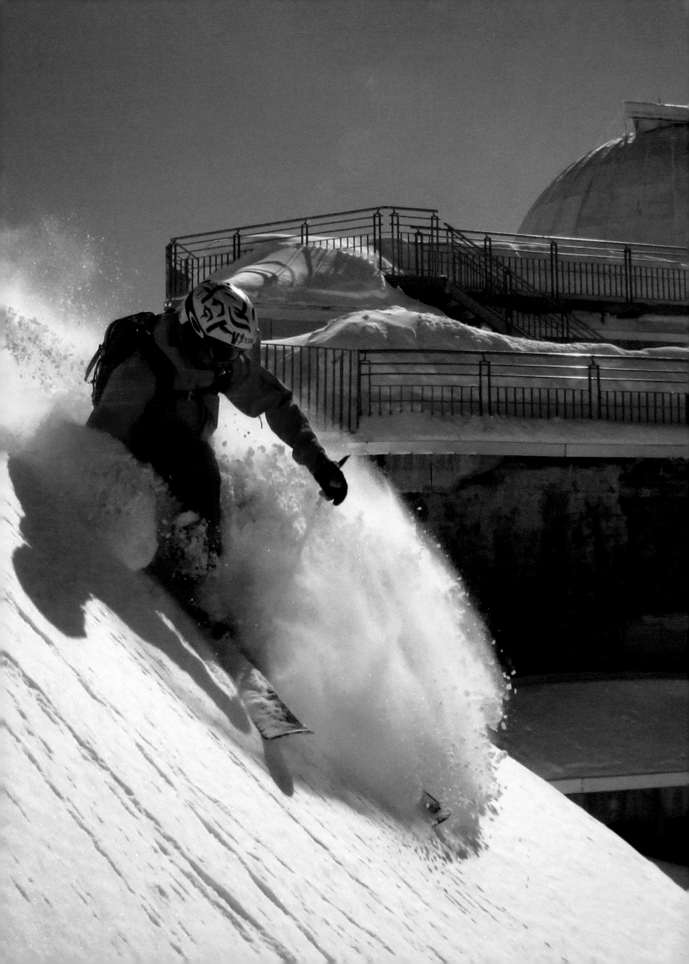

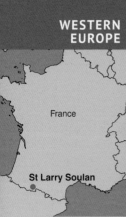

France

St Larry Soulan

Access
Nearest airports:
Lourdes (93km),
Pau (113km),
Toulouse (155km)

Ability Level
Beginner – expert

Season
Dec – Apr

Other Local Activities
Snowshoeing,
snowmobiling, dog-
sledding, ice skating

Resort Stats
Top: 2,515m
Bottom: 1,700m
Vertical: 815m
Lifts: 31
Pistes: 100km

www.saintlary.com

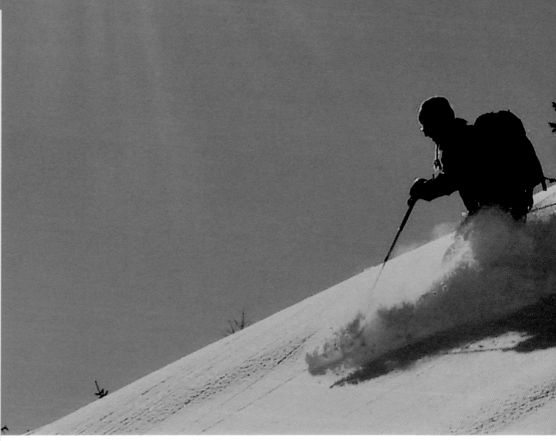

ST LARY-SOULAN, FRENCH PYRENEES
More than first meets the eye

There's a popular misconception that the ski resorts of the Pyrenees are small and therefore somewhat limited in what they have to offer – visit St Lary-Soulan and you'll soon be disabused of that notion.

St Lary-Soulan is one of the biggest resorts in the French Pyrenees with around 100km of pistes, 31 lifts and plenty of decent backcountry terrain, so it will easily keep you going for days if not weeks; and for those who really like variety in their ski trips you're only 2.5-hour's drive from the Atlantic coast and its world class surf – worth considering if you encounter bad snow conditions, maybe...

The skiing is accessed from the pretty village of St Lary (Soulan is a separate hamlet lumped in with St Lary when describing the ski area) via either a gondola or cable car which take you up to St Lary 1700, where there are some decent beginner slopes (you can pay for a pass just for 1700, incidentally).

Above this the fun begins, with a good selection of intermediate pistes, a handful of blacks and, in

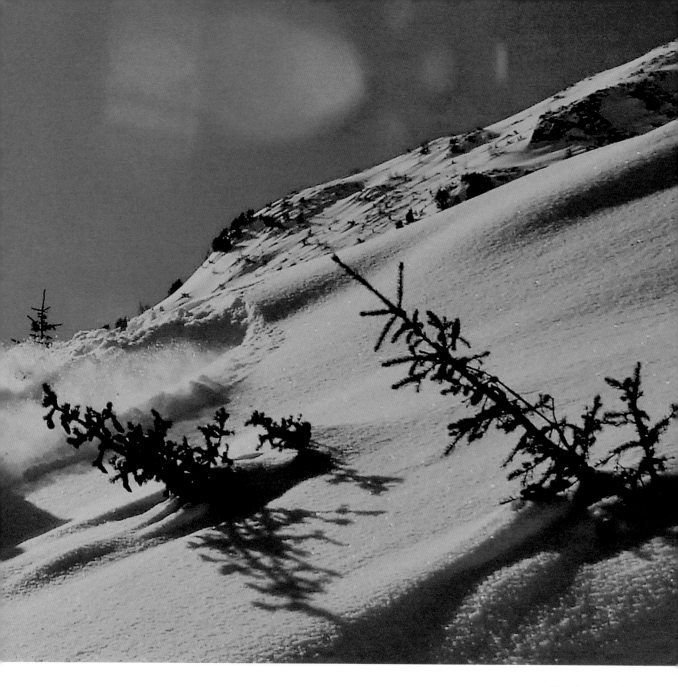

More than enough at
St Lary-Soulan
© Alf Alderson

good snow conditions, some very acceptable off-piste terrain at Soum de Matte and Courne Blanque. This in particular should prove to you that the Pyrenees should not be underestimated – just because the Alps are bigger doesn't mean they're necessarily better, and another great aspect of skiing at St Lary-Soulan is the very relaxed and friendly vibe about the place – it's a resort that doesn't feel quite so serious and severe about its skiing as the likes of Chamonix and La Grave, which is no bad thing since we're here to have fun, after all.

The layout of the terrain – a mixture of open slopes and rocky ridges – also provides you with some fine panoramas of the beautiful Pyrenees National Park, home to brown bears and vultures, although it's unlikely you'll see the former, which are not only very scarce but will also be hibernating for most of the ski season.

You'll also find that the cost of skiing in the French Pyrenees tends to be lower than in the French Alps, and for bon viveurs the restaurants often have more varied fare than the relentlessly cheese-based dishes of the Alps.

All of which combine to make a good case for paying a visit...

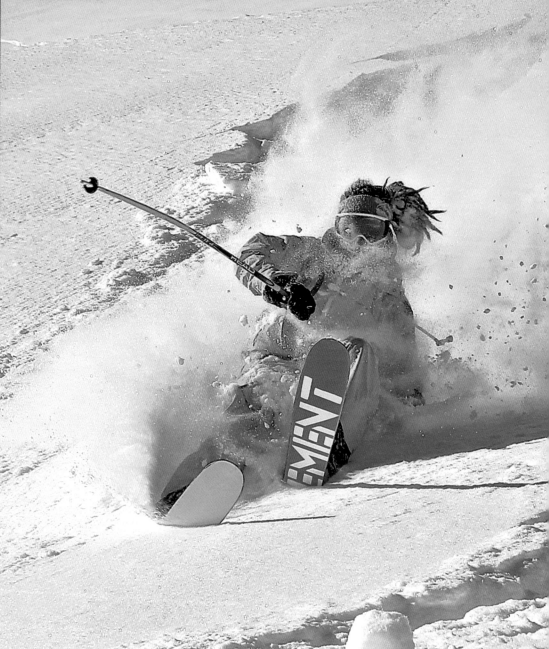

Germany

France

Switzerland

● Monterosa Ski

Italy

Access
Nearest airport:
Turin (110km)

Ability Level
Beginner – expert

Season
Nov – Apr

Other Local Activities
Heli-skiing,
snowshoeing, cross-
country skiing, ice
skating, ice climbing,
hiking

Resort Stats
Top: 3,275m
Bottom: 1,200m
Vertical: 2,075m
Lifts: 37
Pistes: 180km

www.visitmonterosa.
com

MONTEROSA SKI, ITALY
The Italian 'Three Valleys'

Unlike the giant 'Trois Vallées' with its 600km of pistes, Italy's 'three valleys' – Champoluc and the associated two Monterosa Ski resorts of Gressoney and Alagna – have less than 200km of pistes, but bigger isn't necessarily better.

For a start, in the Trois Vallées you'd be hard pressed to ski to a traditional mountain hamlet such as Cunéaz, an old Walser village where the residents traditionally spoke a German dialect called Titsch, as you can here, for in France's mega-resort the old is most definitely out in favour of the new. And Cunéaz serves to emphasise the charm of the Monterosa Ski area generally.

Each valley in Monterosa Ski is made up of one main village and additional smaller hamlets, all of which retain an unspoilt character and an alpine ambience which undoubtedly adds to the ski experience.

And as for the skiing – well, for its size Monterosa Ski packs a hell of a punch; from quiet, grin-

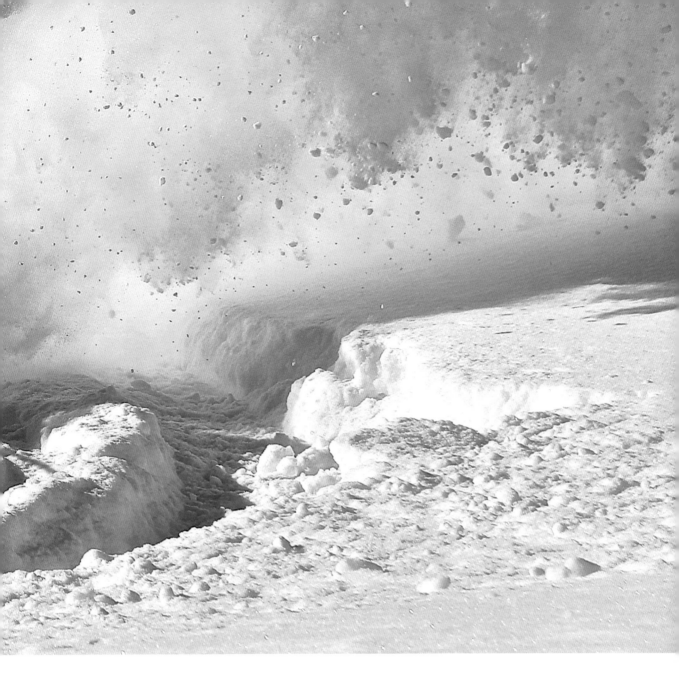

inducing reds, even quieter whoop-it-up blacks to awesome off-piste such as that above the villages of Frachey and Stafal, there's more than enough to go at (not to mention heli-skiing if you're feeling flush).

And then there's the never-less-than-spectacular scenery, with a remarkable array of 4,000-metre peaks always on the near horizon – Matterhorn, Breithorn, Castore, Piramide Vincent, etc., etc. Don't forget your camera – you are, after all, skiing amongst the Monte Rosa Massif (hence the name of the ski area), which is the second highest range in the Alps.

As for the villages that make up Monterosa Ski, Champoluc is the largest and has a certain low-key charm, Gressoney is a rustic little settlement located in the middle of the ski area and as such is well-placed for exploring in all directions, and Alagna is a remote, picturesque old Walser village tucked away beneath impressive peaks which offer some of the best and steepest off-piste terrain in the ski area.

Like many Italian ski resorts things are generally pretty quiet here during the week – and even more so at lunch time, for Italians love to eat, drink and talk (loudly) over a long lunch, which is when you'll have the best chance of getting the slopes to yourself.

And if you hit the area after a good dump, on a fine, sunny day, you'll soon realise that the best things in skiing don't always come in big packages.

Monterosa Ski – Italy's impressive answer to France's Three Valleys © Archivio Fotografico Monterosa Ski

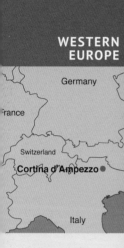

Germany

France

Switzerland

Cortina d'Ampezzo ●

Italy

Access
Nearest airports:
Treviso (140km),
Venice (150km)
Mainline station in
town

Ability Level
Beginner – expert

Season
Dec – Apr

Other Local Activities
Snowshoeing, cross-
country skiing, hiking,
people watching

Resort Stats
Top: 2,930m
Bottom: 1,225m
Vertical: 1,705m
Lifts: 34
Pistes: 115km

www.dolomiti.org

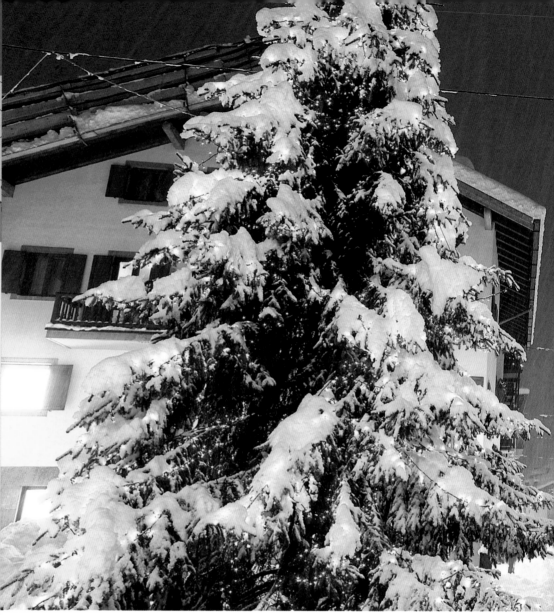

CORTINA D'AMPEZZO, ITALY
Ski amongst the most beautiful mountains on Earth

One of the most exotic names in skiing, one of the most romantic towns in skiing, and one of the most beautiful locations in skiing – Cortina has a lot going for it. Describing the Dolomite Mountains, amongst which Cortina is set, as the most beautiful on Earth may be a big claim, but once seen in the glow of the evening sun you'll never forget them.

And yet many visitors don't come here so much to ski as to be seen – dressed up to the nines in the latest ski wear at some fancy mountain restaurant or strolling the piazza of an evening in furs and make-up (and that's just the men), there's always great people watching to be had either on or off the pistes.

This has its advantages – if you're serious about your skiing you'll rarely find the more challenging slopes too busy, and even the easier pistes can be very sparsely occupied at lunchtime.

That said the options are limited for better skiers unless you use a guide to access the incredibly beautiful backcountry. But for beginners and intermediates it's a wonderful resort – and, as already noted, scenically there are few in the world to compare.

Unfortunately, most of Cortina's ski areas are only linked by bus, which can be a hassly way of

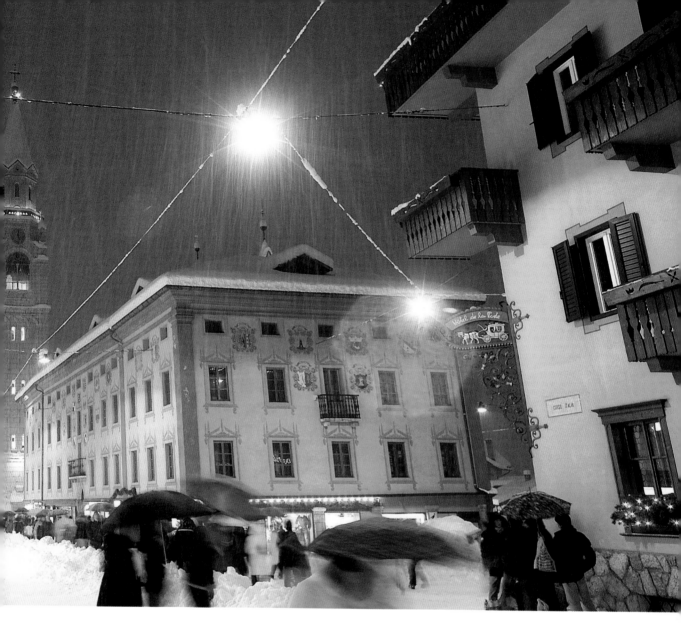

getting to the slopes, especially in ski boots. That said the bus service is free with your lift pass and very efficient. And as an added bonus you also have access to the mighty Dolomiti Superski area, which claims to have 1,200km of groomed slopes spread out across twelve resorts.

Of the various ski areas, the most accessible from town is Faloria, reached via a cable car near the bus station. From here you can access the spectacular terrain of Cristallo with its challenging black run Forcella Staunies, along with some even more challenging off-piste terrain over the back of the mountain.

Just north of town is the small Mietres ski area, which consists mainly of blue and red runs. The most dramatic ski area is Tofana, which rises to 2,830 metres and is reached via a number of linked cable cars from just outside town. From here you can also access Cortina's largest ski area of Pomedes and the popular Socrapes beginners' runs.

Also available on a Cortina ski pass – and well worth a visit despite the 20-minute bus ride to get there – is the spectacular terrain of Cinque Torres, from where you can access the small, north facing Col Gallina area, and the mighty crags of Lagazuoi from where you descend into the Hidden Valley.

All skiers, even committed freeride fiends, will enjoy the lovely Hidden Valley red run (it's only really red at the top) through magnificent mountain scenery and finishing with a horse-drawn lift ride – and before you set off, check out the fascinating First World War tunnels and defences burrowed into Mount Lagazuoi.

Sun or snow, Cortina is a magical ski destination
© bandio.it

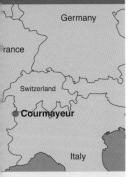

Germany

France

Switzerland

● **Courmayeur**

Italy

Access
Nearest airports:
Geneva (110km),
Turin (150km)
Mainline station in
Pré St Didier (5km)

Ability Level
Beginner – expert

Season
Nov/Dec – Apr

Other Local Activities
Heli-skiing, snow-
shoeing, cross-country
skiing, hiking, ice
climbing, fat biking,
ski mountaineering

Resort Stats
Top: 2,755m
Bottom: 1,210m
Vertical: 1,545m
Lifts: 18
Pistes: 41km

www.courmayeur
montblanc.it

COURMAYEUR, ITALY
In the shadow of Mont Blanc

Courmayeur doesn't just sit in the shadow of Mont Blanc (known hereabouts as Monte Bianco) it also, to some extent, sits in the shadow of Chamonix, which lies on the other (north) side of Europe's highest mountain.

And it really shouldn't, for the setting on Mont Blanc's sunny south slopes is no less dramatic than that of the mountain's French face, with spectacular glaciated crags and peaks looming over the picturesque cobbled streets of the old mountain town, and the skiing is excellent, as well as being less busy than in Chamonix, whilst the mountain restaurants are by and large far superior.

But comparisons can be odious, especially when it comes to ski resorts – everywhere is great on a powder day – so let's move quickly on.

The size of Courmayeur's ski area is relatively modest but the setting is so magnificent that even if you got bored with the skiing you could never get bored with the views, and there's some fantastic off-piste action to be enjoyed on the slopes of Monte Bianco, as we shall hereon call it.

Courmayeur allows skiers of all abilities to enjoy skiing in one of the most spectacular settings in the Alps and, despite having only around 41km of pistes, they're varied and interesting. It's likely to appeal mainly to intermediates who will enjoy the selection of often quite challenging red runs.

The ski area is laid out into two distinct zones – the Checrouit area, which catches the morning sun and is accessed from the Checrouit gondola, and the north-west facing Val Veny area, which is usually best skied in the afternoon when it is in the sun.

Checrouit has a nice array of wide, open mainly red runs and is also dotted with good mountain restaurants for when you need a break. The highest accessible point for piste skiing is 2,624-metre Cresta Youla – from here a series of reds and blues will take you almost 1,400 metres all the way back down to the Dolonne car park just above Courmayeur.

The Val Veny area can be easily accessed from Checrouit too, or by cable car directly. Here you'll find steeper, more challenging terrain with some great black runs mixed in amongst these such as Black 23 and Pista dell Orso. These take you through trees and provide marvellous views of the Monte Bianco massif.

But it's the freeride terrain that is the feather in Courmayeur's ski helmet. The resort has become a bit of a freeride mecca, having hosted the Freeride World Tour in the past, and given the extent and nature of the terrain, particularly on Monte Bianco's wild, glaciated and crevassed slopes (accessed by the spectacular Skyway Monte Bianco rotating cable car – as seen in *Kingsman 2*), it's well worth employing a guide to ensure you make the most of it.

In addition, you can access the famous Vallée Blanche from the top station, although you will have to get yourself back to Courmayeur from Chamonix when you finish.

You can also enjoy heli-skiing from Courmayeur, with a classic outing being the 20km descent down the Ruitor Glacier to Sainte Foy in France, from where you take a taxi to La Rosière (see page 36) then a combination of ski lifts, pistes and taxi back to the resort of La Thuile and, eventually, Courmayeur.

Into the shadows, Courmayeur © Allessandro Belluscio

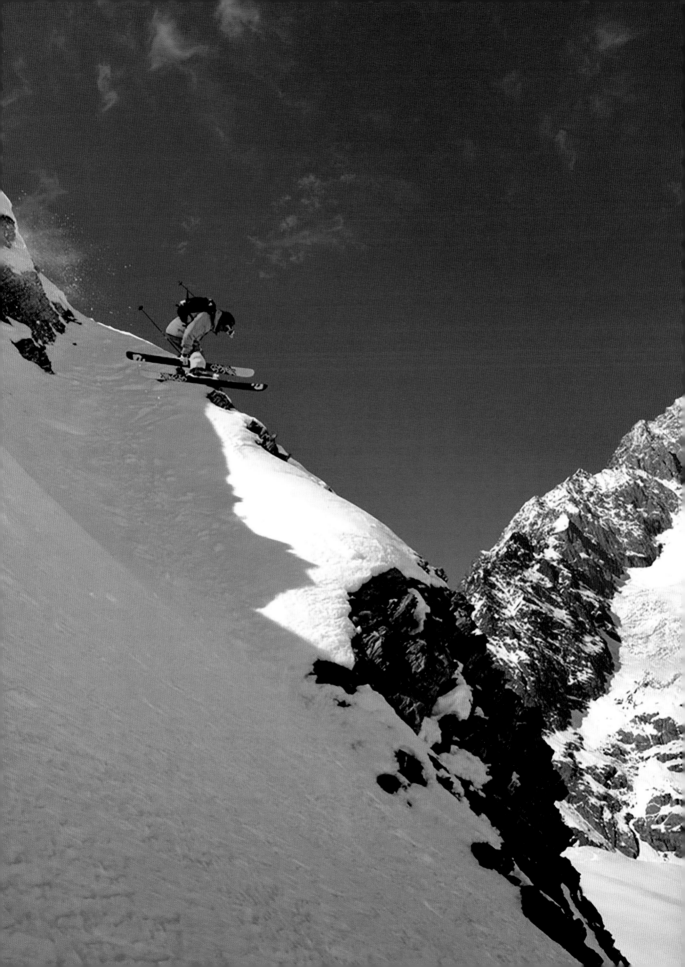

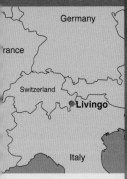

Germany

France

Switzerland

● Livingo

Italy

Access
Nearest airports:
Bolzano (135km),
Innsbruck (180km)

Ability Level
Beginner – expert

Season
Nov – Apr/May

Other Local Activities
Snowshoeing, cross-
country skiing, ice
skating, tobogganing,
dog-sledding,
snowmobiling

Resort Stats
Top: 2,795m
Bottom: 1,815m
Vertical: 980m
Lifts: 30
Pistes: 115km

www.livigno.eu
www.heliski-livigno.
com

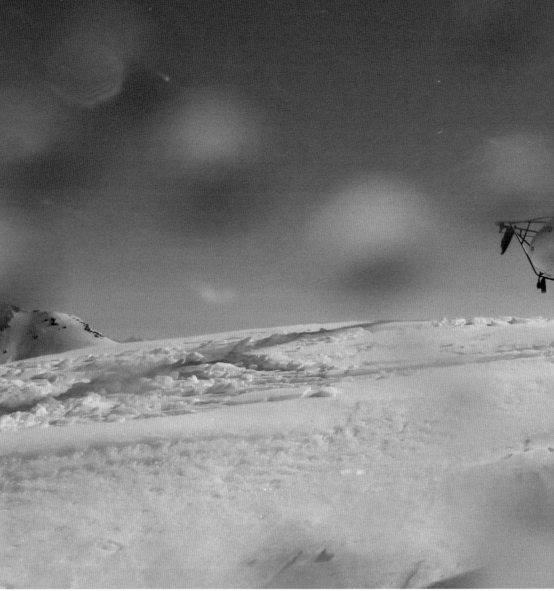

LIVIGNO, ITALY
Flying high

Heli-skiing is, of course, the domain of rich, expert skiers. Or is it? In Livigno you can spend a morning heli-skiing for a fraction of what you'll shell out in better known heli-ski destinations. And what's more, you don't need to be an expert to enjoy it.

There are heli-ski packages available in Livigno for first-time heli-skiers from under €200. You'll need to be a decent off-piste skier, but certainly not an 'expert' and, along with the guarantee of amazing skiing, the deal also includes all the specialist gear (fat skis, avalanche safety gear, etc.) along with advice and tips from your ski guide on how to make the most of your first heli-ski experience.

Livigno's high altitude virtually guarantees great snow conditions, with runs starting from over 3,000 metres and dropping all the way down to 1,800 metres, during which you'll discover the wild, remote peaks of the Stelvio National Park without another skier in sight other than your heli-ski companions.

And, of course, there's the thrill of zooming through the mountains in a helicopter, which is almost as exciting as the skiing.

Clearly things are changing in what was once regarded as a cheap and cheerful destination for skiers

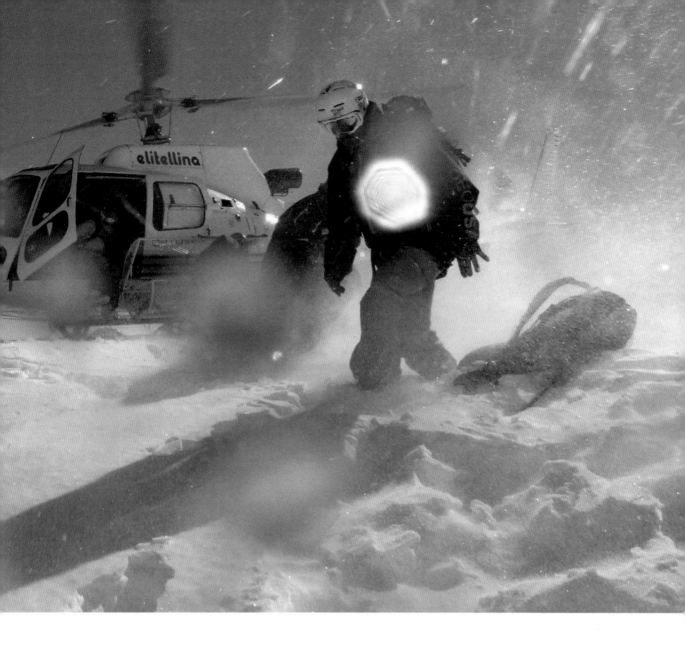

Man-made blizzard above
Livigno © Alf Alderson

looking for undemanding fun on the pistes and plenty of good value après-ski action (although all these are still very readily available in Livigno).

And the resort has also taken the freeride phenomenon on board as well as heli-skiing, making it as easy as possible for visitors to access the plentiful off-piste terrain above the town – a far cry from the past, since up until 2012/13 off-piste skiing was actually banned here.

This has involved opening up a large freeride area on the back of the Mottolino pistes – this remains unpisted but stacks of information on snow conditions, avalanche risk, snow safety and use of safety equipment is made freely available to skiers wishing to access it, whilst some areas are only accessible with a guide.

There's also a free weekly 'lecture' and video every Sunday evening at the local brewery (great venue!) where freeride experts provide you with all the necessary information about riding safely as well as showing you how to check the daily Avalanche Report so you can experience the backcountry as safely as possible.

A detailed daily analysis of snow data is emailed to literally hundreds of local outlets including ski shops and hotels and even broadcast on TV screens on the free local ski buses, and there's info all over the lift stations and slopes on where and how to ski off-piste safely.

So, there's no excuse for not staying as safe as possible when you head off-piste – and there's no excuse for not exploring Livigno's snow-sure backcountry, even if you don't do it in a helicopter.

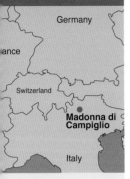

Germany

ance

Switzerland

Madonna di Campiglio

Italy

Access
Nearest airports:
Verona (150km),
Bergamo (180km)

Ability Level
Beginner – expert

Season
Dec – Apr

Other Local Activities
Snowshoeing, cross-country skiing, ice skating

Resort Stats
Top: 2,505m
Bottom: 1,520m
Vertical: 985m
Lifts: 61
Pistes: 150km

www.
campigliodolomiti.it

MADONNA DI CAMPIGLIO, ITALY

Easy does it

If you like your skiing to be fun, but not too challenging, and you want to sample some of the best that Italy has to offer in terms of alpine scenery, you owe it to yourself to check out Madonna di Campiglio.

Beginners and intermediates will love the skiing here, and there's plenty of Italian pizzazz to go alongside it – wander around the pleasant town centre after a day on the slopes and you'll see as much tasteless fur and jewellery on display as in a Milan fashion house.

Lift-accessed skiing in Madonna di Campiglio dates back to the 1930s – renowned for the impeccable quality of its pistes and the preponderance of beginner and intermediate runs, Madonna di Campiglio is the kind of place that will massage your ski ego at the same time as providing great pistes on which to develop your technique.

It's also located beneath some wonderfully scenic mountains, of which the Monte Spinale/Grosté area above the tree line to the east of the town stands out. Over it loom the huge and impressive granite cliffs of Pietra Grande, which dwarf the skiers below – the Graffer blue run starting at the top of 2,504-metre Grosté links in with other blues lower down the mountain to take you on a long, undemanding but exhilarating run all the way back into town.

Another great attraction for intermediate skiers is the opportunity to get out and explore on your skis. Beside Monte Spinale/Grosté, there are two other fine ski areas accessible from the town, Cinque Laghi and Pradalago, both of which have plenty of long blue and red tree-lined cruisers.

All three areas are linked at valley level and from the latter two you can explore the Marilleva and Folgarida areas, where yet again more long, wide cruisers provide fine skiing down into shadowy tree-lined slopes, whilst the Pinzolo area is accessible via a gondola from the Cinque Laghi – here you'll find a nice selection of steep red and black runs and generally good snow conditions.

Beginner skiers will find that Madonna di Campiglio offers a great introduction to the sport – not only does it provide all the character and atmosphere you would expect of a classic alpine resort, it also has some excellent learner slopes at Campo Carlo Magno, and within a couple of days on skis you'll find around half of Madonna's runs accessible to you, some several kilometres in length, and unlike in many resorts a novice skier in their first week can access the top levels of all lifts and find a way down that isn't too demanding.

For more experienced skiers, you can still have fun on a handful of challenging black runs, of which the most exciting are the steep but short Canelone Miramonti just above town and the longer Spinale Diretissima on the opposite side of the valley, whilst the best off-piste is perhaps amongst the trees beneath the Genziana chair – and whatever kind of skier you are, you can enjoy the magnificent views, which are amongst the best in the Brenta Dolomites – and that's saying something.

World-class piste skiing in Madonna di Campiglio © A. Trovorli

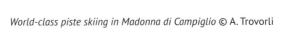

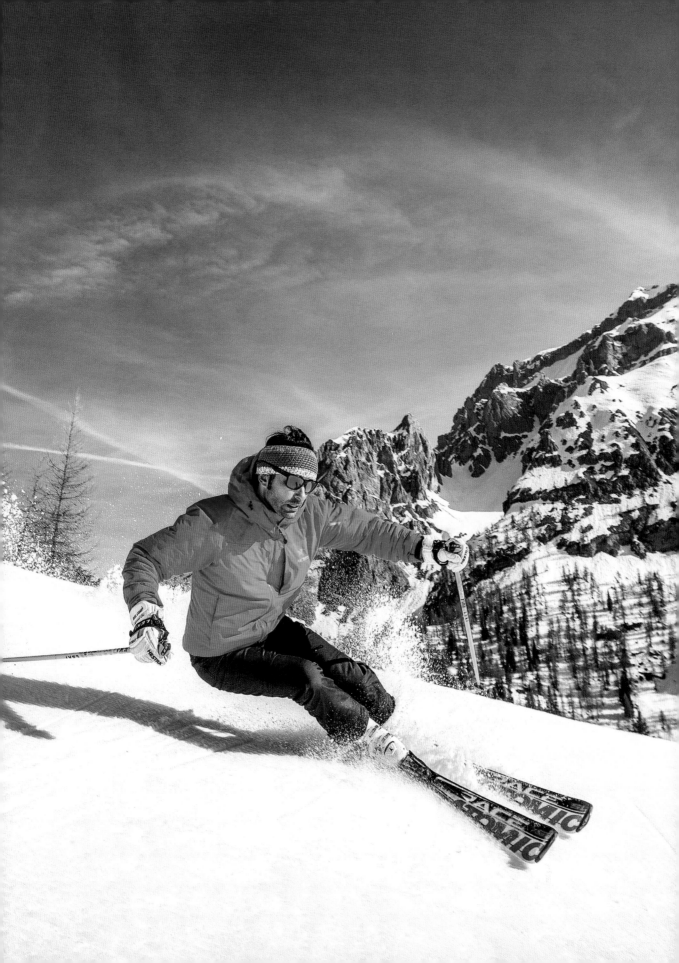

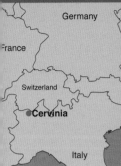

Germany

France

Switzerland

●Cervinia

Italy

Access
Nearest airports:
Turin (120km),
Milan Malpensa
(185km),
Milan Linate (205km),
Geneva (205km)

Ability Level
Beginner – expert

Season
Oct – May

Other Local Activities
Snowshoeing, cross-
country skiing, ice
skating

Resort Stats
Top: 3,480m
Bottom: 1,525m
Vertical: 1,955m
Lifts: 19
Pistes: 160km

www.cervinia.it

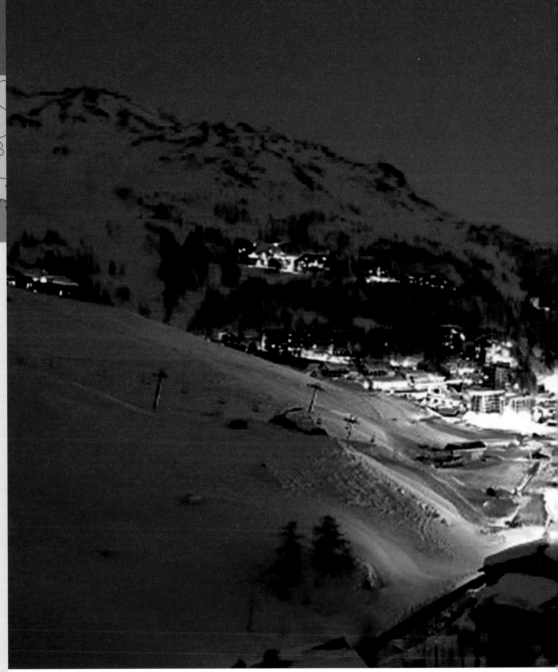

CERVINIA, ITALY
Don't forget your camera

It's easy to end up with a stiff neck when skiing Cervinia – not necessarily from any tumbles in the snow, but from constantly gazing skywards to the spectacular summit of the mighty Matterhorn, which looms over the resort advertising 24 hours a day that this is what a proper mountain should look like.

Hopping off the Bontadini chair at 3,301-metre Theodulpass, the Premier League of 4,000-metre European peaks parade themselves before you, including (in no particular order) Mont Blanc in the distance, Monte Rosa, Liskamm, Breithorn, Dent d'Herens and, of course, the Matterhorn itself.

You don't get the classic view of Matterhorn from Cervinia, that honour is held by Zermatt (page 82) over on the Swiss side of the mountain, which you can readily ski to from Cervinia, but nevertheless it's easy to spend almost as much time gawping in the direction of towering mountains and the various glaciers that tumble down their flanks as in actually skiing.

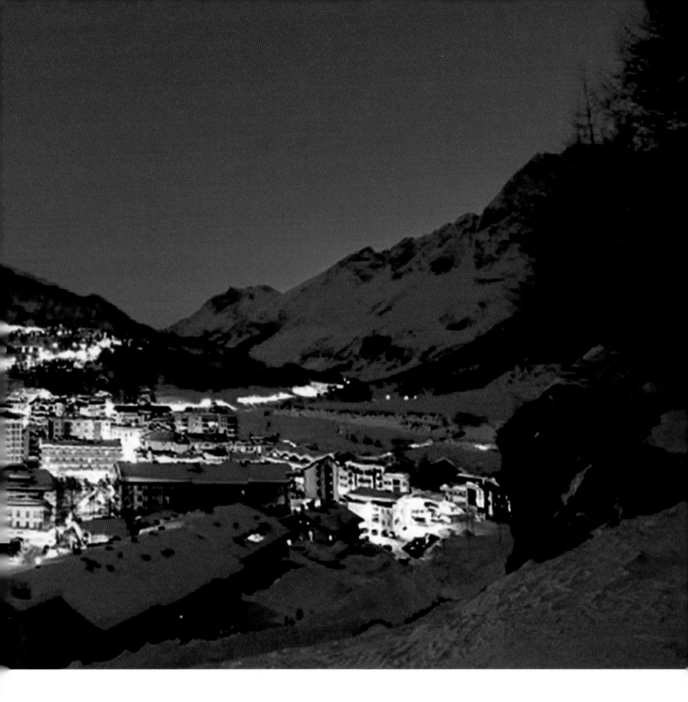

Cervinia – pretty at night,
spectacular during the day
© www.cervinia.it

Almost, but not quite.

The thing about Cervinia is that it's high and wide, it's snow sure (ensuring a very long ski season), it's often sunny and you can generally zoom along to your heart's content, practising your technique or just enjoying the simple pleasure of skiing in a magnificent setting.

It's possible to follow the sun around the slopes on a selection of red and blue runs that will keep anyone smiling – particularly Cervinia's classic red run, the 11km Ventina.

There's nothing especially challenging about the Ventina, any half-decent intermediate skier will handle it with ease, its appeal lies in the fact that it just rolls, twists and turns on and on, seemingly forever, through the most glorious of scenery, with the opportunity to stop and gawp and/or ease tired legs whenever you like. I commend it to you...

But there again, I'd commend pretty much any other red run in Cervinia to anyone who simply wants a fun day out in the high mountains. And if you're looking for something a little bit more challenging, why not head over the border to Zermatt where the slopes tend to be a bit steeper, or check out the off-piste above Plan Torrette, which can remain untracked for days after a fresh dump.

Oh, and one last thing – don't forget your camera...

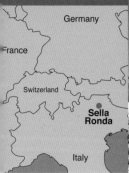

Germany

France

Switzerland

Sella
Ronda

Italy

Access
Nearest airports
to Selva:
Bolzano (50km),
Innsbruck (120km),
Verona (195km)

Ability Level
Intermediate – expert

Season
Dec – Apr

Other Local Activities
Snowshoeing, cross-
country skiing, hiking,
tobogganing, sleigh
rides

Resort Stats
Top: 3,270m
Bottom: 1,005m
Vertical: 2,265m
Lifts: 179
Pistes: 433km

www.valgardena.it

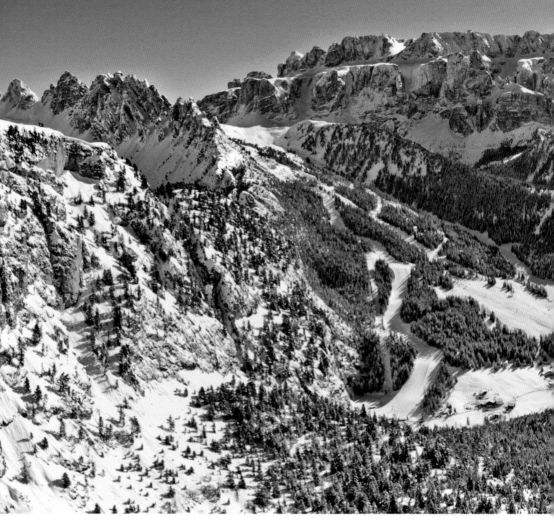

SELLA RONDA, ITALY
One of the world's finest – and longest – lift-accessed ski circuits

The Sella Ronda ski tour is based on an ancient high-level trading route that crosses four of the Sella Massif's main mountain passes, and it can be easily accomplished by any competent intermediate skier in a day. Along the way you'll ski some 23km of fun red and blue runs and ride around 14km on ski lifts, which give you not just the chance to relax between runs but also provide an opportunity to take in the magnificent panoramas as you glide gently uphill.

The route is marked by yellow arrows if you're heading in a clockwise circuit, green if you're going anti-clockwise. Clockwise is most popular and slightly quicker, but some skiers prefer the anti-clockwise route because it's usually less busy.

So grand are the mountains here that all the mechanical jiggery-pokery that you'll be using to get you around is but a blip on the sublime landscapes that it interlaces, and doesn't in any way spoil the view.

The glorious pale yellow and orange limestone peaks, which transform to beautiful warm shades of mauve, pink and purple every dawn and dusk, are a UNESCO World Heritage Site, making them the skier's answer to the Grand Canyon or the Great Barrier Reef.

You can commence the Sella Ronda at any one of a number of pretty mountain villages – Selva,

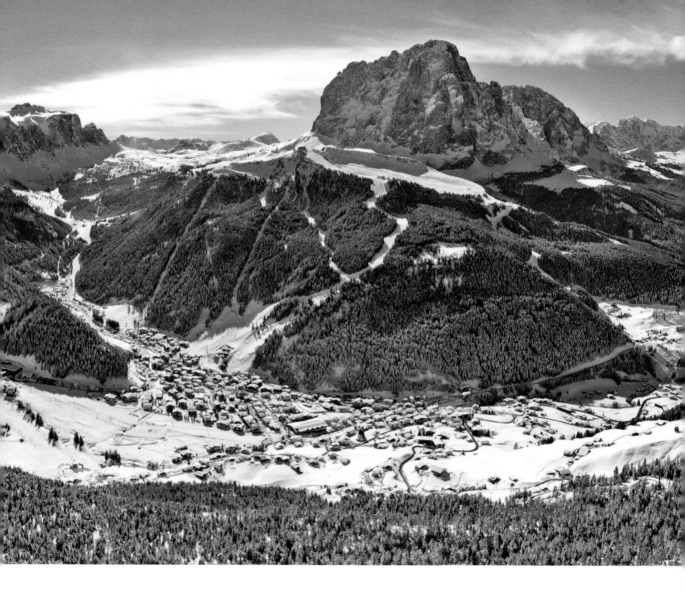

Colfosco, Corvara, Arabba and Canazei are the usual bases. From Selva, for instance it's an easy start, hopping on to what will be one of the day's many ski lifts to ascend to the summit of 2,254-metre Ciampinoi and hit the pistes.

Easy, sunny skiing (the sun shines a lot in the Dolomites) on mostly blue runs will see you approaching the 2,239-metre Pordoi Pass by mid-morning – the views from here are awesome, with the gigantic limestone crags and pinnacles of the Dolomites giving way to shadowy blue lines of mountains stretching away to Austria and Switzerland like an enormous ocean swell.

Beneath the pass you'll see the bulky mausoleum erected to commemorate Italian and Austrian troops who fought each other here between 1915-18 in a little-known theatre of the Great War. The soldiers burrowed into mountainside caves, dug trenches in the snowfields, and created many of the narrow, exposed mountain footpaths known as via ferrata which are now scrambled along each summer by adventurous hikers.

A favoured means of attack in this obscure theatre of war was to fire shells into mountainsides and snowfields above the enemy and bring huge rockfalls and avalanches down on them.

This dismal image will quickly evaporate once you set off again with a rapid, swooping run down to Arabba, from where the Boé gondola transports you to the top of the Passo di Campolongo for yet another fun, fast and undulating red run down into the village of Corvara.

Onwards and upwards, the last leg of the circuit sees you ascending the Passo Gardena for the final long, high speed descent back to Selva, first across wide open alpine pastures before dropping into Val Gardena, which has a long and illustrious skiing history – it's over a century since the first ski races were held locally, and the famed Val Gardena World Cup race takes place here on the steep, camel-backed Saslong World Cup course every December.

A grand day out – part of the Sella Ronda circuit
© valgardena.it

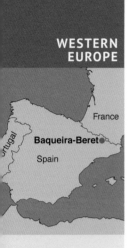

France

Baqueira-Beret

Spain

Portugal

Access
Nearest airports;
Tarbes (136km),
Lleida-Alguaire
(160km),
Toulouse (166km)

Ability Level
Beginner – expert

Season
Dec – Apr

Other Local Activities
Heli-skiing,
snowshoeing, cross-
country skiing

Resort Stats
Top: 2,510m
Bottom: 1,500m
Vertical: 1,010m
Lifts: 28
Pistes: 165km
(Including 'ski routes')

www.baqueira.es

BAQUEIRA-BERET, SPANISH PYRENEES
By royal appointment

Tucked away in a remote corner of the Spanish Pyrenees, Baqueira-Beret may well be one of the most underrated ski resorts in Europe – which could explain why the Spanish royal family has a villa here.

Fortunately royal privilege doesn't extend to getting first lifts and first tracks, although that said even if the entire Spanish royal family decided to take on one of the ungroomed 'itineraries' there would still be plenty of pow left for us mere plebs; a classic is the steep and challenging Escornacrabes, which translates as 'Where Goats Tumble' which, given the legendary sure-footedness of mountain goats, gives you some idea of just how steep it is in places.

Baqueira-Beret is that rare thing, a ski resort with great off-piste terrain that people who like great off-piste terrain rarely visit. They've probably been lured into thinking it's a resort for intermediate and novice skiers, and in many regards it is – there's a very fine selection of red and blue pistes snaking down the three well-connected areas that make up the resort (Baqueira, Beret and Bonaigua), all accessed by a good lift system which seldom sees serious queues, whilst novices will find that the ski schools get good reviews.

But the ski schools shouldn't be eschewed by more experienced skiers looking to head off-piste, as operations such as the Brit-run BB Ski School are regularly praised for the quality of their guiding, and they can also set you up with some of the best-value heli-skiing in Europe.

Another oft-held misconception about the Pyrenees is that they don't get as much snow as the Alps, but Baqueira-Beret regularly receives dumps that many resorts in the bigger mountain ranges to the east would pay good money for – it has had seasons when the base snow level has been as much as 400cm at the end of the season.

And it gets yet better. On a budget? No problem – prices are a third or more cheaper than in swanky resorts like Verbier, whether mountain dining, taking ski lessons or enjoying a night in a tapas bar.

It's worth bearing in mind that the Spanish like to enjoy their après-ski late – 10pm is a common hour to have dinner, following an early evening siesta, and bars and nightclubs will be busy until close on dawn, which is yet again to the advantage of keen skiers since it means the slopes are usually very quiet for the first hour or two after the lifts open as the locals are still partaking of breakfast.

So, by the time they've clipped into their bindings for their first run of the day, you could have scored first tracks on or off-piste and be ready for your morning coffee – or just heading back up the mountain for more of the same.

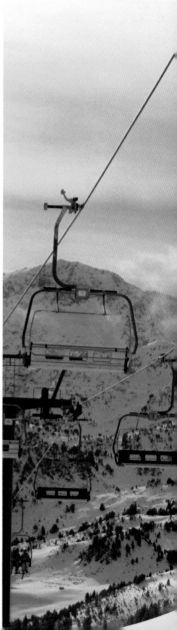

The almost empty chair lift tells its own story © Baqueira-Beret

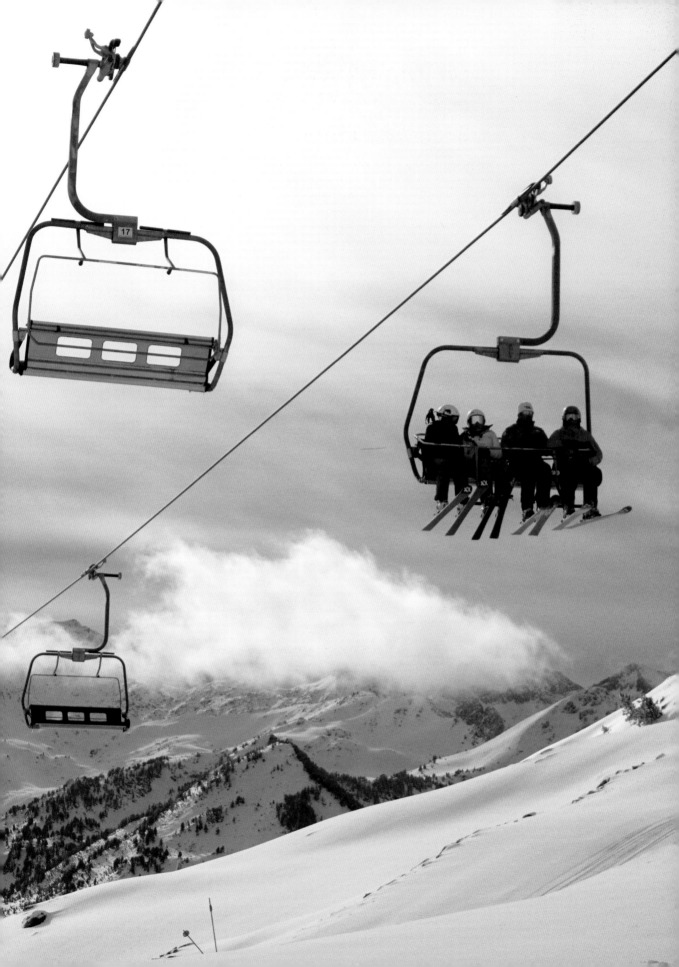

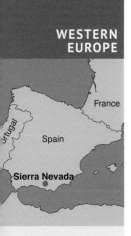

Access
Nearest airports:
Granada (47km),
Malaga (140km)
Nearest train station:
Granada & Malaga

Ability Level
Beginner – expert

Season
Nov/Dec – Apr/May

Other Local Activities
Snowshoeing,
cross-country skiing,
mountain coaster,
tobogganing, snow
tubing, bike-skiing,
skibobbing

Resort Stats
Top: 3,300m
Bottom: 2,100m
Vertical: 1,200m
Lifts: 29
Pistes: 110km

www.sierranevada.es

SIERRA NEVADA, SPAIN
Check out the views

It's a fair bet that there isn't another ski resort in the world that features a different continent on its piste map – for Sierra Nevada, located as it is within view of Spain's Mediterranean coast, and being as high as it is, offers views of Morocco's Rif Mountains – and the piste map makes the most of this unique feature by incorporating both the Med and Morocco into its design.

Given the sunny climate here there's a pretty good chance you'll get to see both the Med and the Rif Mountains – and you're even close enough to the sea to ski in the morning and swim in the afternoon.

Despite the close proximity of Spain's famous holiday beaches, Sierra Nevada (once known perhaps more appropriately as 'Sol-y-Nieve' or 'Sun and Snow') is high enough to be skiable from late November to early May in a good season.

Sierra Nevada's terrain is made up of four areas that are well-linked and lend themselves to intermediate skiers looking to cruise around in warm sunshine and come home with a goggle tan – there are only seven black runs (plus a terrain park) out of an impressive total of 131 pistes, although there is some very passable off-piste to be had in the right conditions.

That said there are also a couple of marked ski touring routes, one from the Virgen de las Nieves chairlift lower station which climbs for 920 vertical metres and 6.2km to the Laguna chairlift upper station near the summit of Veleta, and a second in the Loma de Dilar Area.

The resort's highest point is 3,300 metres, making Sierra Nevada one of the highest ski resorts in Europe, and it also has the longest vertical in Spain – 1,200 metres. From here some of the best red runs take you down through the Laguna de las Yeguas valley and the Valle de San Juan, the latter meandering pleasantly all the way to the stylish, modern base station of Pradollano.

The mountain is usually pretty quiet during the week, but can be busy at weekends when locals come up from nearby Granada and Malaga. Because of the altitude the slopes are all above the tree line, and as such winds can be an issue, sometimes closing the lifts, which gives you a good excuse to visit the nearby city of Granada which is only an hour away and famed for its impressive fortified Alhambra Palace, elaborate Roman Catholic cathedral and great tapas bars.

So, skiing, sea swimming and a bit of culture (and maybe shopping if that's your thing) all on the same trip – Sierra Nevada can genuinely say it has something for everyone.

Sierra Nevada: Pista Olimpica © www.sierranevada.es

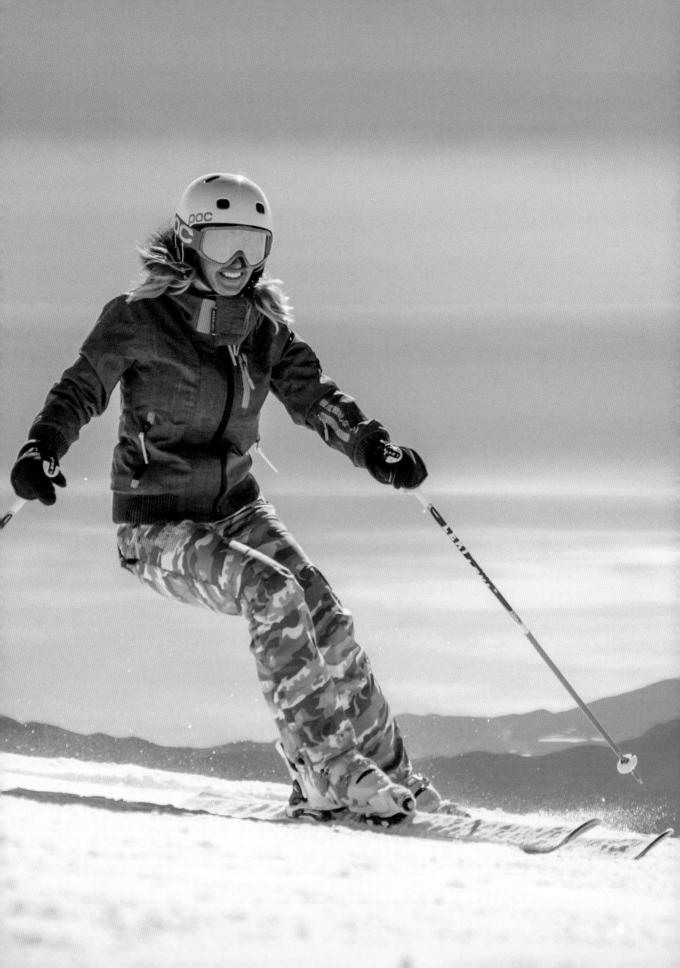

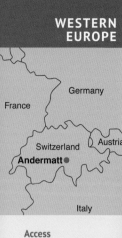

Germany

France

Switzerland · Austria

Andermatt ●

Italy

Access
Nearest airports:
Zurich (109km),
Lugano (110km)
Train station in the
town

Ability Level
Beginner – expert

Season
Nov – May

Other Local Activities
Snowshoeing,
cross-country skiing,
tobogganing, snow
tubing (Sedrun)

Resort Stats
Top: 2,965m
Bottom: 1,445m
Vertical: 1,520m
Lifts: 19
Pistes: 102km

www.andermatt.ch

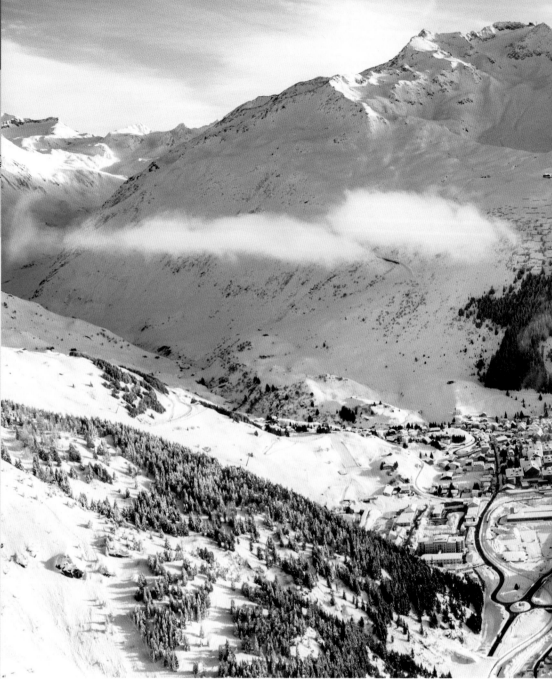

ANDERMATT, SWITZERLAND
Double the fun

Up until a few years ago Andermatt was a small, picturesque, sleepy sort of ski town that attracted skiers looking to take on its steep blacks, fantastic array of off-piste terrain and ski touring.

Then in 2013 a series of luxury developments began to take place on the outskirts of the charming old village, funded by Egyptian billionaire Samih Sawiris on the back of a 130 million Swiss Franc upgrade to the ski area, eventually leading the place to almost double in size. This included new ski lifts, allowing better and faster access to the slopes – whether all this has been for the better depends on who you're talking to, but the slopes and the great skiing are still there, if busier than before.

Things got even bigger and better when Andermatt (now known by the rather convoluted name of SkiArena Andermatt-Sedrun) was linked to the neighbouring resort of Sedrun in 2018/19 to create

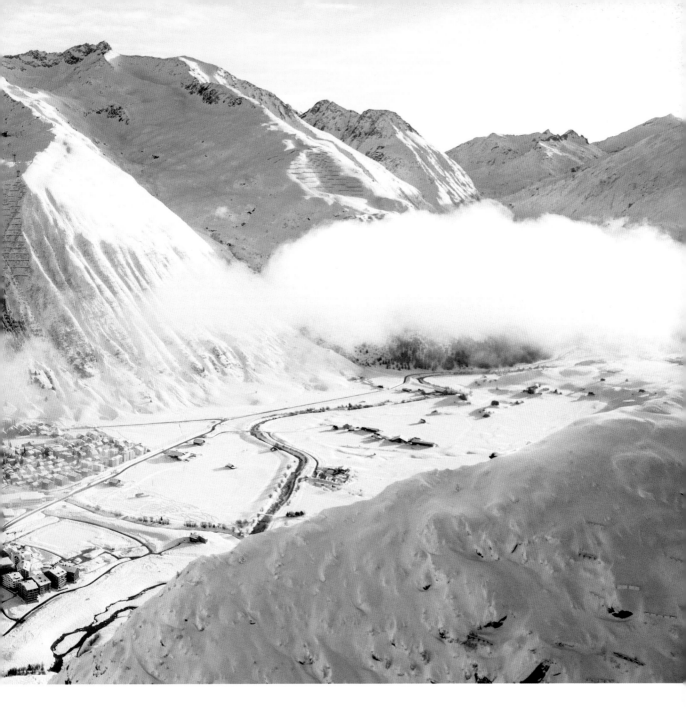

the largest ski area in central Switzerland; this included ten new and upgraded ski lifts (mostly large, high speed chair and gondola lifts) so traditionalists may not be best pleased – the Andermatt of old is no longer really there – but if you welcome everything newer, bigger and faster then you'll love the upgrades, the more so because you can now access more of the slopes, and more quickly.

The area is famed for its generous quantities of soft, deep powder, and as such especially attracts more adventurous skiers, although that's not to say there's nothing for intermediate skiers – the focal point of the resort, 2,965-metre Gemsstock has some fun pistes as does the lower peak of Natschen on the opposite side of town, but it's the aforementioned Gemsstock that is the focal point of the action with its steep, snow-sure and predominantly off-piste terrain.

It offers a north-facing bowl with a mix of off-piste, piste and itineraire routes, all of them steep and exciting and with as much as 900 metres of vertical; perhaps the best way to discover Andermatt is to spend a day or two warming up on the in-bounds terrain and then hire a guide to discover what is some of the best backcountry in Switzerland.

Andermatt has almost doubled in size in recent years
© Valentin Luthiger

Germany

France

Switzerland   Austria
Davos-Klosters●

Italy

Access
Nearest airports:
Zurich (160km),
Friedrichshafen
(155km)
Train station in both
towns

Ability Level
Beginner – expert

Season
Nov – Apr

Other Local Activities
Snowshoeing, hiking,
cross-country skiing,
tobogganing, ice
skating (Europe's
biggest natural ice
rink), climbing wall

Resort Stats
Top: 2,845m
Bottom: 810m
Vertical: 2,035m
Lifts: 56
Pistes: 320km

www.davos.ch
www.klosters.ch

DAVOS-KLOSTERS, SWITZERLAND
Fit for a prince

Davos and Klosters are neighbouring resorts in Switerland's Grisons region, with long histories dating back to the very beginning of skiing in the Alps in the 1880s. Sir Arthur Conan Doyle further popularised the area by writing about his ski adventures here in 1894, and there then followed an invasion of well-heeled British winter sports enthusiasts which to some extent has continued to this day, with Klosters in particular being well known as a favourite haunt of Prince Charles.

The popularity of the two resorts is well justified, with some 320km of well-maintained pistes which are particularly good for intermediate and advanced skiers, magnificent mountain scenery, an efficient lift and transport system and the options of hectic nightlife in the busy town of Davos or an altogether quieter and more genteel experience in Klosters, which is essentially no more than a pretty alpine farming village.

On the slopes you're spoilt for choice, with several different ski areas to choose from. The biggest and most popular is the Parsenn, with upwards of a hundred pistes and long, exhausting runs which, snow conditions permitting, will take you down to Serneus and Kublis, some 12km and 2,000 vertical metres away.

The Parsenn area, which is at the heart of the skiing in Davos-Klosters, can be accessed from both resorts for a superb range of wide, open blue and red runs which will flatter your technique, whilst stronger skiers can continue on a couple of black options all the way back down to Davos Dorf at 1,560 metres.

It's intermediate skiers who will enjoy the upper slopes of both resorts most, since these are criss-crossed almost entirely by blue or red runs, some over 10km long.

If you're looking to venture off-piste this is a great area to be in. From easy little adventures in the powder either side of the groomed runs to quite serious backcountry expeditions such as the circuit from the Madrisa to Gargellen at the head of the Montafon Valley, or the exciting backcountry terrain off the back of the autonomous Rinerhorn area, there are plenty of options, whilst the separate but lift-linked Pischa area has in recent years reinvented itself as one of the largest freeriding regions in Europe.

When the skiing is over, Davos is the place to head for if you want more action – although not the prettiest of towns (it consists of a six-kilometre strip of hotels, shops, restaurants and houses along the valley bottom from Davos Dorf to Davos Platz), there are plenty of bars and clubs that rock until the early hours; over in Klosters things are considerably quieter, with après-ski often consisting of nothing more exciting than tea and cakes, whilst dining out can eat up the dollars in spots like the Michelin-starred Walserstube – unless you're a prince, of course.

Bumps galore at Davos © Alf Alderson

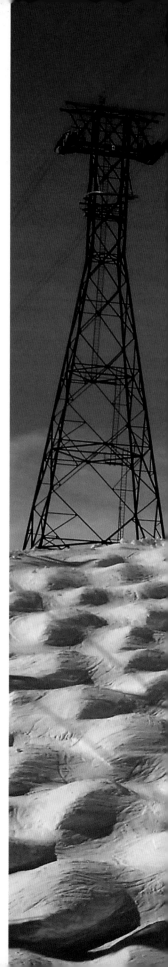

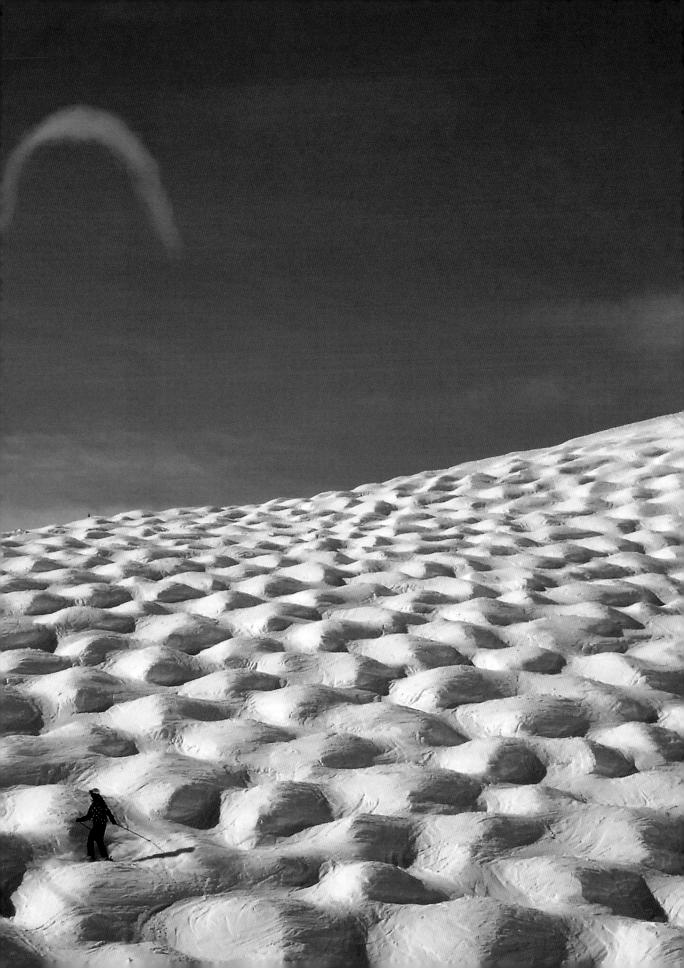

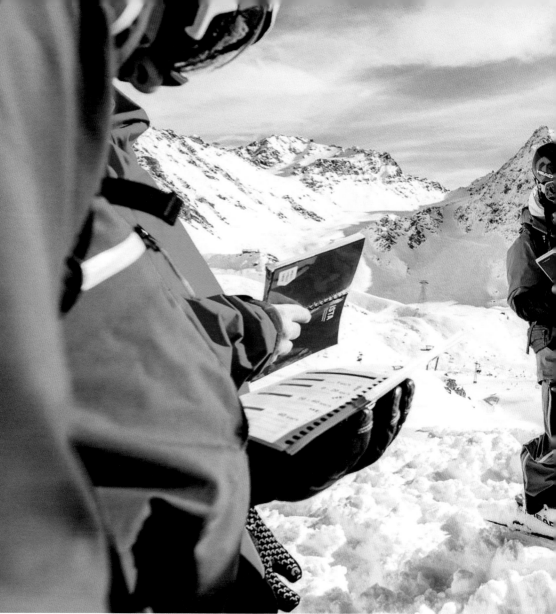

Germany

France

Austria

Switzerland

● Verbier

Italy

Access
Nearest airports:
Sion (55km),
Geneva (160km),
Zurich (280km)
Train station below
the resort in Le
Châble

Ability Level
Beginner – expert

Season
Nov – Apr

Other Local Activities
Snowshoeing,
cross-country skiing,
tobogganing, ice
skating, curling, dog-
sledding, hiking

Resort Stats
Top: 3,330m
Bottom: 1,500m
Vertical: 1,830m
Lifts: 92
Pistes: 412km

www.ista-education.
com/en
www.verbier.ch

VERBIER, SWITZERLAND
Playing it safe in freeride country

Verbier is renowned as the final stop on the Freeride World Tour, so it goes without saying that there's lots of world class off-piste terrain here. But how do you ski it as safely as possible?

In order to learn you could do worse than take part in one of the International Snow Training Academy's avalanche safety courses, which are held here – and elsewhere in the Alps – regularly each winter.

Before we go further, a few cold, hard facts – some 90 percent of avalanches affecting skiers are triggered by the skiers themselves, and on average 200 recreational skiers die every year in avalanche incidents in the Alps, eighty percent of whom are male, between the ages of 35-55.

You may be pleasantly surprised to find that the introductory ISTA Course – called 'Discovery' – involves a good deal of skiing rather than just tramping around with transceivers and digging in the snow – it's avalanche risk prevention rather than what to do after a slide has happened that is the meat and bones of the programme.

The course, indeed the International Snow Training Academy, is the brainchild of freerider Dominique Perret, who in 2000 was voted 'Freeride Skier of the Century' by his peers. It was set up in 2014 after a

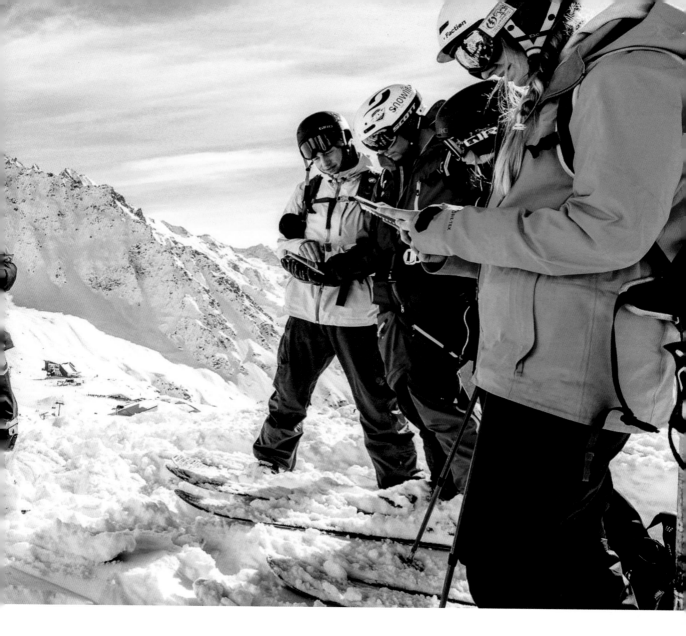

spate of avalanche deaths in the Alps and media accusations of irresponsibility amongst skiers riding away from the pistes, with the programme being developed in Lausanne by forty experts in everything from snow science and mountain rescue to education and communication.

The 'Discovery' course will introduce you to the basics of travelling safely in avalanche country; you start off with the instructors assessing the competence and ability of your group in skiing off-piste terrain, then go on to such fundamentals as studying the snowpack for stability and learning the basics of sun, wind and terrain features on snow stability as you ski around the slopes above Verbier.

The course takes in all manner of safety essentials, from how to measure slope angle using your ski poles to how to dig a snow pit to assess the stability of the snowpack; you'll even consider the effect you have on the flora and fauna of the areas where you're skiing.

It's only at day's end that transceivers, probes and shovels are put into action, with an exercise in which you're given 15 minutes to locate a hidden transceiver and dig it out (15 minutes being the point at which survival rates for a buried victim drop drastically).

However, Dominique emphasises strongly that: "This is a situation you never, ever want to find yourself in" which underlines the importance of understanding the risks as much as knowing how to use your rescue gear.

The course is a fun, but at the same time serious, day in the mountains, in which you learn a lot, and also ski quite a bit – so it certainly ain't boring. And most importantly, you'll discover that the best way to survive an avalanche is to learn how to avoid ever getting caught in one in the first place.

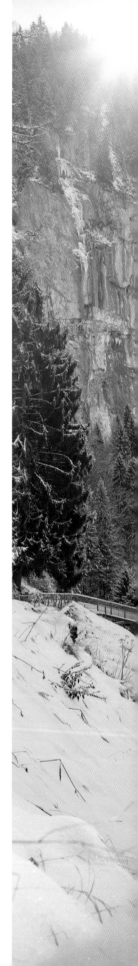

Germany

France

Switzerland   Austria

Mürren●

Italy

Access
Nearest airports:
Bern (65km),
Zurich (150km)
Train station
below the resort in
Lauterbrunnen

Ability Level
Beginner – expert

Season
Dec – Apr

Other Local Activities
Snowshoeing,
cross-country skiing,
tobogganing, ice
skating, paragliding,
hiking

Resort Stats
Top: 2,970m
Bottom: 1,650m
Vertical: 1,320m
Lifts: 17
Pistes: 54km

www. murren.ch

MÜRREN, SWITZERLAND
As Swiss as a cuckoo clock

Mürren is what skiers and non-skiers alike think of when they think about skiing in Switzerland – a pretty, car-free village easily accessed by rail, steeped in skiing tradition and surrounded by spectacular alpine scenery; it's the kind of place that as a skier you visit once and never want to leave.

The views from the village are absolutely staggering – look across the deep valley beneath Mürren and you'll see the vertiginous, glacier-draped, iconoclastic peaks of the Eiger, Mönch and Jungfrau glaring down at you. Mountaineering history was made on their towering north faces and they still offer a daunting challenge.

Skiing history was made in Mürren – the British more or less 'invented' modern skiing here, with Sir Arnold Lunn organising the first slalom race in 1922, whilst the first package winter holidays came here 12 years earlier, organised by Lunn's father Henry.

From this developed the Kandahar Ski Club in 1924, which introduced the infamous 'Inferno Downhill' to Mürren in 1928. The race is still held and is, in fact, the longest downhill in the world, starting from the Schilthorn at 2,970m and finishing, when conditions permit, in Lauterbrunnen at 800m, a course of over 14.9km. The race is so popular that it's limited to 1,850 competitors, starting at 12-second intervals throughout the day.

You can only get to Mürren by cable car from the train station down in the valley, which further adds to the charm. From the village various lifts take you up onto the slopes, with the cable car to Birg being the main attraction since it accesses the higher slopes including the famous 2,970-metre Schilthorn via a second cable car.

Here you'll find Piz Gloria restaurant, which revolves 360 degrees every hour to provide amazing panoramas whilst you dine; there's also a free James Bond exhibition based on the film *On Her Majesty's Secret Service*, which was shot here in 1969.

All this and we haven't even mentioned the recreational skiing yet! The classic descent is the 1,300-metre Schilthorn, a black from the top of the eponymous peak which takes in a variety of terrain and – as ever in Mürren – great views from top to bottom.

There's a decent selection of blue and red cruisers too, although you'll probably want to explore further afield with visits to Wengen and Grindelwald (page 80), both of which are linked to Mürren by a mix of piste, ski lifts and cog railway.

How very Swiss...

As Swiss as it gets – heading into the mountains by train
© MySwitzerland.com

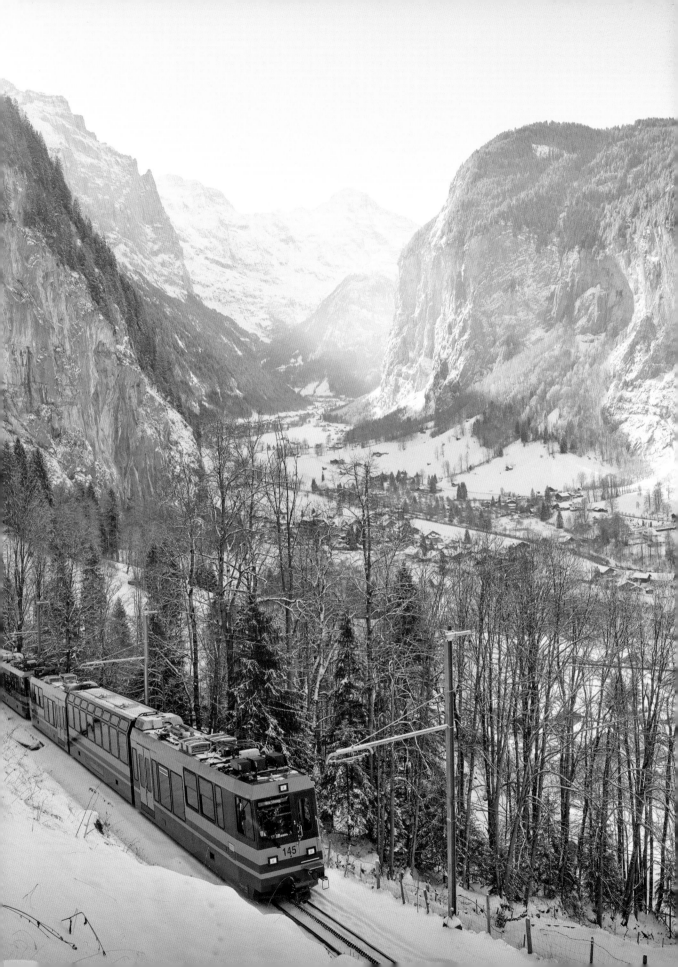

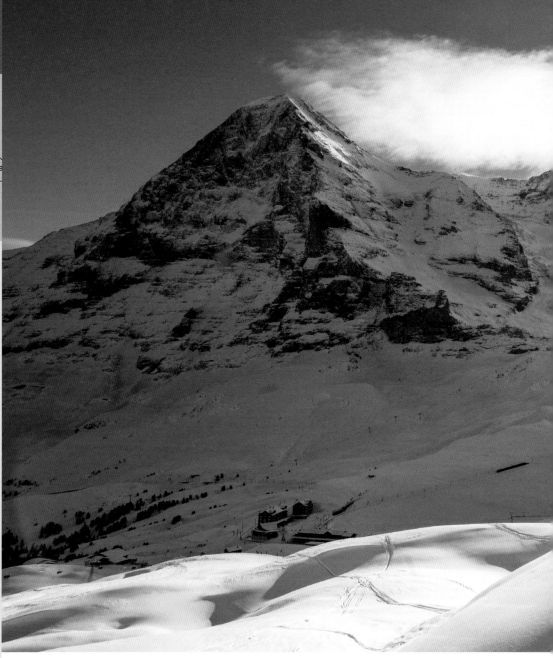

France

Germany

Switzerland Austria

Grindelwald

Italy

Access
Nearest airports:
Bern (70km),
Zurich (155km)
Train station in town

Ability Level
Beginner – expert

Season
Dec – Apr

Other Local Activities
Snowshoeing,
cross-country skiing,
tobogganing, hiking

Resort Stats
Top: 2,500m
Bottom: 945m
Vertical: 1,555m
Lifts: 28
Pistes: 170km

www.grindelwald.ch

GRINDELWALD, SWITZERLAND
A tangible presence

Grindelwald is one of the most spectacularly located mountain towns in the world. Massive 4,000-metre ramparts of rock, ice and snow loom above the town – the glaciated peaks of the Weisshorn, Schreckhorn, Eiger, Mönch and Jungfrau create an immense wall that casts shadows into the valley for much of the day in winter and exudes a tangible presence over the town.

The Eiger's north face in particular stands out – you can ski right beneath it, and are made to feel totally insignificant by a mountain wall so big it creates its own weather.

Perhaps surprisingly, given the daunting reputation of its mountains, the skiing around Grindelwald is not as challenging as that of other historic alpine centres such as St Anton and Chamonix. But it does have a unique charm, largely tied in to the fact that much of the skiing is accomplished via the local rail network.

Shiny bright locomotives and carriages that look like the models for a child's train set link

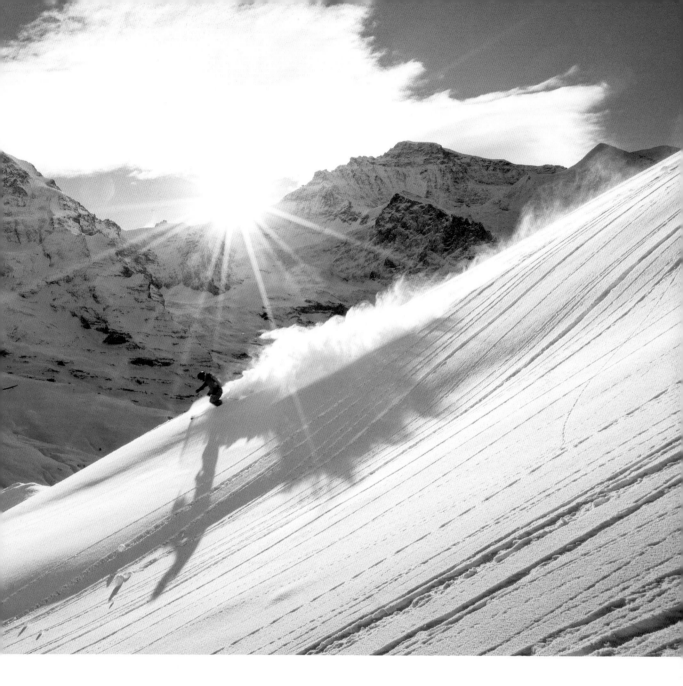

Grindelwald with the resorts of Wengen and Mürren, as well as connecting with the mainline system. They haul bogeys for ski storage so you can trundle up to stations such as Kleine Scheidegg underneath the Eiger's north face in comfort, clamber out, clip into your skis and head for a selection of easy red and blue runs, with the occasional black thrown in almost as an afterthought. From Kleine Scheidegg, you can also head to the start of the Lauberhorn, one of the World Cup's most prestigious downhill ski courses; and the train will actually take you through a tunnel in the Eiger to the station at the Jungfraujoch which, at 3,450 metres, is the highest in Europe.

The train stops on the way up so you can gaze out from galleries carved in the vertiginous north face of the Eiger at incredible mountain views, whilst from the top station you get dramatic panoramas across the Aletsch Glacier, a UNESCO World Heritage Site.

But back to the skiing. Besides being a photographer's dream, Grindelwald is particularly good for intermediate skiers, who can enjoy a fine range of blue and red runs in the Kleine Scheidegg-Männlichen area, or on the opposite side of the valley in the First ski area, where you're not directly beneath the towering rock walls of the Eiger and co and the extra distance allows you to view the mountains in all their glory.

Racing for the train – a skier heads for Kleine Scheidegg above Grindelwald
© MySwitzerland.com

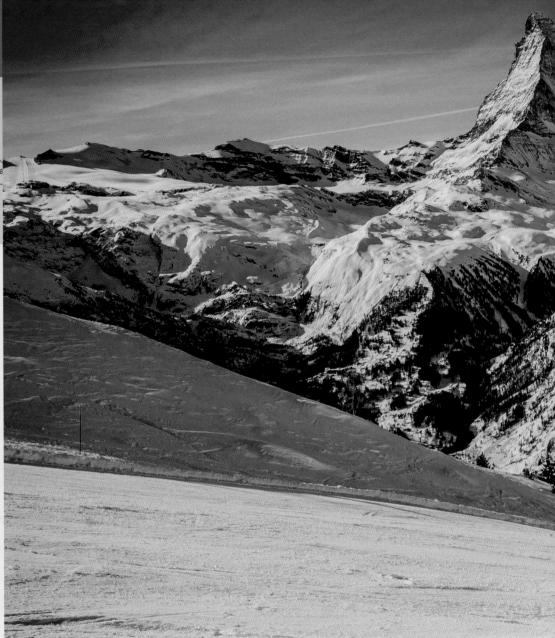

France
Germany
Austria
Switzerland
Zermatt
Italy

Access
Nearest airports:
Sion (80km),
Geneva (240km),
Zurich (250km)
Train station in town
Non-residents' cars
not allowed in the
village

Ability Level
Beginner – expert

Season
Year round

Other Local Activities
Heli-skiing,
snowshoeing, ice
skating, curling,
tobogganing, hiking

Resort Stats
Top: 3,820m
Bottom: 1,620m
Vertical: 2,200m
Lifts: 35
Pistes: 200km

www.zermatt.ch

ZERMATT, SWITZERLAND
Skiing in Toblerone country

It's unlikely you'll look at the Matterhorn, which soars above Zermatt like a child's drawing of a mountain, and think of chocolate bars, but if you should the one that ought to come to mind is Toblerone, since its triangular shape was apparently based on the instantly recognisable outline of the Matterhorn...

Anyway, arcane chocolate-themed trivia aside, Zermatt ranks alongside the likes of Chamonix (page 28) and Lake Louise (page 174) as on one of the world's most dramatically located mountain towns; it doesn't seem to matter how many times you ski here, the jagged, imposing bulk of the Matterhorn rising into the sky like a mighty dagger will never fail to impress.

Possibly the most famous mountain in the world, it was first climbed in 1865 as teams of mountaineers from Britain and Italy, massively aided by local guides, competed to be the first to reach the improbably pointy summit.

The Brit team narrowly made it, led by the irascible Edward Whymper, but at a massive price – four

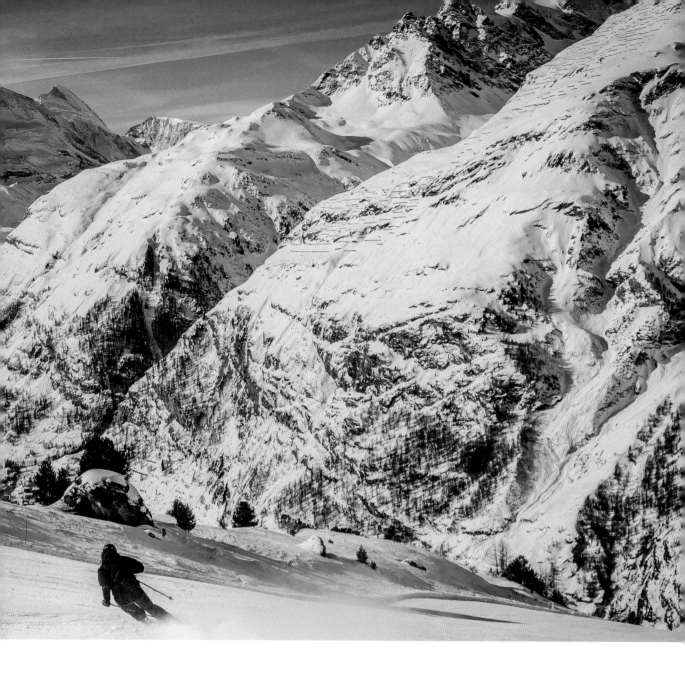

of their party of seven died after their climbing rope snapped, and the body of one, Douglas Hadow, still remains somewhere on the mountain. You can see the infamous snapped rope along with other ancient climbing gear in Zermatt's fascinating museum, which is well worth a visit should you have a down day.

Zermatt is one of those ski resorts that pretty much has it all – not just spectacular scenery, but a fine range of slopes which are some the highest in Europe, plenty of dramatic freeride terrain, the option of heli-skiing, an attractive mountain town mixing the old and modern and offering good nightlife, great mountain restaurants, reliable snow at altitude and a link to Cervinia in Italy – but make sure you don't miss the last lift back to Zermatt – if you do you're looking at €300-plus for the taxi ride home.

About the only downside to skiing here is the cost – nothing is even remotely budget-priced in Zermatt; that said, Cervinia is much cheaper so you could cut your costs by staying there and making day trips to Zermatt as and when the mood takes you.

Zermatt's four ski areas are reached via a mix of funiculars, cog railways, gondolas and cable cars and offer seemingly endless miles of beautiful pistes, whilst in between and above these is a superb range of off-piste options to cater for everyone from newbies to experts; the 'itineraires' you'll see on the piste map are marked and controlled for avalanche danger so offer a good introduction for freeriders; and if you can't bear to live without snow, there's also year-round glacier skiing.

The Matterhorn never fails to impress when you ski Zermatt
© Valon's Wallis Promotions
Tamara Berger

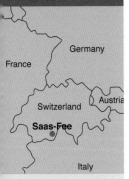

Germany

France

Switzerland · Austria

Saas-Fee

Italy

Access
Nearest airports:
Sion (75km),
Geneva (225km),
Zurich (225km),
Milan (180km)

Ability Level
Beginner – expert

Season
Nov – Apr
Limited summer
skiing

Other Local Activities
Snowshoeing, cross-
country skiing, ice
climbing, ice skating,
curling, tobogganing,
hiking

Resort Stats
Top: 3,500m
Bottom: 1,800m
Vertical: 1,700m
Lifts: 21
Pistes: 100km

www.saas-fee.ch

SAAS-FEE, SWITZERLAND
Enjoying the high life

With skiing, as with most other things in life, we all have to learn somewhere, sometime – and as far as skiing is concerned Saas-Fee is a pretty good bet for first timers and novice skiers looking to improve technique and confidence.

This is because it has the ideal combination of snow-sure slopes (thanks to a winning mix of glaciers and altitude – the highest intermediate red runs start at a literally breath-taking 3,500 metres) and long, gently-angled slopes, not to mention a beginner's area set aside from the main slopes where you can make your first turns without more experienced skiers whizzing past you at intimidating speeds.

Indeed, Saas-Fee is so snow sure that it also opens in the summer, when you'll find around 20km of groomed pistes on the glacier along with one of the best summer freestyle parks in Europe.

The resort also provides the ideal introduction to alpine culture in that it's a pretty, traditional, car-free Swiss mountain village surrounded by spectacular 4,000-metre peaks, thus encompassing a 'proper' ski holiday in one neat package. Needless to say, the views get better the higher you go, but even if you spend all week on the lower beginner slopes you can't fail to be impressed by the panoramas.

Most of the skiing is between 2,500 metres and 3,500 metres, and this impressive altitude provides a pretty good snow guarantee, although it can have its downsides in bad weather since strong winds and heavy snow fall may result in lift closures.

Fret not though, there's plenty to do on down days considering the relatively small size of the resort, from snowshoeing to splashing around in the large indoor leisure centre or a visit, perhaps, to the world's largest ice caves or a tour of the local brewery.

Another world beater is the Threes!xty Restaurant at the resort's high point, Allalin – it's the world's highest revolving restaurant and given the array of mighty peaks and glaciers that can be seen from it you may spend most of your lunch staring out of the window as you go round and round.

Whilst any half-decent skier will love hooning around on the wide array of red and blue runs on offer at Saas-Fee, there are some more challenging 'itineraries' for more experienced skiers and some very decent off-piste terrain, whilst ski touring is getting bigger by the year here – however, you need to be wary of crevasses on non-pisted sections of the glacier, so a guide is recommended.

Everyone from beginners to experts like Aaron Durlester will enjoy Saas-Fee
© db.pc.keystone-sda.ch / Schweiz Saastal Tourismms AG

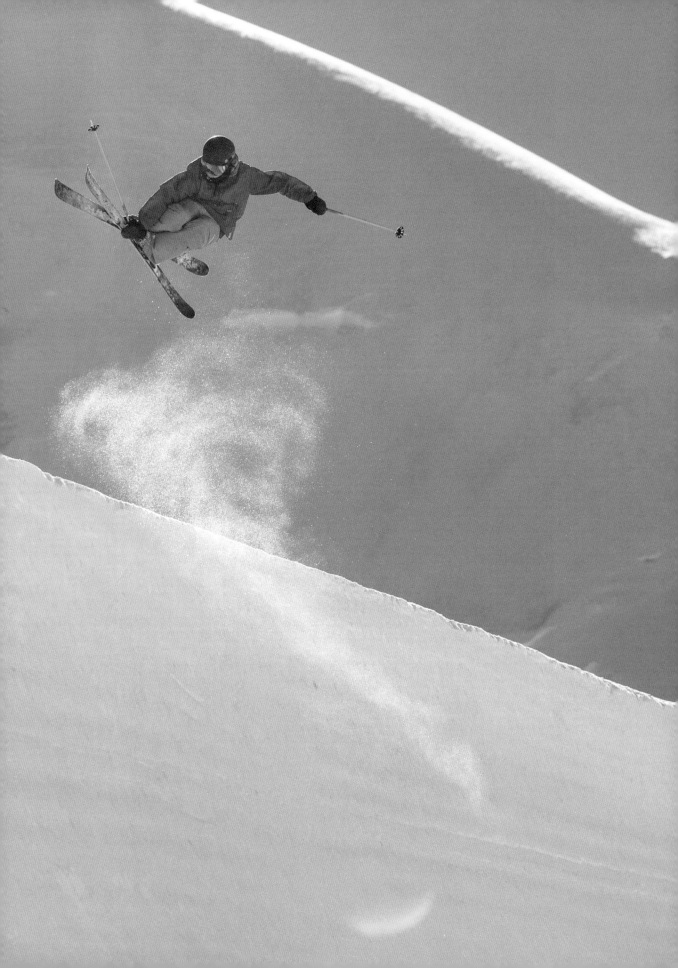

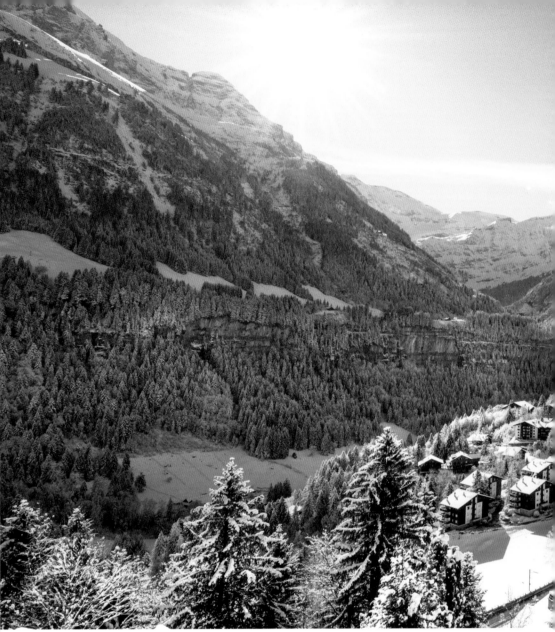

Access
Nearest airports:
Sion (65km),
Geneva (120km)

Ability Level
Beginner – expert

Season
Dec – Apr

Other Local Activities
Snowshoeing, cross-country skiing, ice climbing, ice skating, hiking

Resort Stats
Top: 2,275m
Bottom: 950m
Vertical: 1,325m
Lifts: 196
Pistes: 650km

www.regiondentsdum
idi.ch

CHAMPÉRY, SWITZERLAND
Border hopping in the Swiss Alps

For intermediate skiers Champéry is hard to beat. It has that perfect mix of plenty of blue and red runs between the four small interlinked satellite stations (Planachaux, Les Crosets, Champoussin and Morgins) and a lovely, rustic mountain village in which to relax at the end of a hard day on the slopes.

Plus an extra little – or not so little – nugget to top it all off. For Champéry sits on the Swiss side of the Portes du Soleil, the second biggest ski area in the world with some 650km of pistes and almost 200 lifts. Knock all that lot off in a week and you deserve a medal.

Besides Champéry, the Portes du Soleil consists of around ten other ski resorts including the French big-hitters Avoriaz, Morzine, Les Gets and Châtel, so those skiers who like to cover the ground not only have heaps of variety to go at but they also have two countries to ski in (no passport is required to travel between the two either).

The Portes du Soleil is actually named after the pass connecting Morgins to Les Crosets, above Champéry – when plans for this enormous ski area were unveiled in 1964 it was set to be called the 'Haute Route des Familles', but Jean Vuarnet, the 1960 Olympic downhill champion and Morzine native,

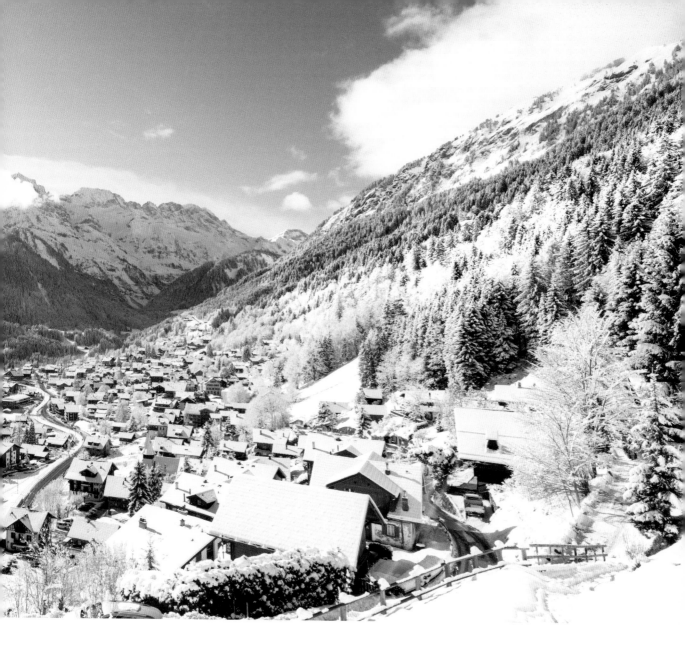

Champéry at its inviting mid-winter best © jbbieuville

lobbied for alternatives, of which Les Portes du Soleil was the winner (although it has to be said that the original suggestion is pretty apt since the Portes du Soleil does contain skiing to suit any avid ski family down to the ground).

But back to Champéry. Another of its benefits is that it gets plenty of sun, although this can obviously affect the snow if there are too many rays hitting the slopes for too long – in which case simply head over to France, where there's a good chance you'll find better conditions.

You'll also encounter some great scenery on the way – the resort sits beneath the spectacular, craggy ridge of the Dents du Midi. And if your skiing is above intermediate level, don't think this ain't the place for you – head for the infamous 'Swiss Wall' beneath the Pas de Chavanette, an 'itineraire' that develops into an enormous bump run that will trip up all but the best, and for the amusement of others is located right beneath a chair lift.

In Morgins you'll find the region's first 'Rando-Parc', consisting of seven ski touring routes of varying difficulty, taking from half-an-hour to 2.5 hours to complete and with an average height difference of 600 metres – a great introduction to ski touring (aka ski randonée) if you've never tried it.

It's also easy to access Avoriaz from Champéry, which is well worth a visit if only to see the 'like it or loathe it' modernistic wood-clad high rises that it's famous for – not your traditional, Champéry-like alpine settlement by a long way.

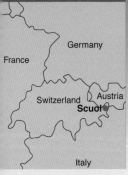

France
Germany
Switzerland
Austria
Scuol
Italy

Access
Nearest airport:
Zurich (180km)
Train station on edge
of town

Ability Level
Beginner – expert

Season
Dec – Apr

Other Local Activities
Snowshoeing, cross-
country skiing, hiking

Resort Stats
Top: 2,750m
Bottom: 1,250m
Vertical: 1,500m
Lifts: 15
Pistes: 80km

www.scuol.ch

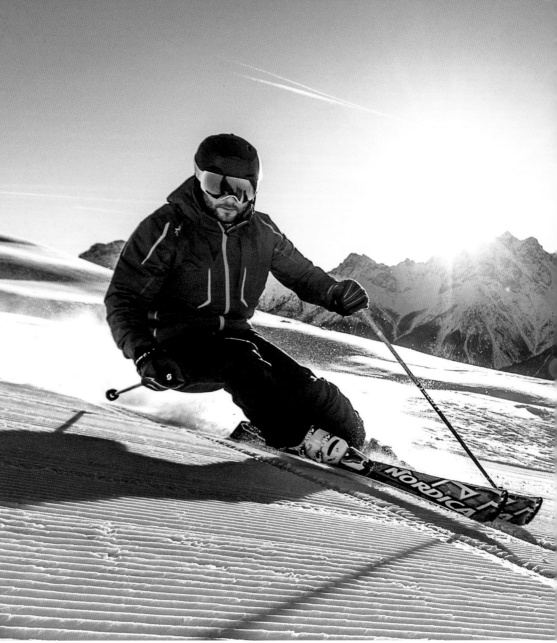

SCUOL, SWITZERLAND
Back to Scuol...

Depending on how you travel, getting to the delightful old alpine spa town of Scuol, close to Switzerland's eastern borders with Austria and Italy, involves a meandering train journey through glorious mountain scenery, including passing through the Vereina Tunnel, which at 19.5km in length is the world's longest metre-gauge tunnel.

Popping out on the far side of the tunnel feels like you've arrived in a different country; hamlets and villages display an Italianate architecture rather than the traditional Swiss chalet-style encountered to the west of the tunnel, a feature of which is wall paintings called sgraffito, while the place names – Scuol, Ardez, Ftan, Funtana – are of Romansh origin since you're now in the Engadin region, heartland of Switzerland's fourth language.

Ski guide Peder Rausch has lived all his 60-plus years here, and Romansh is his first language;

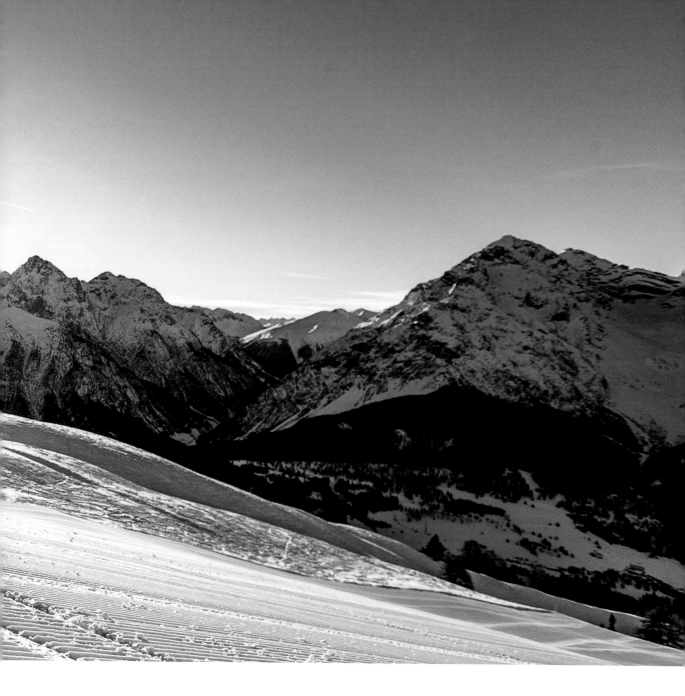

Scuol – at the end of the line
© Andrea Badrutt, Chur

when he translates a few pertinent Romansh words ('alpina' – small hill; 'alpetta' – medium-sized hill; 'alpuna' – large hill; 'muntogna' – mountain) you may decide Romansh isn't all that difficult; but when you hear Peder speak to his many friends on the slopes in his native tongue you'll be lost in seconds. But it all adds to the romance (sorry) of the region.

Scuol acts as the rail terminus for the Vereina Line and has an end-of-the line feel about it, but in a positive way – arriving here is like discovering your own little ski area. Most of the skiers are locals and the atmosphere is friendly and garrulous on the slopes and in the slope-side bars and restaurants.

It's the kind of place that is made for exploring – an enticing mix of red and blue pistes allow you to whizz around what is a very decent-sized ski area as well as heading for the linked settlements of Ftan and Sent (a free ski bus will bring you home) and lovely, long meandering runs like the Pista del Sömmi ('Dream Piste') from the top of 2,710-metre Salaniva are almost like ski touring without the strain of the climb, whilst the off-piste potential is plain to see, with plenty of open terrain at all angles easily accessible from the pistes along with a good lick of tree-skiing lower down the mountain.

And you don't need to understand Romansh to read the piste map either...

Germany

France

Switzerland Austria

Disentis

Italy

Access
Nearest airports:
Zurich (178km),
Friedrichshafen
(183km),
Milan (186km)
Train station in town

Ability Level
Beginner – expert

Season
Dec – Apr

Other Local Activities
Snowshoeing, cross-
country skiing, hiking

Resort Stats
Top: 2,830m
Bottom: 1,150m
Vertical: 1,680m
Lifts: 10
Pistes: 60km

www.disentis-sedrun.
graubuenden.ch

DISENTIS, SWITZERLAND
Where is everyone?

While a ski resort with very few skiers is clearly a very good thing, there's also something slightly unsettling about this if you're used to the hordes on planks that is common to most well-known ski areas.

So, plodding up to the cable car that accesses Disentis' slopes on a sunny Monday morning in January, it would be understandable if you felt a little ill at ease by the almost total absence of other skiers, especially considering that the local slopes have recently had a fresh dump of powder.

Adi Schürmann, a cheerful local ski guide, will soon set your mind at rest though. "It's always like this in January. We're a bit off the beaten track, so outside of weekends it's never very busy; which is all the better for us."

Join Adi and head for Disentis' high point of 2,833 metres, below the craggy summit of 3,027-metre Péz Ault (which entails riding five lifts which vary from the aforementioned cable car to chairs and drags) and it's quite possible you'll still be wondering where everyone is by the time you get to the top. Perfect.

Glancing at the piste map, you'd be forgiven for thinking Disentis is a fairly limited in terms of its terrain, since it only has 10 lifts in total, which access a modest number of mainly red and blue pistes; but what is hard to gauge on paper is its impressive 1,680 metres of vertical and vast expanse of freeride terrain that lies above the treeline and is accessible from the ski lifts; you can easily spend a couple of days or more riding here and not take the same line twice.

Typical are descents such as those down the Val Gronda, Val Acletta and Val Segnas, three alpine valleys that wend their way down from high, open terrain into wooded lower slopes before crossing wide meadows to bring you out at the main cable car station back in town.

The pitch tends to be steeper towards the top, although never scarily so, after which things mellow out with lovely, undulating terrain that eventually flattens out somewhat as you hit the trees (not literally one would hope) lower down.

Disentis itself is pretty small and unassuming and not the kind of place you go if you're looking for banging nightlife or fancy restaurants – there's a pretty laid back, local vibe, and many skiers are return visitors; and after a couple of days skiing here it's easy to see why.

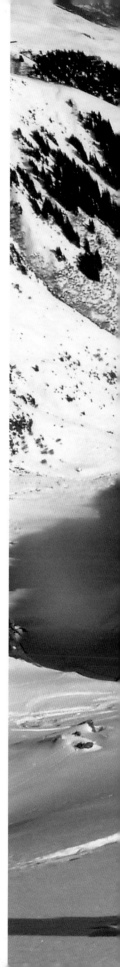

Adi Schumann gives it a big thumbs up before heading down to Disentis
© Alf Alderson

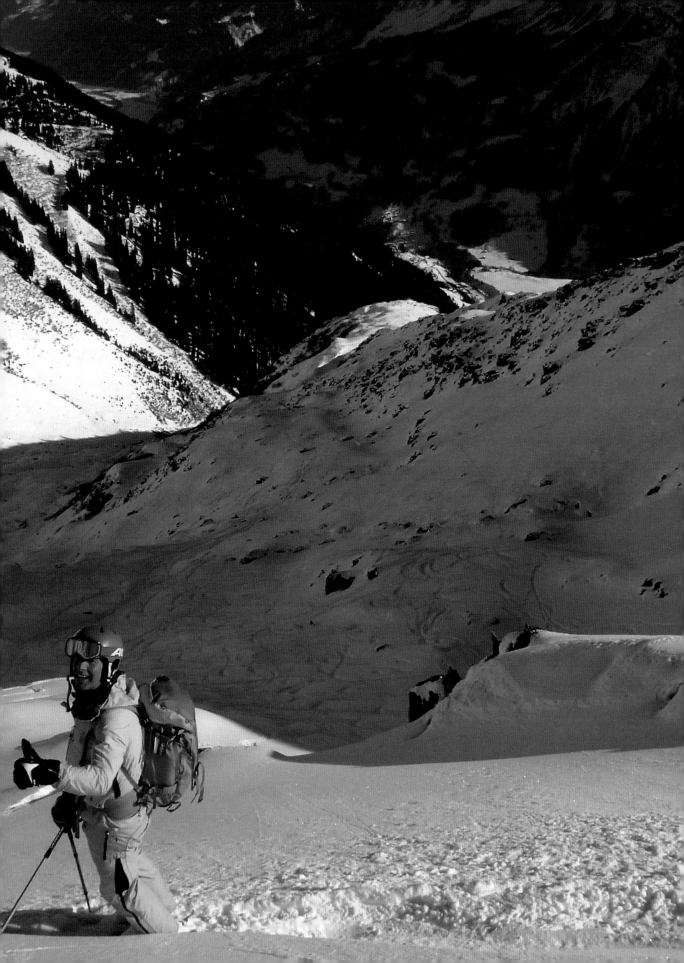

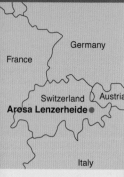

France

Germany

Switzerland Austria
Arosa Lenzerheide ●

Italy

Access
Nearest airports from Arosa:
Zurich (150km),
Friedrichshafen (155km)
Train station in Arosa

Ability Level
Beginner – expert

Season
Dec – Apr

Other Local Activities
Snowshoeing, cross-country skiing, hiking, ice skating, curling, tobogganing, sleigh rides, ballooning, paragliding

Resort Stats
Top: 2,865m
Bottom: 1,230m
Vertical: 1,635m
Lifts: 42
Pistes: 225km

www.
arosalenzerheide.
swiss

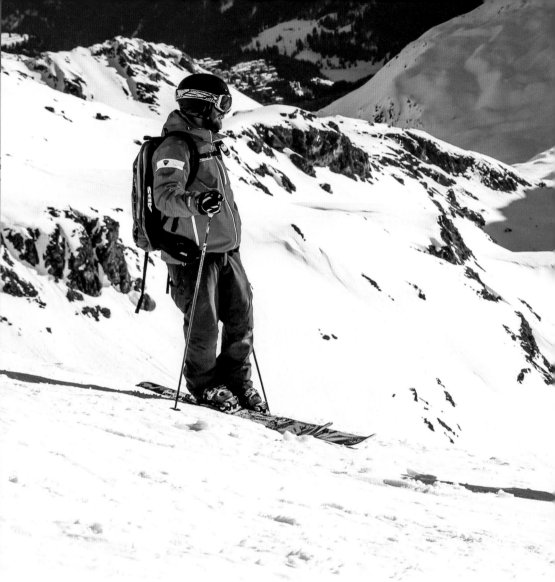

AROSA LENZERHEIDE, SWITZERLAND
Don't look down

Many skiers arrive in Arosa by train; should you decide to do so, here's a bit of advice – don't bother with newspaper, magazine, book, tablet or any other form of reading material for the journey.

For the chances are you'll spend the entire trip with your nose squashed against the window, taking in the spectacular landscapes through which your cute red train is chugging on the 1,100-metre climb from the regional capital of Chur up to Arosa.

The line clings to vertiginous mountain slopes, wends beneath frozen waterfalls and towering crags, weaves its way through snow-bound forests and past picturesque alpine villages and teeters across improbably high and narrow bridges where anyone suffering from vertigo definitely shouldn't look down.

As for the skiing – well, Arosa was recently linked to the neighbouring resort of Lenzerheide via a cable car which takes you over a yawning void from the 2,511-metre peak of Hörnli to 2,546-metre Urdenfürggli.

Prior to this its modest 70km or so of pistes were not really enough to keep avid skiers satisfied for a full week (although there's plenty of fine freeride terrain too), but the link to Lenzerheide's 155km of pistes means that there's now more than enough skiing to suit anyone, not to mention a vast array of alternatives from hiking to ballooning if you want to take a break from skiing.

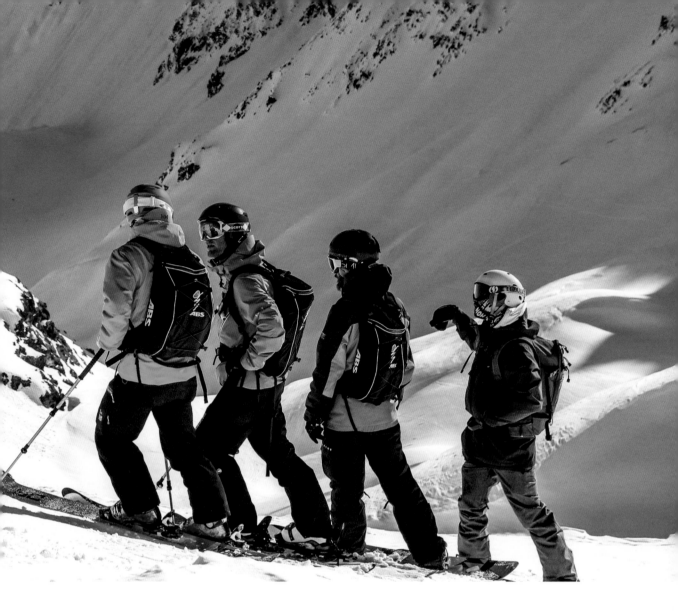

A great way to make the most of the slopes is to ski Arosa's sunny south facing terrain in the morning then pop over to Lenzerheide around lunch when the mix of north and south facing slopes are all catching the rays too.

A fine selection of steep, sunny black and red pistes offer themselves up beneath Arosa's high point, 2,653-metre Weisshorn, accessed by a fast cable car, and, once the morning shadows have retreated, there are some fine reds to be explored beneath Hörnli; and both mountain summits have restaurants where you can enjoy the obligatory morning coffee with spectacular views when the legs start to complain.

It's from Hörnli that you access Lenzerheide, where one of the highlights is a fast, hooning black run called, rather uninspiringly, Piste 72, but this is the Swiss way of doing things – and who really cares what a run is called if it's this much fun? From the top of the Stätzerhorn chair at 2,421 metres Piste 72 is wide, steep, open and takes you right past the Chilihütta, where what may well be the finest chiliburgers in the Alps are to be found and eaten when lunchtime approaches.

Returning to Arosa you get the chance to have a good look at the settlement of Lenzerheide since some of the pistes and one of the ski lifts runs literally right through the town, revealing a mix of broad, stocky, stone chalets and more modern apartment blocks in contrast to the traditional timber mountain restaurants and shepherds' huts that dot the mountainsides above.

This is one of the endearing features of skiing in Switzerland – you're in a place where skiing is such a fundamental part of the national character and infrastructure that ski runs slice through the middle of rustic old settlements and modern towns and traffic is expected to give way to people on planks – as it should.

Preparing to drop into some of Arosa Lenzerheide's great freeride terrain
© elvis.somedia.ch

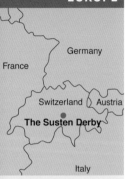

Germany

France

Switzerland Austria

The Susten Derby

Italy

Access
Nearest airports:
Bern (117km),
Zurich (133km)

Ability Level
Intermediate – expert

Season
The Susten Derby is
held every April

www.sustenderby.ch

THE SUSTEN DERBY, BERNESE OBERLAND, SWITZERLAND
A bit of a habit

You may think that not everyone is cut out to be a ski racer, but the Susten Derby thinks differently. One of a burgeoning number of ski touring races now taking place across the Alps, it consists of a 1,100-metre climb on climbing skins to the summit of the 2,960-metre Obertaljoch in the Bernese Oberland from the start point above the Steingletscher Hotel on Sustenpass, between the towns of Wassen and Meiringen, followed by a blast back down to the start point.

The event is a very inclusive out and back 'race' which anyone is welcome to attend. The majority of entrants take part in a 'fun' race (there's a 'serious' category for more serious skiers too) which involves kids and families, skiers and snowboarders.

You can, of course, take the whole thing very seriously – perhaps even aim for a podium place – but for a good number of entrants the only ambitions is not to finish in any worse a position than last. This means you can make a relatively leisurely ascent of slopes that vary from gentle to steep – but not too steep – and never offer anything other than spectacular mountain vistas, stopping regularly to try to breathe normally/take in the views/eat large quantities of chocolate and generally immerse yourself in the perverse pleasure that is ski touring.

There's a sense of satisfaction about ascending a mountain under your own steam that a ski lift can never provide – the fabled 'earn your turns' philosophy that underpins so much of ski touring has a lot to recommend it, even if it may cause discomfort, blisters and excessive perspiration.

And because you're doing it with a whole bunch of like-minded, smiley souls the camaraderie of the event provides a very inclusive feel to it all. The keenies will, of course, reach the summit of Obertaljoch in considerably less than the three-hour or so average time, stopping ever-so-briefly to check in with the course marshals before hammering back down to the finish point (the fastest competitor's descent times may be little more than three-minutes; the slowest may take ten-times longer).

If you're not in it to win it there's much to be said for taking a break once you get to the race's high point and chew on an energy bar while you enjoy the magnificent views – blue-green serrated lines of huge peaks and ridges fade into the distance, whilst glaciers creak their way between the higher mountains of the central Swiss Alps.

And, of course, there's the 1,100-metre descent to look forward to, at the end of which you'll be cheered across the finish line like an Olympian (well, almost).

There's an après-race shindig in the spring sunshine outside the Steingletscher Hotel in which fast and slow, young and old, fit and fat mingle together to recall their race experience, and, no doubt, to agree to meet again at the same time, same place next year – because like so many similar events, the Susten Derby can become a bit of a habit. Even if you almost end up coming last (and I speak from personal experience on that score...).

Getting into the habit – Simon Murray Henwood slogging upwards in the Susten Derby
© Alf Alderson

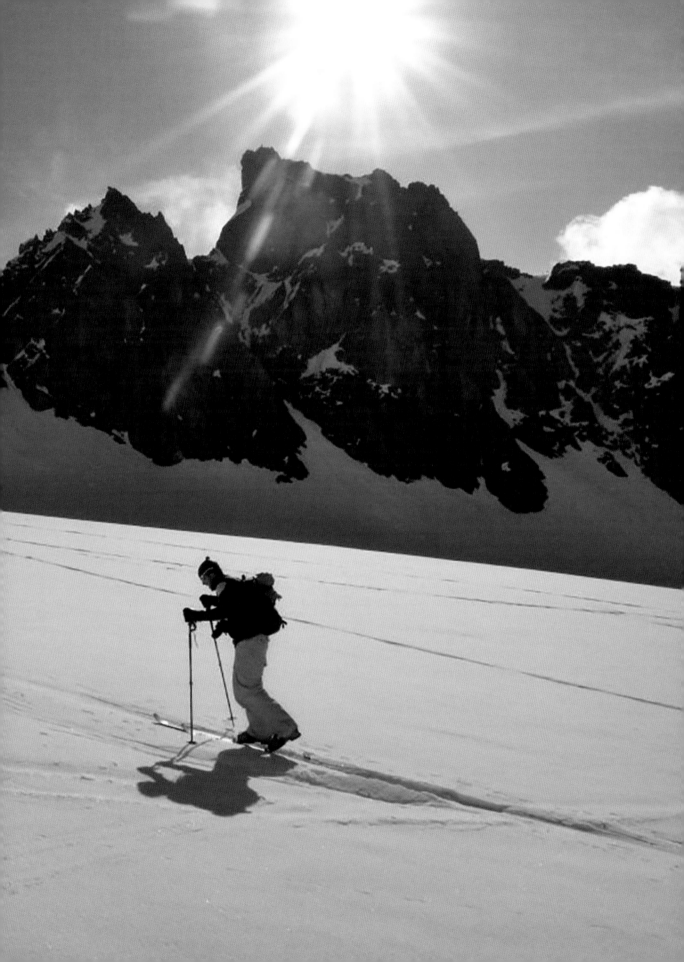

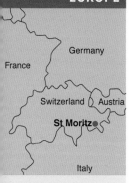

France
Germany
Switzerland Austria
St Moritz●
Italy

Access
Nearest airports:
Zurich (220km),
Friedrichshafen
(210km)
Train station in resort

Ability Level
Beginner – expert

Season
Oct – May

Other Local Activities
Heli-skiing,
snowshoeing, cross-
country skiing, hiking,
ice skating, curling,
tobogganing, sleigh
rides, Cresta run, polo
etc., etc.

Resort Stats
Top: 3,305m
Bottom: 1,770m
Vertical: 1,535m
Lifts: 22
Pistes: 100km

www.stmoritz.ch

ST MORITZ, SWITZERLAND
Bring on the glitz, it's St Moritz

Is there any town in winter sports more associated with the alluring combination of glamour, danger and wealth than St Moritz? And although this is a book about skiing, it would be perfectly easy to write about St Moritz without mentioning skiing at all (don't worry, I won't).

But I will mention in passing that if you have friends or family who don't ski you could bring them here and they'd have a whale of a time – albeit an expensive one – without ever needing to clip into a pair of ski bindings.

If cricket, horse racing or polo on snow appeal to you, this is the place to be. There's even a mountain with funicular access (Muottas Muragl) that's been set aside just for snowshoeing and tobogganing. And then, of course, there's the famous Cresta Run, a last bastion of braying upper-class Britishness where you can pay 600 Swiss Francs for five runs as a beginner unless you're a woman, in which case you '... may use the Run strictly by invitation, at the discretion of the Committee and under the supervision of the Secretary (or his nominee) at selected times of the season'; yes, the 20th century has yet to arrive in Cresta land, never mind the 21st.

As for the skiing, well, beneath some of the most spectacular peaks in Switzerland – and that's saying something – is some fine off-piste terrain which doesn't tend to get tracked out as quickly as that of more hard-core resorts such as Verbier. There's some enjoyable, challenging backcountry terrain accessible from the resort's two high points of 3,055-metre Piz Nair and 3,305-metre Piz Corvatsch, along with a popular and scenic glacier descent from beneath Piz Bernina to Morteratsch (best done with a guide). There's also heli-skiing if you haven't spent all your money on snow polo and Cresta runs.

And if off-piste action isn't your thing, fret not, for St Moritz is laced with enjoyable red and blue runs, particularly in the Corvatsch-Furtschellas area where you can easily spend a day whooping around the red runs and, having got your ski legs, finish off with a descent of the scenic Hahnensee back to St Moritz – yes, it's a black, but it's an easy one and completing it in style will allow you to justify taking out a second mortgage for a martini (shaken, not stirred) in the casino later in the day...

Living in the past – vintage action on the slopes of St Moritz © stmoritz.com

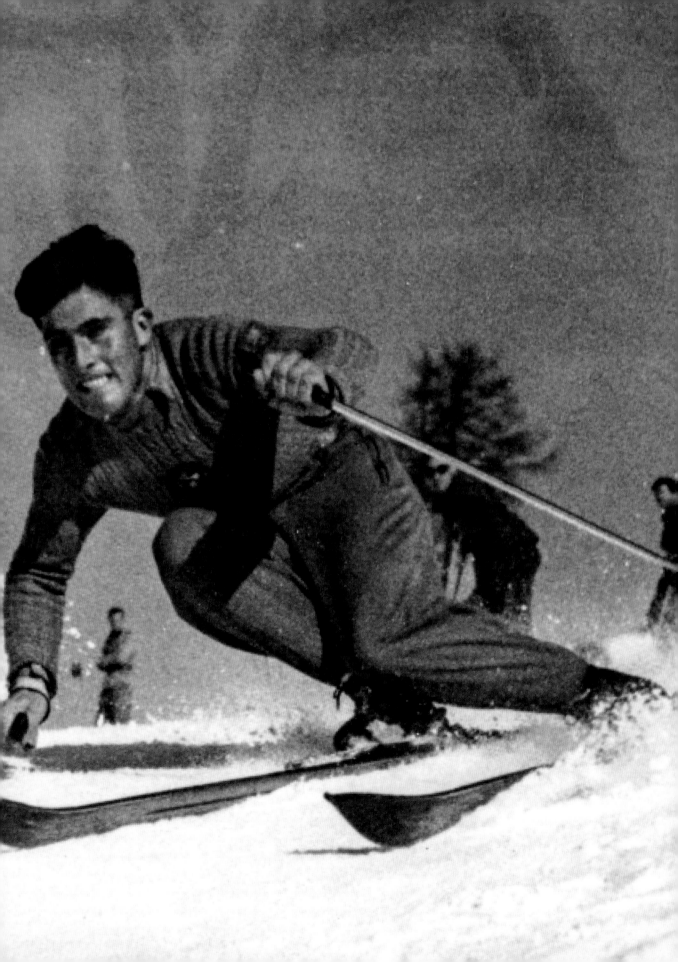

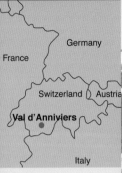

France
Germany
Switzerland Austria
Val d'Anniviers
Italy

Access
Nearest airports:
Sion (45km),
Geneva (200km)

Ability Level
Beginner – expert

Season
Dec – Apr

Other Local Activities
Snowshoeing, cross-
country skiing, ice
climbing, hiking

Resort Stats
Top: 3,000m
Bottom: 1,340m
Vertical: 1,660m
Lifts: 43
Pistes: 220km

www.valdanniviers.ch

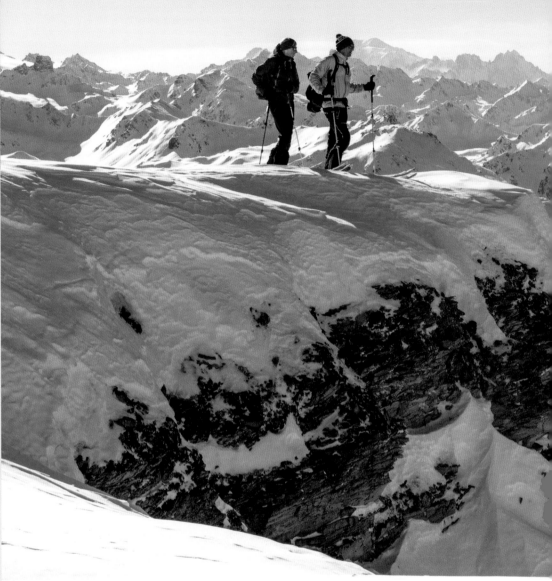

VAL D'ANNIVIERS, SWITZERLAND
Slowing things down

The Val d' Anniviers is a deep valley the sides of which are home to five picturesque Swiss mountain villages (St Luc, Chandolin, Zinal, Grimentz and Vercorin) which make for an ideal destination if you're looking to get away from it all.

The villages are quiet, cute and hassle free and access to the slopes is, in lots of cases, very old school – T-bars seem to be the transport of choice here (although there are several modern lifts too).

Whilst all the ski areas are linked by either ski lifts or free ski buses, the majority of visitors are likely to forget about little Vercorin, since it offers limited skiing (although the few slopes it does have are often almost deserted) and head to the other four villages.

Grimentz in particular is a cracker of a place to visit, especially if you're into freeriding and ski touring; it's renowned for the extensive amount of off-piste terrain, which varies from snow-sure, open alpine slopes to great tree-skiing lower down the mountain, the latter of which is a real bonus if the

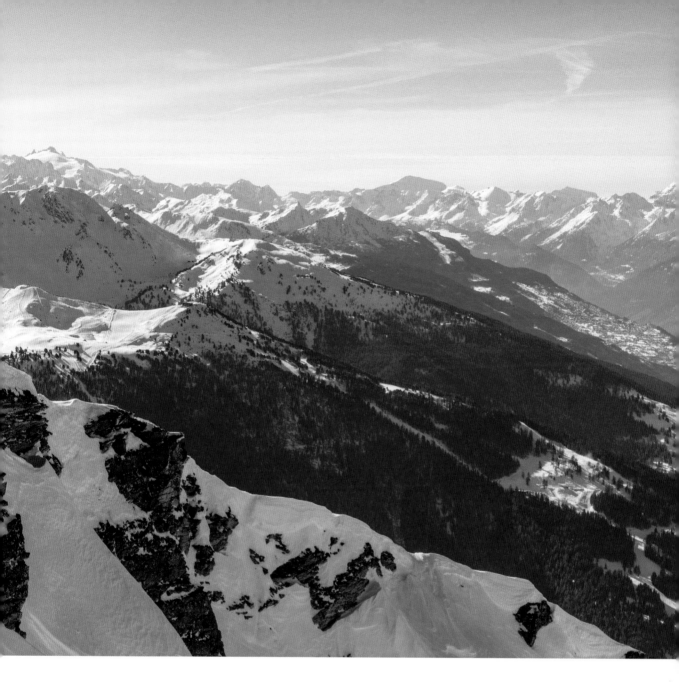

weather turns bad; and having just dismissed Vercorin as hardly worth a visit, you may be pleased to end up there if you take the 1,500-vertical-metre off-piste run all the way from Grimentz' upper slopes down to Vercorin (you'll need to get a bus back).

Zinal is linked to Grimentz by bus and cable car and, since the slopes here face a roughly easterly direction, it too is quite snow sure. Whilst there's some great fun to be had on the relatively short red runs that make up the majority of the piste skiing, and some fantastic views (including the Matterhorn) from the higher slopes, one of the 'must do' runs here is the Piste du Chamois, a long black with 1,300 metres of vertical that also offers plenty of side country fun for skiers looking for a bit more of a challenge.

Over on the sunny, west-facing side of the valley, St Luc and Chandolin (again both linked by ski lifts) are a better bet for intermediates with their fine collection of long, cruisy reds, one of which, from the top of 3,000-metre Bella Tola, offers over 1,200 metres of 'vert'; and there are some seriously steep black and 'itineraire' options if that's your thing.

So, a good way to discover the Val d'Anniviers is to ski the sunny slopes of Zinal and Grimentz in the morning, then take the free ski bus to St Luc-Chandolin for the afternoon sun to make the most of the rays.

Taking it easy, for a while at least, above Val d'Anniviers
© media-photos.valais.ch
Yves Garneau

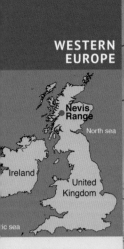

Nevis Range

North sea

Ireland

United Kingdom

ic sea

Access
Nevis Range is seven miles from Fort William, which has good road and rail access

Ability Level
Beginner – expert

Season
Dec – April but opening and closing dates are very weather dependant

Other Local Activities
Paragliding, cross-country skiing, mountain biking/fat biking

Resort Stats
Top: 1,221m
Bottom: 640m
Vertical: 581m
Lifts: 12
Pistes: 20km

www.nevisrange.co.uk

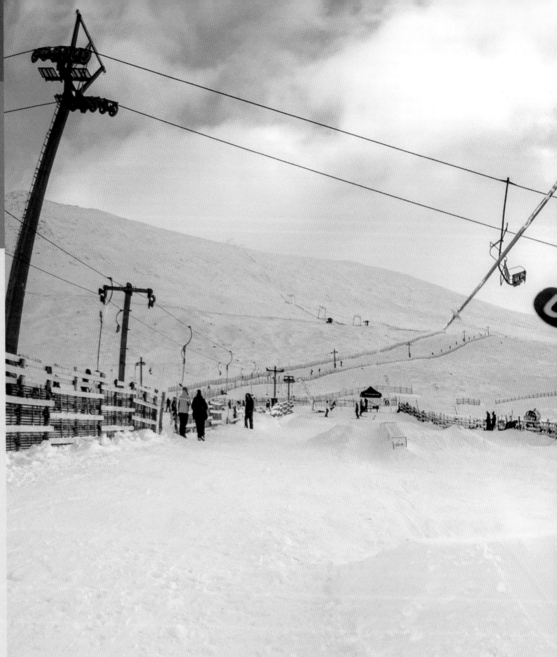

NEVIS RANGE, SCOTLAND

On a good day...

Skiing in Scotland invariably comes with the rider: "It's as good as the Alps if you catch it on a good day." And indeed, it can be almost as good as the Alps when the snow is deep and powdery and the sun is shining; however, these conditions are the exception rather than the norm, which explains why the majority of British skiers head overseas for their mountain experience.

However...

... if you live close to the Scottish mountains or are in the area after a good dump it would be madness not to check out the skiing and, in this respect, the Nevis Range, Scotland's newest ski area (it dates back to 1989, with more recent upgrades including Britain's only six-seater gondola) is a fine option.

This is Scotland's highest ski area, topping out at 1,221-metre Aonach Mor, from where Britain's highest peak Ben Nevis (1,345m) is readily visible, along with inland panoramas that are reminiscent of

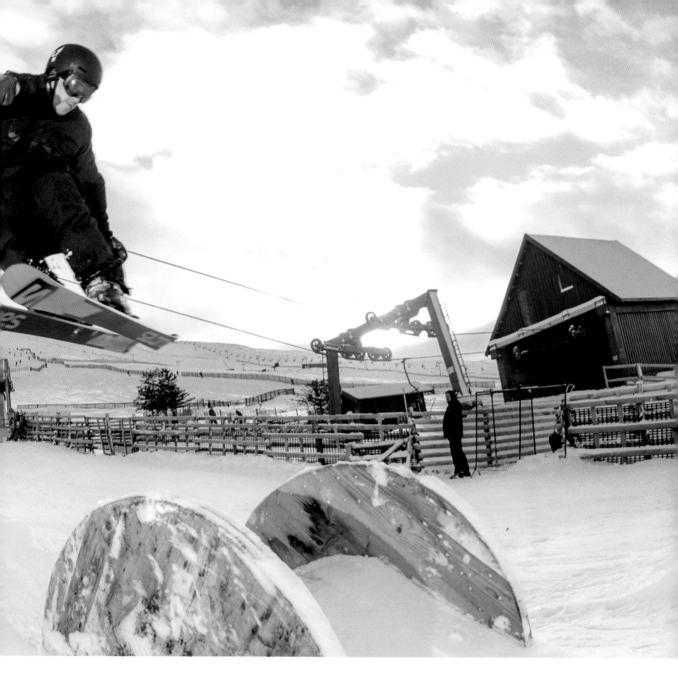

Making the most of it on Scottish pow © Ski Scotland

Scandinavia, whilst westwards the views are unique – Scotland's glorious west coast and its islands and highlands stretch away into the distance; on a sunny day it's worth visiting just for the view.

Once you've tired of the scenery, experienced skiers will doubtless find themselves heading for the infamous Back Corries, a wilderness area which was opened to skiers in the mid-1990s, and which can provide some of the finest and most easily accessed backcountry skiing in Britain.

There are marked 'itineraries' as in the Alps, and if you're in any doubt about what you might be getting into, simply ask at the ski patrol station above the Corries – as Head of Nevis Range Ski Patrol Jeff Starkey advises: "We tend to give visitors informal advice on the best runs according to the conditions. We also run freeride clinics and Back Corrie workshops specifically tailored to the conditions you'll find here."

If you prefer something a little less challenging the majority of pistes are blue and red, with a good smattering of easy greens, making the area ideal for novice and intermediate skiers as well as offering plenty for experts too.

Of course, with Scotland's famously temperamental maritime climate there's inevitably a large element of chance when it comes to scoring the place at its best, but if you do – well, didn't someone say it's almost as good as the Alps...?

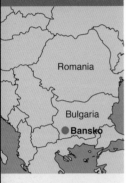

Romania

Bulgaria
● Bansko

Access
Nearest airport:
Sofia (160km)

Ability Level
Beginner –
intermediate mainly

Season
Dec – Apr

Other Local Activities
Ice skating,
paragliding,
snowmobiling

Resort Stats
Top: 2,600m
Bottom: 990m
Vertical: 1,610m
Lifts: 14
Pistes: 75km

www.banskoski.com

BANSKO, BULGARIA
Bulgaria's biggest and best

Bansko features high on many a list of budget ski options and, while the overall skiing experience isn't generally as slick as that of resorts in the Alps or Rocky Mountains, it's improving all the time.

The resort saw a surge of modern developments including fast new lifts and improved accommodation back in 2004, since when there have been more improvements which ensure it remains Bulgaria's number one ski resort in terms of both size and facilities. And perhaps the most important feature of all is provided free by Mother Nature – the region, which is in the Pirin National Park (and as such there has been some understandable opposition to some of the developments since the wilder areas of the park are home to bears and wolves amongst other animals) tends to have more reliable snowfall than the country's other resorts.

The skiing consists primarily of red and blue runs which snake down from the open upper slopes of the impressively pointy Mount Todorka (2,746 metres) and then through trees before winding up back at the base in town (where unfortunately you can often encounter long lift queues); it will suit all but the most picky of intermediate skiers, and there are also some challenging blacks including the Tomba to Bunderishka (depending on how old you are you may remember the flamboyant Italian ski racer after which it's named).

But that's not to say there isn't plenty of off-piste action to be had too. Indeed, Bansko has featured on the Freeride World Tour qualifiers (as well as FIS World Cup alpine ski races), and is Bulgaria's most popular freeride and ski touring destination. Even so, you'll have a good chance of scoring fresh tracks if you decide to explore the backcountry here – it gets tracked out considerably less quickly than the popular resorts of the Alps and Rockies.

As a recognised budget ski option, you may have to keep check of your alcohol intake on nights out in the town if you want to make the most of the skiing though. Bansko is renowned for its cheap and cheerful nightlife, including the 'mehanas', traditional Bulgarian inns in the old part of town which serve up roast meat, wine and beer in huge quantities and at low prices.

There's a lot to be said for keeping your skiing cheap and cheerful of course, which means there's a lot to be said for Bansko (and there is five-star accommodation if you really must have the best – try the Florimont, with its casino, or the Kempinski Grand Arena and its amazing spa).

And catch Bansko after a fresh dump of powder and you could end up scoring five-star skiing at three-star prices.

Getting high in Bansko

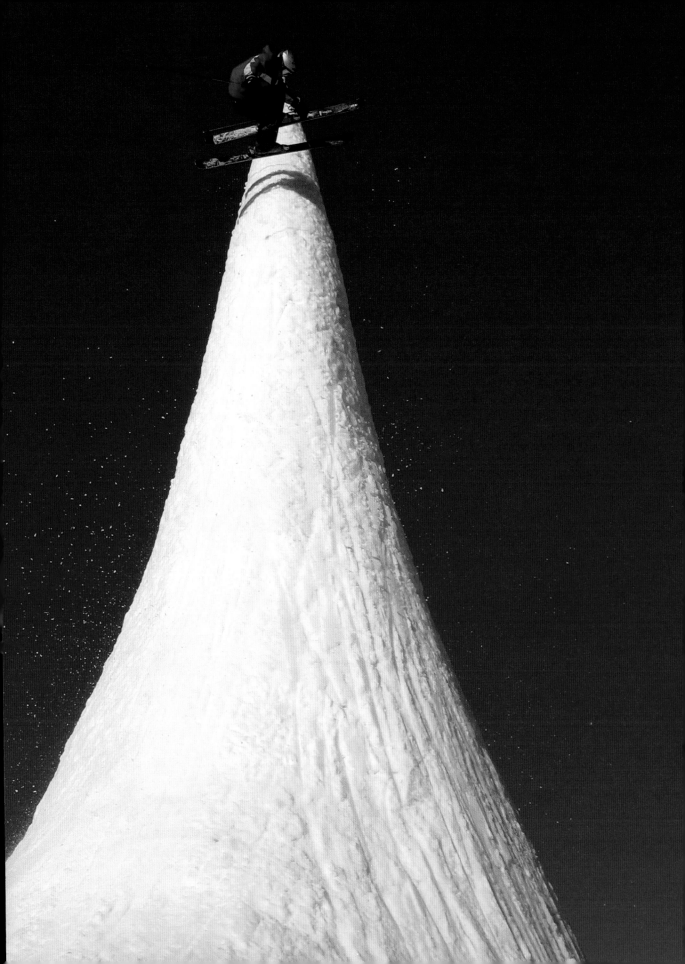

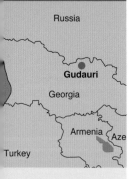

Russia

Gudauri

Georgia

Armenia Aze

Turkey

Access
Nearest airport:
Tbilisi (120km),
Kutaisi (295km)

Ability Level
Beginner – expert

Season
Dec – Apr/May

Other Local Activities
Cat-skiing, heli-skiing,
cross-country skiing,
snow tubing

Resort Stats
Top: 3,276m
Bottom: 1,993m
Vertical: 1,283m
Lifts: 15
Pistes: 35km

www.gudauri.info

GUDAURI, GEORGIA
Lapping it up

Georgia's biggest and best-established ski resort made the headlines in 2018 when footage of a chair lift running backwards at high speed went viral on the internet. Fortunately, no one was seriously hurt, and, well, mistakes happen – anyone who chooses to give Gudauri a miss on the basis of this one incident is making a big mistake.

The resort is only a two-hour drive from Georgia's eclectic capital city of Tbilisi, along the historic Georgian Military Road, which crosses the Jvari Pass into Russia at 2,379 metres; its strategic importance has seen the route used by travellers, traders and invaders from Pliny the Elder to the troops of Imperial Russia and the Soviet Union, and today it grumbles to the sound of endless convoys of trucks carrying goods from Central Asia to Europe and vice versa.

Gudauri has the happy-go-lucky feel of a resort where the skiing isn't too serious – it's popular with novices from Georgia and Eastern Europe along with Arabic visitors who are often seeing snow for the first time. That said, there is plenty of steep and challenging side-country terrain and designated freeride areas where you can be as serious as you want if that's your thing, and there's also the option of good-value cat- and heli-skiing too.

Sitting beneath 3,276-metre Mount Sadzele West, and with ridge after ridge of high mountains fading away into the north, Gudauri also offers a lovely array of intermediate level pistes that are wide, open and invite you to blast down at full speed.

Wending your way past machine-gun toting, but nevertheless friendly, security guards at the bottom of some of the lifts (perhaps a throwback to the Soviet era?), the pistes invite you to repeat lap after lap, maybe eventually whizzing down to Gondola Square in 'New Gudauri' which, as the name suggests, is a recent addition to the resort, akin to a small suburb a few hundred metres above Gudauri itself, where a range of hotels, cafes, bars, shops and ski hire can be found.

New Gudauri has been developed by the Canadian company Ecosign Mountain Resort Planners, and as such has a North American feel to it; enjoying a coffee at the Drunk Cherry Bar you could easily be at a ski resort in the Rocky Mountains as music ranging from hip-hop to Miles Davis fills the air and bearded hipsters in the latest ski fashions slouch with self-conscious cool against the most convenient wall.

Back on the mountain, and moving away from the pistes, expansive, treeless slopes allow you to weave your way pretty much wherever you please, with fantastic views of the High Caucasus, the biggest and wildest mountain range in Europe, opening up the higher you go.

For skiers who want to explore further afield Gudauri's freeriding and backcountry potential is high, and the terrain is considerably less busy than that of the Alps and Rockies – which is probably why it's becoming a bucket list destination for many.

Dropping into Gudauri's quiet backcountry © gudauri.info

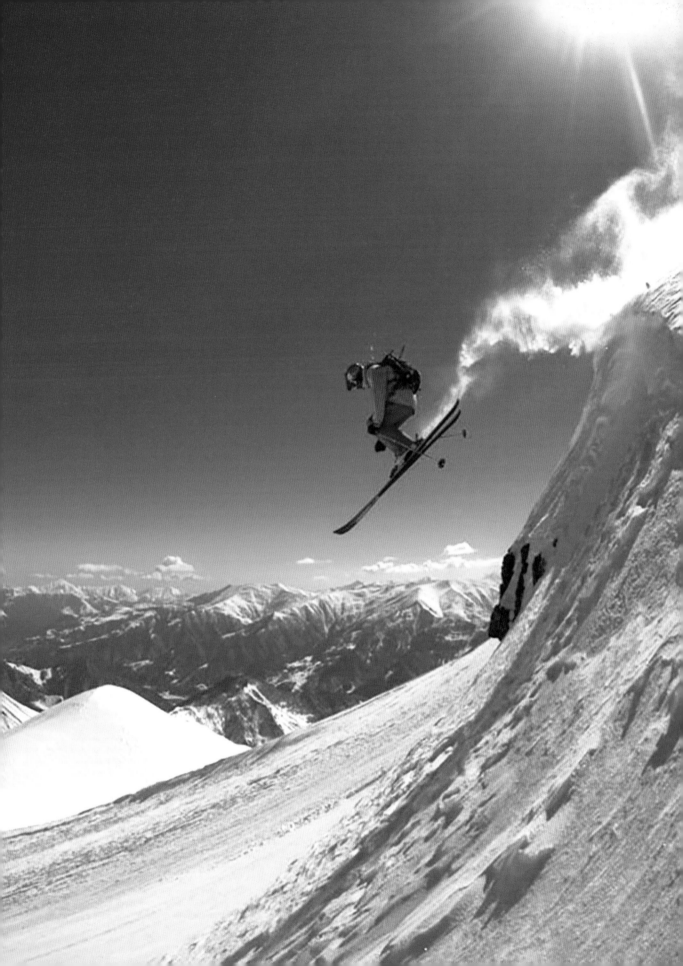

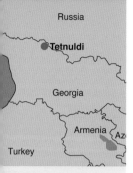

Access
Nearest airports:
Mestia (small
airstrip, 15km),
Kutaisi (240km),
Batumi (256km),
Tbilisi (430km)

Ability Level
Beginner – expert

Season
Dec – Apr

Other Local Activities
Heli-skiing, cat-skiing,
paragliding, horse
riding

Resort Stats
Top: 3,160m
Bottom: 2,265m
Vertical: 895m
Lifts: 5
Pistes: 13.4km

www.tetnuldi.com

TETNULDI, GEORGIA
Wine, dumplings and very, very good skiing

Whilst a pedant might take issue with whether Georgia is actually in Eastern Europe – the Greater Caucasus mountains amongst which Tetnuldi lies are generally considered to be at the geographic 'intersection' of Europe and Asia – there's no doubt that Tetnuldi is right out there when it comes to ski resorts.

In unfavourable weather conditions it can only be accessed by a nine-hour drive along increasingly potholed roads from the cosmopolitan capital city of Tbilisi (where most visitors arrive) up the deep Enguri Gorge, dammed during the Soviet era, through thick forests that are home to brown bears, wolves and lynx, beneath rugged mountain peaks higher than anything in the Alps until you eventually arrive at the base for skiing here, the historic 'townlet' of Mestia (in good weather it's a short flight from Tbilisi to the airstrip in Mestia, but good weather is at a premium in the Caucasus).

Mestia is famed for its Svan towers, sturdy stone-built defensive structures rising several storeys into the sky that date back to the 12th-13th centuries and are now listed as UNESCO World Heritage sites; they give the place a distinct 'Game of Thrones' feel and are well worth a visit, as are Mestia's small but lively bars and restaurants serving delicious traditional Georgian dishes such as khachapuri (a kind of Georgian pizza) and khinkali (meat dumplings eaten by hand) along, of course, with excellent wines in the country that was the birthplace of viticulture.

When you're eventually ready to go skiing it's another half-hour drive from Mestia along a snowbound dirt track only accessible by 4WD vehicle to reach Tetnuldi ski resort, which lies in the shadow of 4,858-metre Mount Tetnuldi, one of four Georgian peaks higher than Europe's loftiest point, Mont Blanc.

Given its relative inaccessibility it's no surprise to find that Tetnuldi's four chairlifts and attendant slopes are usually very scarcely populated. Combine this with consistently good snow and almost 1,000 vertical metres of terrain to slide down and the long drive to get here suddenly becomes very worthwhile, despite there being only 13km of marked pistes – because that's not what you come here to ski. It's the backcountry that's the big attraction here – don't let the sparsely detailed piste map put you off, there's far more to Tetnuldi than first meets the eye.

The resort has only been operating since 2014, so has yet to really make a mark on the international ski scene – visitors tend to be either locals from Mestia, city-dwellers from Tbilisi or a sprinkling of international guests mainly from neighbouring Russia and Europe.

You'll meet local skiers over lunch in the sparsely decorated restaurant at the base of the ski area (there's no accommodation in resort at present), where a quick "გამარჯობა" ("Gamarjoba" – "Hello" in Georgian) is invariably followed by the response: "Where are you from?"

The off-piste terrain can be challenging and is best explored with a guide, but in return for taking on the challenge you get to enjoy deserted slopes, deep powder and truly wild and spectacular alpine panoramas.

This is all easily accessed from the lifts, whilst the slopes between the handful of easy pistes also offer some very fine powder skiing. From the open expanses of high alpine landscapes beneath the top chairlift at 3,160 metres, the terrain eventually descends into wooded glades, all of which generally remain innocent of crowds; but don't expect it to stay that way for ever, since Georgia is rapidly becoming the ski destination for the discerning skier.

Mount Ushba, the 'Matterhorn' of the Caucasus © BaBu. Luka MamulaiDze

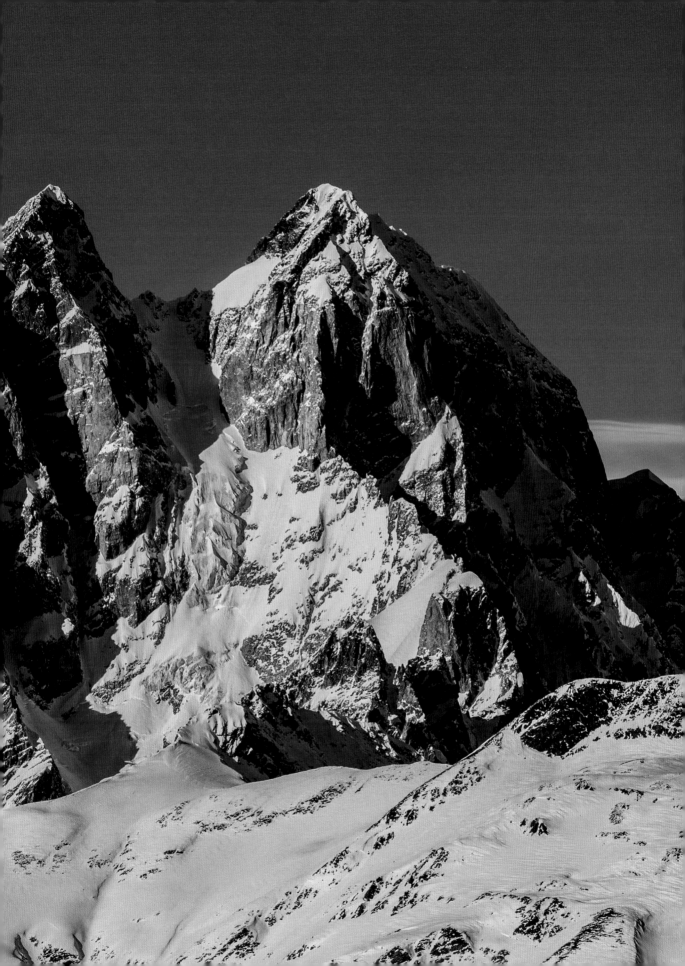

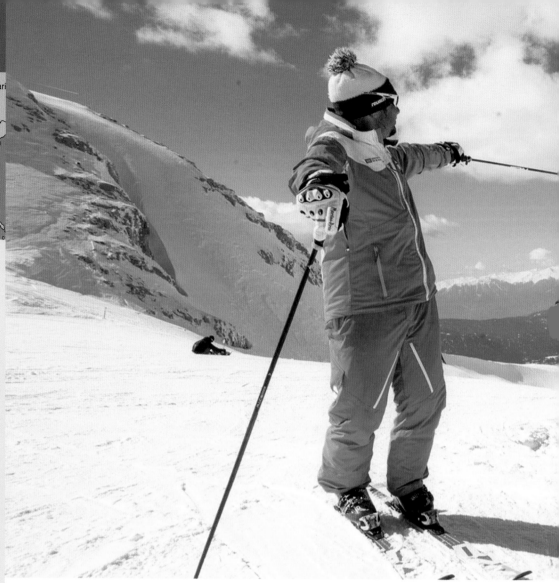

Bulgari

North Macedonia

Albania

Greece

Mount Parnassos

Access
Nearest airport:
Athens (180km)

Ability Level
Beginner – expert

Season
Dec – Apr

Other Local Activities
Ski touring & visiting
historical sites

Resort Stats
Top: 2,300m
Bottom: 1,600m
Vertical: 700m
Lifts: 17
Pistes: 36km

www.discovergreece.
com

MOUNT PARNASSOS, GREECE
Skiing with the gods

Greece is far from being the first place you'd consider for a ski trip, but it has a number of ski resorts that often have surprisingly good conditions. Mount Parnassos is the biggest of them, and as such offers the best range of facilities – along with the unique opportunity to ski with views of olive groves and the dazzling blue waters of the Gulf of Corinth and the Euboic Sea (which, let's be honest, most of us have never even heard of).

And, this being Greece, you're surrounded by classical history – the UNESCO World Heritage Site of Delphi is just to the south and well worth a visit, perhaps the more so in winter when it won't be overrun by tourists.

But back to the skiing... Parnassos Ski Centre consists of two linked ski areas, Fterólakka and Kellária. The former dates back to 1976, the latter to 1981, with the link between the two being completed in 1986/87.

This created a modestly-sized ski area which has been developed further to now offer around 36km of pistes, the majority of which are blue and red and come with appropriately Greek names, such as Hermes and Aphrodites (both blue) and Odysseus, a tough red with a couple of nice, steep sections. Four of the pistes have been approved by the FIS for international competitions.

In recent years a number of ungroomed 'ski tours' have been developed (akin to 'ski itineraries' in the

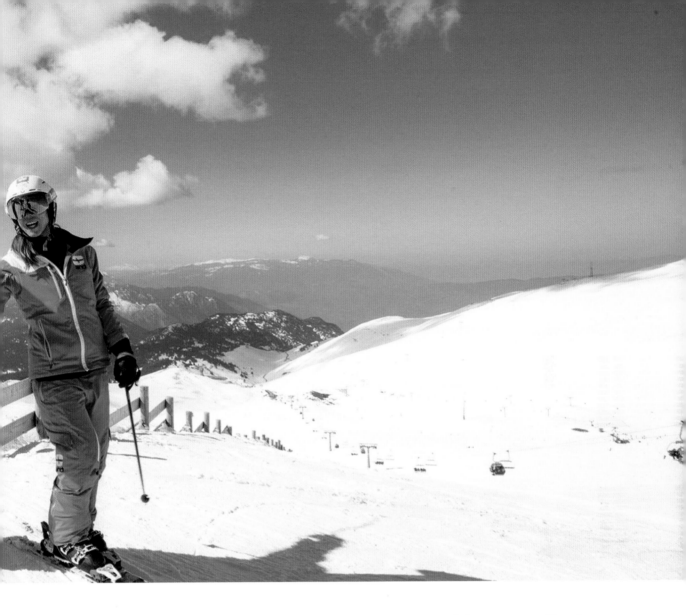

Alps); since the ski scene at Parnassos tends to be very relaxed it means the plentiful off-piste terrain is invariably quiet and remains untracked for far longer after a dump than it would at an equivalent-sized resort in the Alps. There's a good range of freeride, backcountry and ski touring options, and the quality of them is good enough for the Freeride World Tour to have held a qualifying event here.

To get a feel for what Greece has to offer skiers it's well worth checking out *A Line in the Snow*, a lovely short film about the Greek ski touring scene. As Giorgos Rokas, a Greek mountain refuge guardian says in the film: "Greece is a ski touring paradise... I think it's going to be a major destination in the future for ski touring."

We shall see...

There's no slopeside accommodation at Parnassus, so visitors have to stay in one of a variety of villages between 20-45 minutes away, of which Arachova is the best option for its attractive setting and good range of hotels, bars and restaurants.

For most overseas skiers there's the obvious concern over snow quality and quantity when visiting Greece given the country's reputation for hot, sunny weather and beach life, and to be fair even though Mount Parnassos and its neighbouring peaks rise to around 2,500 metres the southerly location means that the snow conditions can't really match those of the Alps.

However, if you're looking for a little adventure and can travel at the last minute it's well worth keeping an eye on the weather charts and snow reports for the possibility of making a lightning strike on Parnassos; or, since the resort is only 180km from Athens, it's gotta be worth taking a pair of skis along if you're in the city for any length of time in winter – or just head up to the mountain and rent your gear for the day.

Mount Parnossos – an unexpected combination of Greek sun and snow
© discovergreece.com

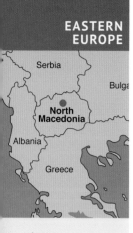

Access
Nearest airport:
Skopje (63km from
Popova Shapka)

Ability Level
Intermediate –
expert

Season
Dec – Apr

Other Local Activities
Ski touring & visiting
historical sites

Resort Stats
Vary depending upon
operator

www.powerhounds.
com

NORTH MACEDONIA
An eclectic mix of skiing, terrain and culture

There are a handful of ski resorts in North Macedonia, of
which the largest are Popova Shapka and Mavrovo, which
have around 11 ski lifts each and between 20-25km of pistes,
so you wouldn't make them the focus of a week or more of
skiing.

However, given that they're less than 100km apart you
could get two or three days of decent skiing by visiting both
– but all this is really beside the point, since the reason most
visiting skiers come to North Macedonia is cat-skiing in the
wild and remote Šar Mountains close to the Albanian border
– the highest peak, Mount Korab, rises to an impressive 2,764
metres, and the peaks here a well-placed to pick up ample
winter precipitation descending upon them from the north.

Indeed, Eskimo Freeride in Popova Shapka is the oldest cat-
ski operation in Europe and offers an eclectic mix of skiing,
majestic nature and gastronomical and cultural experiences
along with a massive 10,000 hectares of alpine and forest
terrain. They have an impressive seven cats which allows
groups to be well mixed in terms of ability and preferred ski
terrain.

South of Popova Shapka near Bogovinje, Shar Outdoors
operates a recently opened cat-skiing operation based out of
two mountain huts, as well as running the highly regarded
Balkans Cat Ski Safari, taking in the best of North Macedonia
and neighbouring Kosovo.

Also in North Macedonia is SF Freeride, which operates
within the Pelister National Park, where the rich array of
wildlife includes bears, roe deer, wolves, lynx, chamois, wild
boars and several species of eagles – keep your eyes peeled,
you never know what you might see whilst hooning down a
powder field.

North Macedonia is a far cry from the kind of
commercialised skiing you'll find in the Alps – one of the
major package operators for the area, Powderhounds,
succinctly sums it up: "When you cat-ski here you are in one
of the last European wildernesses. There are no mountain
huts with disco music serving beer, and once away from
the Popova Sapka ski area there is very little infrastructure.
Despite this, you can still expect great culinary and local
cultural experiences."

And, one huge plus point – it'll cost you less than half the
price of similar cat-ski experiences in North America.

Powederhounds also advise that if you're considering
a ski trip here you should be aware of the fact that North
Macedonia is far from being "... a fully sanitised Western
European ski destination" and as such "... is best suited to
skiers with a worldly, open mind and a sense of adventure."

If that sounds like you, what are you waiting for?

One of the last European wildernesses
© Dane Freeride Kosovo Powerhounds

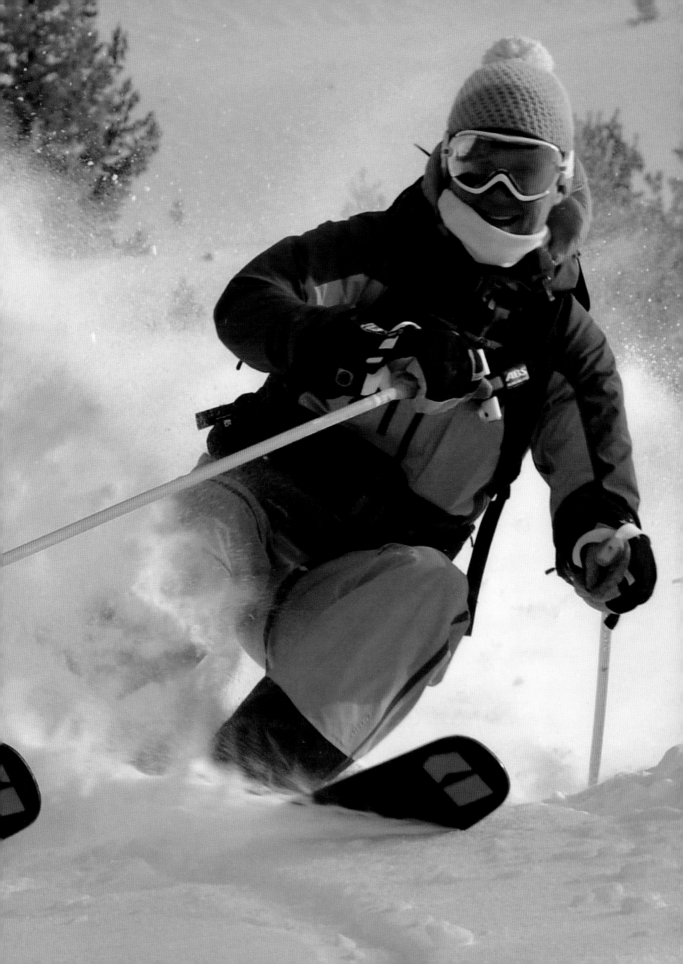

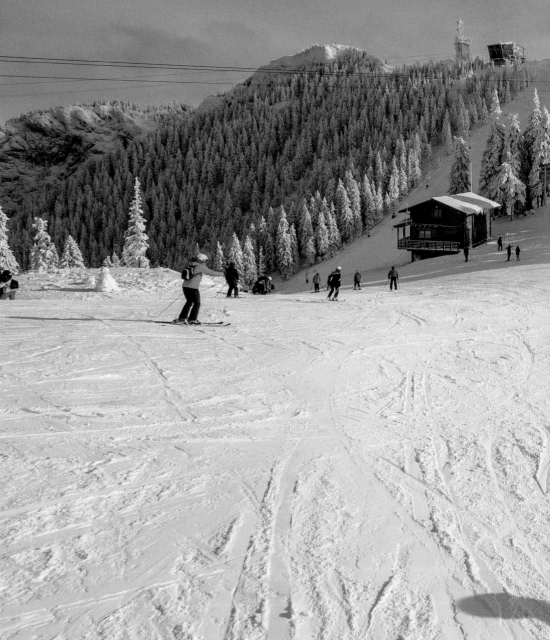

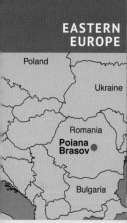

Poland

Ukraine

Romania

Poiana Brasov ●

Bulgaria

Access
Nearest airport:
Bucharest (188km)

Ability Level
Beginner –
intermediate

Season
Dec – Mar

Other Local Activities
Snowshoeing

Resort Stats
Top: 1,800m
Bottom: 1,050m
Vertical: 750m
Lifts: 9
Pistes: 24km

www.poianabrasov.
com

POIANA BRASOV, ROMANIA
A winning combination

Experienced skiers may raise an eyebrow at the inclusion of little Poiana Brasov in this book but, if you're looking for your first ski experience, and / or you're on a tight budget, it has a lot to offer – and I speak from the experience of being in both of those positions when I first skied here.

Website reviews of the resort regularly consist of novice skiers raving about the quality of the ski instruction, the friendliness of the locals, the low costs and the beauty of the Carpathian Mountains, which is a pretty winning combination by any standard.

The resort dates back to 1951, when it hosted the World Student Winter Games; needless to say, for the next few decades it was pretty much out of bounds to visitors from Western Europe, Romania being locked behind the Iron Curtain as it was. But following the Romanian revolution in December 1989 the country was able to gradually open up to tourism in the 1990s, and few places went for it more than

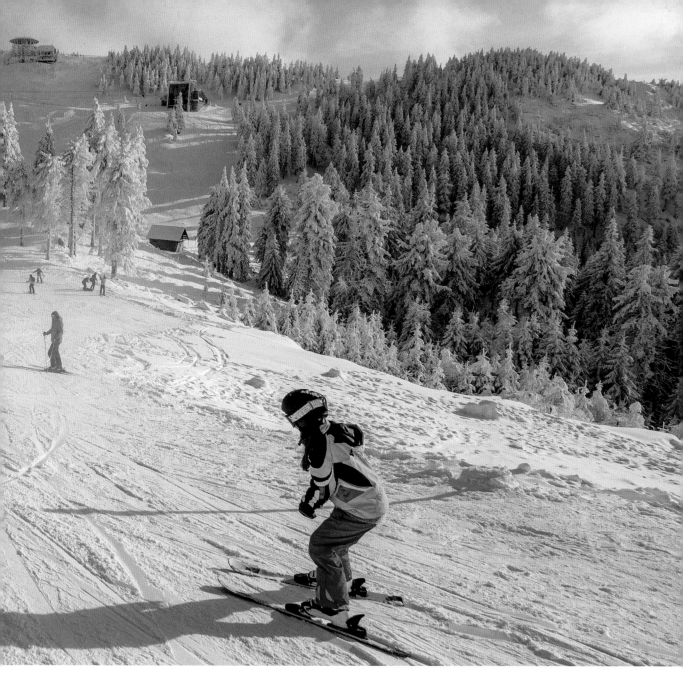

Poiana Brasov.

The architects and designers of the resort looked west to see how it was done in the Alps, and in recent years there has been a large investment in improving the slopes, snow-making, lifts and accommodation, and although the resort is small by worldwide standards so are the prices – look to spend around €100 for a five-day lift pass, for instance.

Of course, you ain't gonna get anything comparable to a French mega-resort for this price – as the stats opposite show the skiing is very limited for better skiers (although the off-piste terrain can remain relatively untouched for days at a time) but Poiana Brasov isn't trying to offer a great holiday for skiers looking to cruise massive distances on piste or hit epic backcountry powder fields.

What it does offer novice skiers in particular is a chance to experience the sport without breaking the bank. On top of that you get to ski in one of the wildest and least-spoiled mountain ranges in Europe, you can take day trips to Dracula's castle (yes, really) or the nearby medieval city of Brasov, and you can drink far too much of an evening without having to take out a second mortgage.

Plus, you'll probably come back a way better skier than you were before you visited, and what's so wrong with that…?

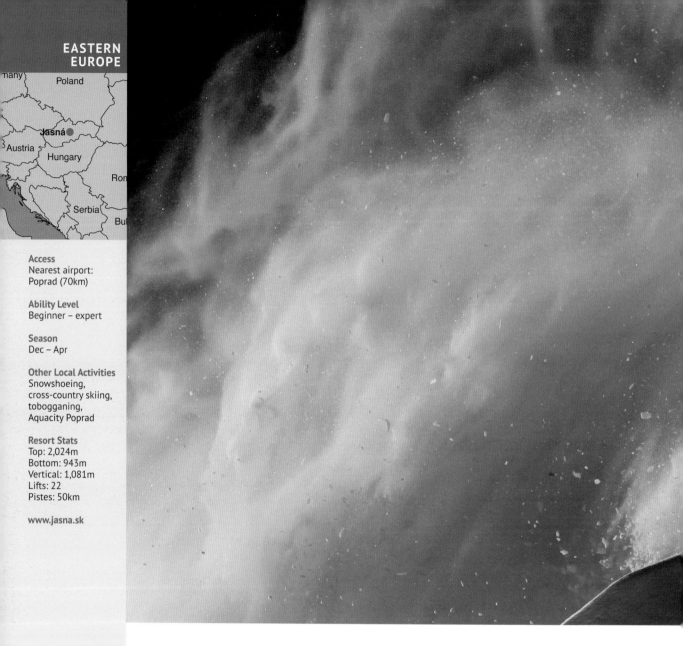

Poland

Jasná●

Austria

Hungary

Germany

Ror

Serbia

Bul

Access
Nearest airport:
Poprad (70km)

Ability Level
Beginner – expert

Season
Dec – Apr

Other Local Activities
Snowshoeing,
cross-country skiing,
tobogganing,
Aquacity Poprad

Resort Stats
Top: 2,024m
Bottom: 943m
Vertical: 1,081m
Lifts: 22
Pistes: 50km

www.jasna.sk

JASNÁ, SLOVAKIA
Enjoy the good vibes

From the top of Jasná's high point, 2,024-metre Mount Chopok, you can look down on what is the largest ski resort in Central Europe, and one that can readily compete with the small to medium-sized resorts of the Alps and North America in terms of ski area, vertical and snow quality – and it's a hell of a lot cheaper to ski here.

And don't be fooled into thinking that because you're skiing in the Low Tatra mountains you're missing out on what's available in the High Tatra mountains, which lie less than an hour's drive to the north – despite the name, the three resorts in the High Tatra (Tatranská Lomnica, Starý Smokovec and Štrbské Pleso) are significantly smaller in size than Jasná.

So, back to Jasná. Its 50km of pistes contain a well-balanced mix of beginner, intermediate and advanced runs and, whatever level of ability you have, you'll undoubtedly enjoy blasting around them and taking the occasional budget-friendly break in one of the mountain restaurants that dot the slopes (don't miss the Von Roll on Chopok's north side, which is built around an old lift station, after which it's named – the architects retained the sixty-year-old winding mechanism as the centrepiece of the dining

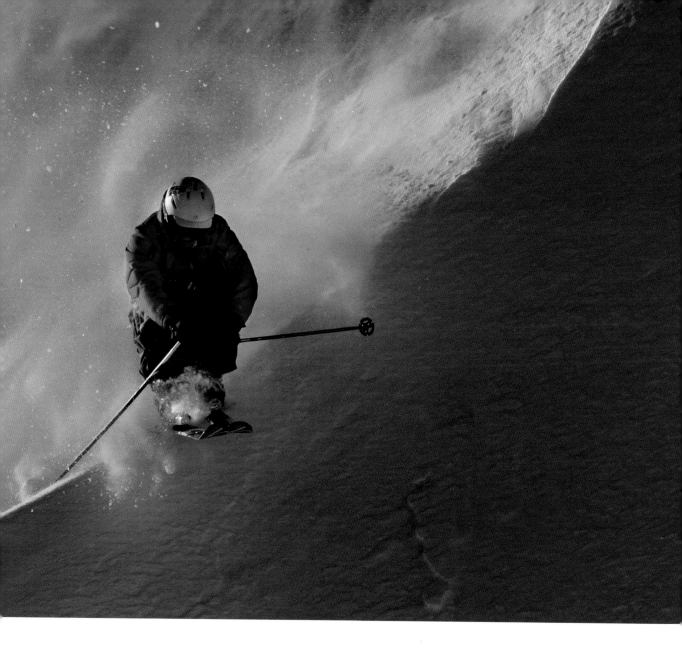

area, and this along with a roaring fire and fine food will endear it to anyone wanting to refuel before heading back onto the mountain).

But the pièce de résistance at Jasná is the freeride terrain. A dozen or so freeride zones await you, and there's even a 'freeride manual' for the ski area with info on said zones, so you can pick out the area best suited to your abilities.

The freeriding is, loosely speaking, split between the north and south sides of Chopok, which are very different in nature, with steeper and more challenging terrain – including a few couloirs – on the north side, and less steeply angled bowls and open faces on the south side; indeed, Jasná's terrain is so good that the qualifying rounds of the Freeride World Tour have been held here several times.

Along with good skiing there's also a good vibe in Jasná, with the locals being as keen, friendly and enthusiastic as you'll meet anywhere, and although the amount of terrain is quite modest by the standards of European and North American mega-resorts there's more than enough snow-based fun here to keep anyone going for a week, especially when you consider that you can easily take a day trip to the smaller resorts of the High Tatra mountains too.

And if you have a down day, or feel like a break from the skiing, the nearby city of Poprad is well worth a visit, if only for its fine bars and beers, although it also boasts the huge Aquacity Poprad, a water park and spa with thirteen pools and no end of water-based jollity.

Snow, water, beer and good vibes all wrapped up in one neat package – hard to beat really...

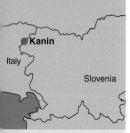

Austria

Kanin

Italy

Slovenia

Access
Nearest airport:
Ljubljana or
Klagenfurt (Austria)
depending on ski
resort

Ability Level
Beginner – expert

Season
Dec – Apr

Other Local Activities
Snowshoeing, cross-
country skiing, hiking,
tobogganing

Resort Stats
Vary depending upon
resort

www.slovenia.info

KANIN AND CO, SLOVENIA
Flagging it up

"What does 'Kanin and co' mean?" you may ask, and not unreasonably. Well, given the small size of Slovenia's thirty or so ski resorts it seems reasonable to start with the highest and – arguably – the best of the country's resorts, Kanin, and move on from there – hence the 'co'.

That said, Kanin was actually closed for a time a few years back, but thankfully it has now reopened and offers some very acceptable skiing just outside the Triglav National Park in the Julian Alps on Slovenia's western border with Italy; indeed, you can actually ski into Italy from Kanin (and vice-versa) since it's linked to the small Italian resort of Sella Nevea.

(Whilst we're on the subject of Triglav National Park, it's named after Slovenia's highest peak, which tops out at 2,864 metres and is the only mountain in the world to appear on a national flag, sitting as it does in the top left-hand corner of the Slovenian flag – which kind of shows how central mountains are to everyday life in Slovenia.)

Kanin is close to several other ski hills, amongst which are Vogel, with its beautiful lake setting, Krvavec, which has some of Slovenia's steepest slopes, and Kranjska Gora, perhaps the country's best-known ski area (despite not being the biggest) thanks to having a World Cup slalom run. And then some miles to the east is Maribor-Pohoroje – amongst others – above Slovenia's outdoor capital of Maribor; this is the largest ski resort in the country, although it has less than 50km of pistes. And then there's Planica, where you can go ski jumping should you so wish...

The skiing options are relatively limited when compared to neighbouring Austria and Italy but, if you're prepared to drive, Slovenia can make for a great ski road trip since most ski areas are less than an hour apart, and – the real clincher – you can buy a 'Julian Alps International Ski Pass' for around €200 a week which gives you access to 14 ski resorts in three countries (Slovenia, Italy and Austria) which between them offer 260km of slopes at altitudes of between 550 and 2,293 metres. And some even offer views over the sparkling blue waters of the Adriatic.

Along with this fun selection of dinky little ski hills you'll also discover in Slovenia some truly beautiful scenery, a very friendly and hospitable culture and a refreshing absence of lift queues – indeed, during the middle of the week it's not that unusual to find the slopes almost deserted.

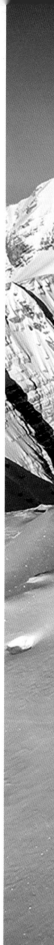

Glorious solitude at Kanin © Katja Pokorn

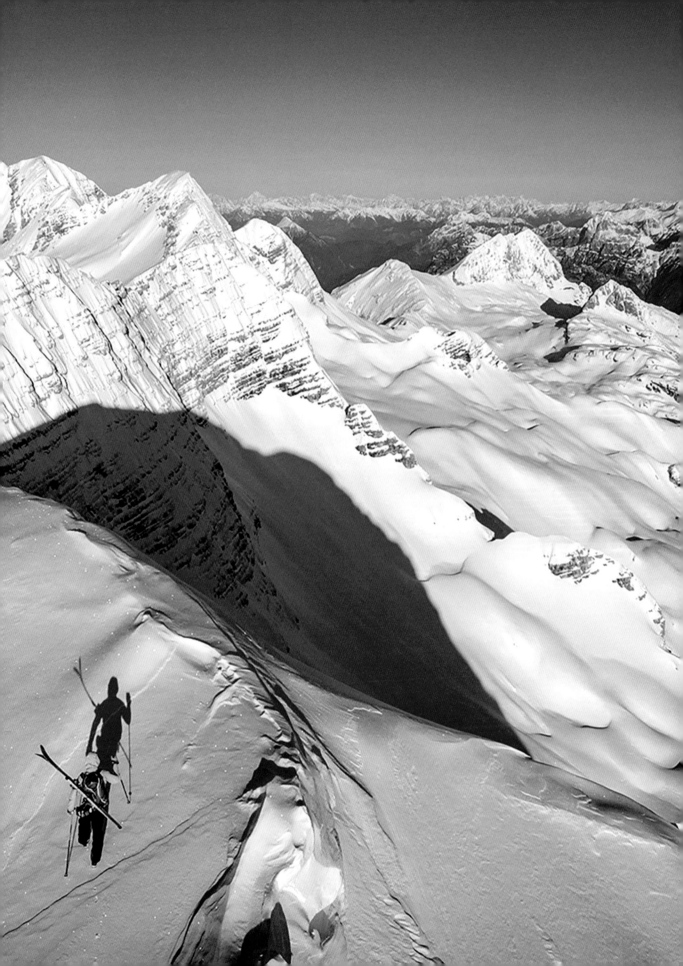

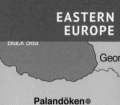

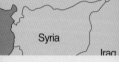

Palandöken●

Turkey

Syria

Iraq

Access
Nearest airport:
Erzurum (16km)

Ability Level
Beginner – expert

Season
Nov/Dec – Apr/May

Other Local Activities
Heli-skiing, cross-country skiing

Resort Stats
Top: 3,192m
Bottom: 2,100m
Vertical: 1,092m

www.skiturkish.com

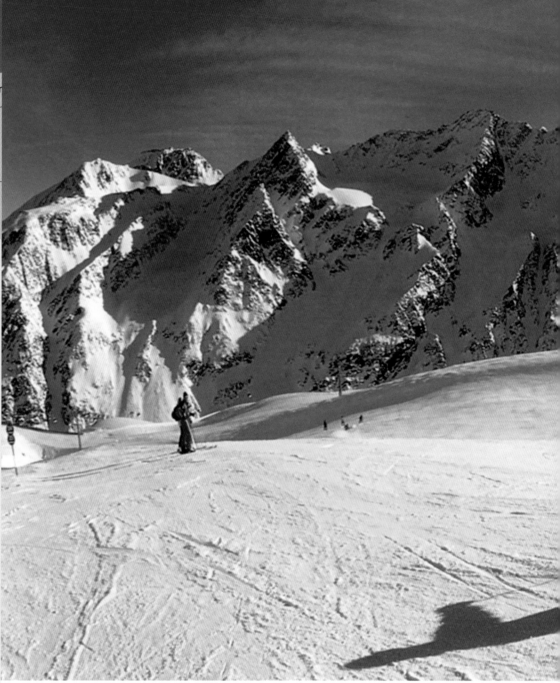

PALANDÖKEN, TURKEY
Turkish delight

Turkey has some fifteen different ski resorts, spread liberally around the country, all the way from close to the shores of the Mediterranean and Aegean to Palandöken in Eastern Anatolia.

Since Palandöken is one of the biggest Turkish resorts as well as being the highest at 3,125 metres it makes a good option if you plan to ski in this exotic nation. It's made even more exotic by the fact that you're unlikely to run into that many western skiers, with the majority of visitors being Turkish, Russian and Ukranian, and most seem only too keen to meet skiers from further afield and compare notes.

Palandöken also offers some of the longest and steepest pistes in Turkey, with a decent mix for all abilities – wide, open beginner, intermediate and advanced pistes dot the mountain pretty equitably in a ski area that could readily pass for a small-to-medium sized European resort, and there's also a

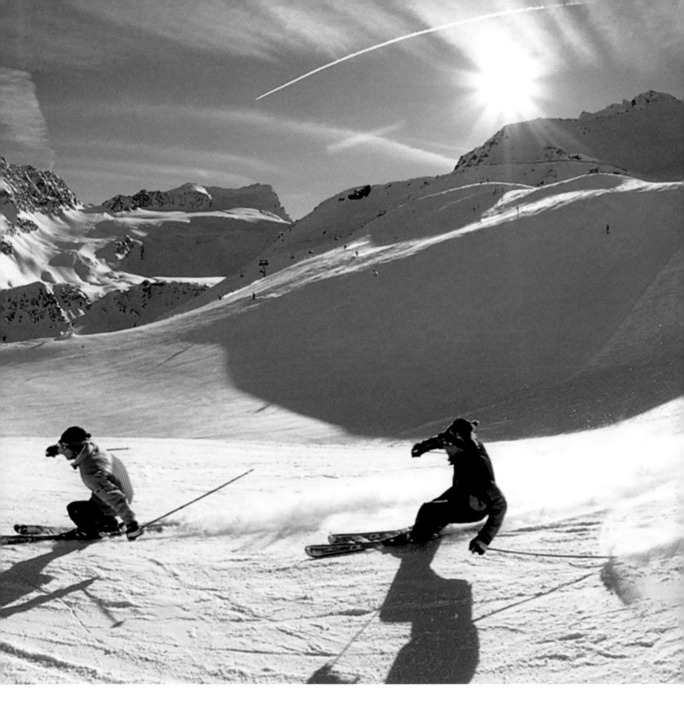

smaller neighbouring resort, Konakli which, whilst not linked, can be accessed by shuttle bus or taxi.

It's worth noting that most of the skiing at Palandöken is above the tree-line, which can cause problems with visibility in bad weather, although there are three good-value mountain restaurants where you can shelter from the elements should the need arise.

In addition, there's plenty of freeride terrain, including five off-piste itineraries, and since off-piste skiing isn't anywhere near as popular here as in the west you can expect to find fresh tracks all day long after a dump. And that fresh powder often stays in good condition for longer than in the Alps due to the combination of high altitude, heavy snowfalls and a continental climate that is low in humidity.

Another bonus of Palandöken's location is that you're literally just a few minutes' drive from the 6,000-year-old city of Erzurum. A visit should be on your list of things to do on a down-day since it is so far removed from the towns and cities you'll experience in more 'regular' ski resorts. Established in Roman times and once on the Silk Road, Erzurum has some splendid mosques and madrasas to wander around along with shops and markets where you can pick up bargain souvenirs.

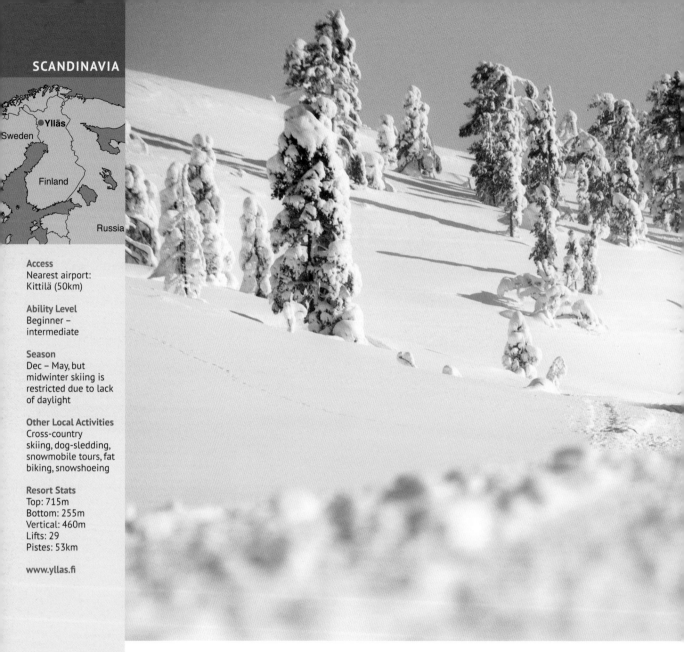

Sweden
●Ylläs

Finland

Russia

Access
Nearest airport:
Kittilä (50km)

Ability Level
Beginner –
intermediate

Season
Dec – May, but
midwinter skiing is
restricted due to lack
of daylight

Other Local Activities
Cross-country
skiing, dog-sledding,
snowmobile tours, fat
biking, snowshoeing

Resort Stats
Top: 715m
Bottom: 255m
Vertical: 460m
Lifts: 29
Pistes: 53km

www.yllas.fi

YLLÄS, FINLAND
Break out the skinny skis

Despite the fact that Ylläs is Finland's largest ski resort, it's not really the downhill skiing that is the attraction here, but the cross-country skiing. With well over 300km of marked trails snaking out across the local peaks, valleys, forests and lakes (and some 15 trailside cafés in which to warm up / cool down and refresh) it dwarfs the 53km of downhill pistes.

This makes Ylläs a great destination for those skiers who like to vary the kind of planks they ride upon. And it's also very family friendly too, since the majority of pistes are suited to novice and intermediate skiers (there are also four snowparks if that's your thing) and outside the main season in February the slopes tend to be pretty quiet.

The gently rounded hills rise bare above forests and lakes and are less vertiginous and savage than major mountain chains such as the Alps, but they have their own chilly charm – for it can get very cold this far north, with minus 30°C being quite common.

There's a real feeling of being in the far north when you ski in Ylläs, and this is exacerbated by the

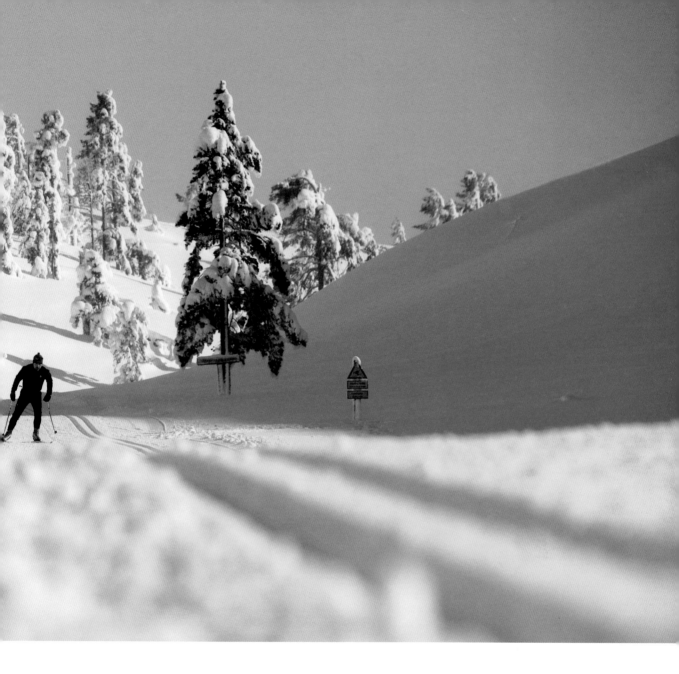

Cross-country at Ylläs
© www.yllas.fi

fact that in mid-winter daylight hours are limited, if not non-existent due to the high latitude; on the plus side, the Northern Lights can be seen regularly, and towards the end of the ski season daylight hours are much longer than in the Alps.

The resort rises to a high point of 715 metres (with 460 metres of vertical) from where you can ski down to either Sport Resort Ylläs on one side of the mountain or Ylläs-Ski on the other, in each of which you'll find everything including ski schools, restaurants and shops.

Check with the ski schools if you're looking to enjoy some off-piste skiing – beside the 'side country' either side of the pistes the surrounding 'fells' (as opposed to mountains) also offer some good backcountry entertainment and this far north the snow can stay in good condition for long periods.

Given the popularity of cross-country skiing in this part of the world, and the excellent facilities available in Ylläs, it's well worth considering having a go on skinny skis too if you've never tried it. There's a huge variety of trails to suit all abilities with wind shelters, huts and the aforementioned cafés along the way for when you need a break – or just want to stop and take in the silence and the scenery.

And 38km of the trails are illuminated – there's something magical about being out in the forests in deep winter at night, particularly when the snow is falling.

The Finnish fells may be small in comparison to the Alps or Rockies, but when you catch them as the Northern Lights put on a show overhead they're every bit as wild and wonderful.

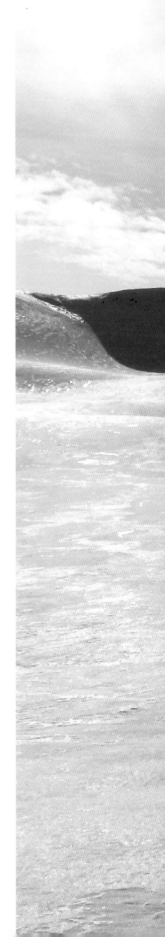

Access
Nearest airport to
Húsavík: Akureyri
(76km)

Ability Level
Advanced – expert

Season
May – Jun

Other Local Activities
Whale watching

Resort Stats
Top: 1,000m
Bottom: Sea level
Vertical: 1,000m
Lifts: None
Pistes: None

www.bergmenn.com

Í FJÖRÐUM, ICELAND
Ski and sail on the edge of the Arctic

So, this is a bit different – using a two-mast, 60ft wooden schooner as a ski 'chalet'. But it makes admirably good sense if you're ski touring amongst the wild and magnificent landscapes of northern Iceland.

The peaks of the Í Fjörðum region are easily reached in just a few hours sailing from the busy whale watching centre of Húsavík, which despite a modest population of just 2,500 souls is one of the largest settlements on Iceland's north coast – indeed, a boat is by far the best way to access Í Fjörðum, a perpetually snow-capped landscape of mountains and moorlands that is virtually inaccessible by vehicle and which has no settlements other than an occasional remote, abandoned farmhouse or an equally remote 'summer house' here and there along the shoreline.

Iceland offers the chance to ski amongst landscapes that you just don't find in the Alps or Rockies; where else can you stand atop a mountain and look down on the ocean, the small dot of Flatey Island just offshore, further north the outline of Grímsey Island through which passes the Arctic Circle, and beyond nothing until the pack ice of the Arctic Ocean?

And although ski touring is obviously quite hard work in itself, there's never any rush to ascend the slopes, since with almost 24 hours of daylight when the ski touring season gets under way in early May it doesn't really matter what time you head off into the hills – even if you got 'benighted' it would only be for about 90 minutes.

Days follow a regular pattern. Rise to bright sunlight glinting on the waters of whichever bay you're anchored in, down a huge breakfast and then transfer to shore in the boat's tender. Once ashore hike for a few hundred metres up to the snowline (although in a good winter the snow will come right down to the beach), clip in to your bindings then settle in for several hours of skinning up to your chosen summit.

Yes, it may be a slog, but every time you stop for a breather you're greeted by views of elemental sub-Arctic landscapes – sky, snow, sea, it's about as primal and as glorious as it can get and it more than repays the effort.

Most of the mountains that stand guard along this stretch of Iceland's north coast top out at around 1,000 metres, which means that once you reach your chosen summit you've earned a descent as long as those in many decent-sized ski resorts.

But unlike most ski resorts this descent will be with just a handful of friends on untracked spring snow, with no sign of humankind to be seen anywhere...

Inaccessible by vehicle, so arrive by boat © Alf Alderson

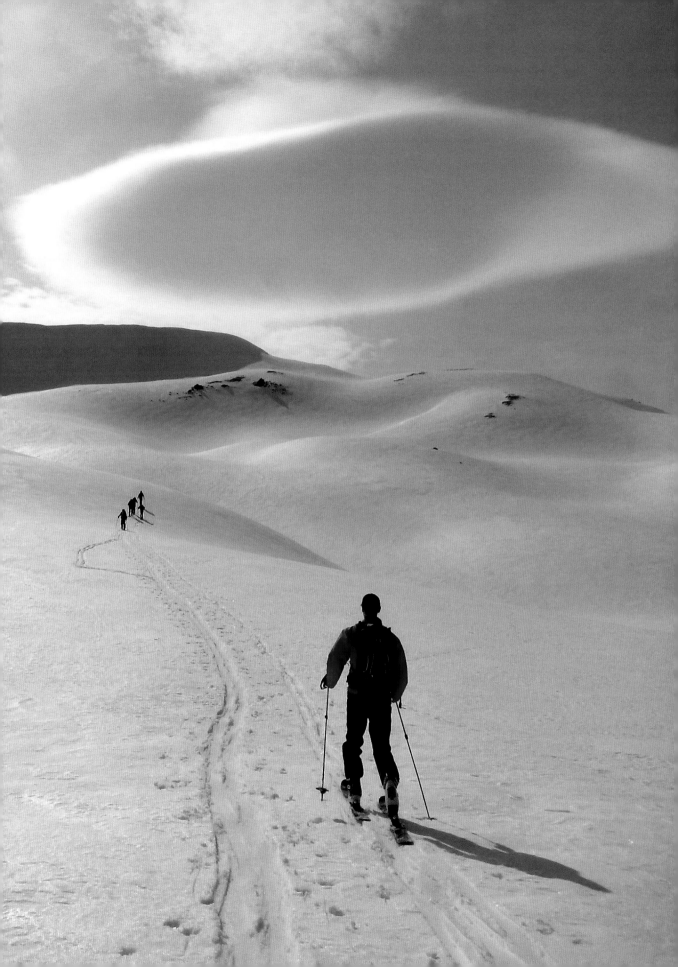

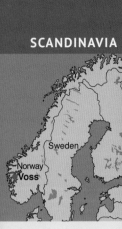

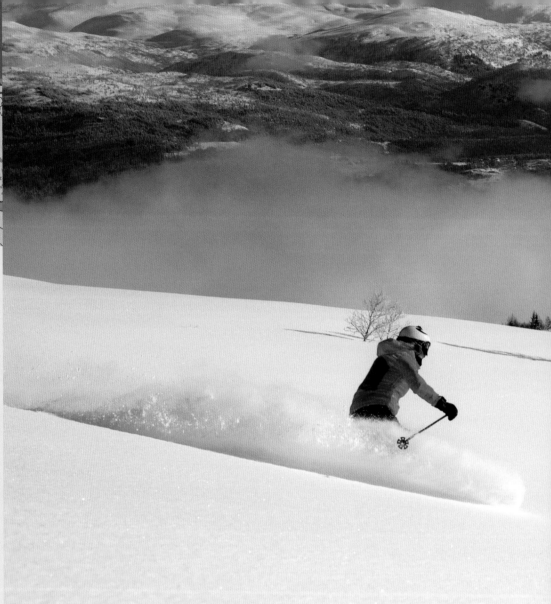

VOSS, NORWAY
Ride the whalebacks

Voss ski resort is relatively small in size (40km of groomed pistes), but there's enough skiing and other winter activities here to occupy most people for several days. The mix of downhill runs accessed by the modern new gondola from the lakeside town is adequately varied and offers sublime sunset views across the region's vast whaleback mountains.

For many skiers it's the wild, Arctic feel of the mountain landscape that is a major draw when skiing in Voss. As with most Scandinavian ski resorts you don't get the high and rugged character that is a key feature of, say, the Alps, but a more open and exposed landscape presents itself, with fine views north towards the Jotunheimen mountains and, closer to hand, of the town of Voss and the often frozen waters of Vangsvatnet. You can also ski under floodlights three nights a week, which adds an entirely new element to the ski experience.

This region's huge, rolling hills mean that whilst there are still some challengingly steep slopes, the predominantly gently-angled terrain appeals more to novices and intermediates.

Indeed, the ski instruction, based in Bavallen and at the top ski station of Hangursbanen, is renowned

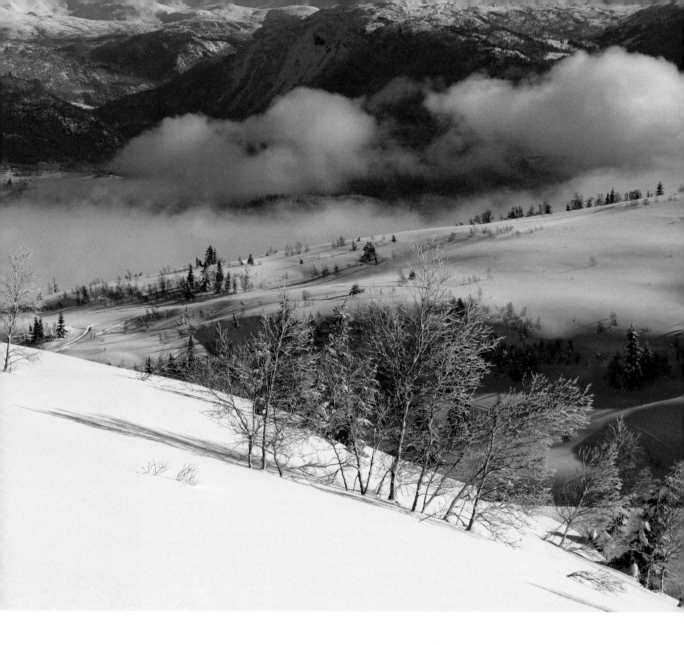

Cruising Voss' whalebacks
© Eric Østlie

(and this being Norway everyone speaks perfect English). Kids in particular are especially well catered for, but something that expert skiers could usefully try here is signing up for some telemark lessons with the ski school since Norway is, of course, the home of telemark skiing and the coolest rider on the slopes will often be 'free-heeling'.

The resort has three distinct summits (Hanguren, 810 metres; Slettafjellet, 917 metres and Horgalleten, 964 metres); lording it above these is 1,411-metre Lønahorgi, which you have to hike up if you want to tackle its slopes.

A modest 654 metres of vertical is mainly criss-crossed with green, blue and red runs along with a couple of blacks, and there's a decent-sized terrain park; the majority of the pistes wend their way down to Bavallen; this is just outside the main town of Voss, which cannot be reached on the pistes.

It's well worth taking a day away from skiing for some sightseeing. Sound boring? You'll soon change your tune if you catch the train from Voss to the nearby Flåm Railway, which descends 866 metres from the mountains via twenty tunnels to bring you out on the shores of mighty Sognefjord, one of the most spectacular fjords on Earth.

When the skiing is over, things tend to be relatively sedate – perhaps not surprising given the stratospherically high price of booze in Norway, but you might find some decent action at the Top Spot at Fleischers Hotel or the Pentagon at the Hotel Park; or just save your energy (and your money) to enjoy the slopes the following day – after all, how often do you get to ski in Norway?

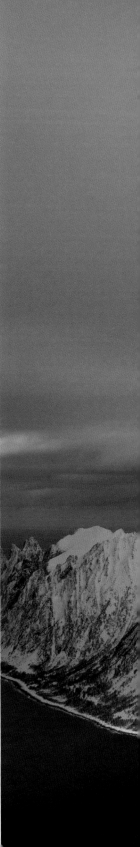

Access
Nearest airport:
Tromsø (207km)

Ability Level
Advanced – expert

Season
Nov – May, but
midwinter skiing is
restricted due to lack
of daylight

Other Local Activities
Snowshoeing, cross-
country skiing

Resort Stats
Top: 1,000m
Bottom: Sea level
Vertical: 1,000m

www.hamnisenja.no

SENJA ISLAND, NORWAY
Isolated skiing in the far north

There are no ski resorts, no ski lifts and no marked trails on
Senja – which makes it perfect for anyone looking for a true
backcountry experience in the Arctic, since what this gorgeous
island off Norway's north-west coast does have is lots of
impressive mountains that rise up from the steel-blue waters of
the Atlantic Ocean into a sky that is regularly a mass of swirling
snow.

Thanks to its remote location Senja's mountains see relatively
few skiers, which means that in return for the effort of hiking up
the slopes you can enjoy descents down wide, open, untracked
powder fields and through sheltered birch forests with just a few
friends, whilst the clank of ski lifts and hubbub of skiers that are
part and parcel of the Alps and Rockies in winter simply isn't an
issue.

True, Senja's mountains are only modest in altitude – the
highest point on the island is just over 1,000 metres – but
since they soar straight up from sea level that's more than
enough 'vertical' to keep any skier happy, and it's this dramatic
conjunction of coastline and mountains that makes for such a
special experience.

You may, for instance, find yourself approaching the summit
of a peak such as Litjemoa, which at around 800 metres doesn't
sound all that exciting; but to get there you'll be negotiating a
reassuringly wide ridge with mind-blowing views – on one side
enormous crags plummet down to the black waters of a deep fjord
whilst on the other lines of ocean swell can be seen rolling onto
craggy shores and deserted beaches.

And because you're so close to sea level there are no issues
with altitude either – simply adopt a slow and steady pace as
you gradually rise above the valley floor into a world of white,
expansive snow fields and even more expansive horizons.

When you eventually get to descend, these snow fields will be
empty of any tracks other than those you left whilst climbing up
and, given Senja's location north of the Arctic Circle, deep powder
is common, so it's pure bliss to hoon back down to sea level.

A fine base for adventures such as this Hamn i Senja, an old
fishing station which dates back to the 17th century and has a
permanent population of around ten plus a very comfortable hotel
complete with outdoor hot tub from which you can admire the
peaks you've been playing on.

In the 1880s over 650 people lived in Hamn and the man
running affairs, one Adolf Lund, was regarded as a local 'king' and
even had two tame sea eagles for pets. Senja may no longer have
a 'king', but adventurous skiers can enjoy riding fit for royalty on
this Arctic island's quiet, empty slopes.

On top of the world in more ways than one © Fredrik Schenholm

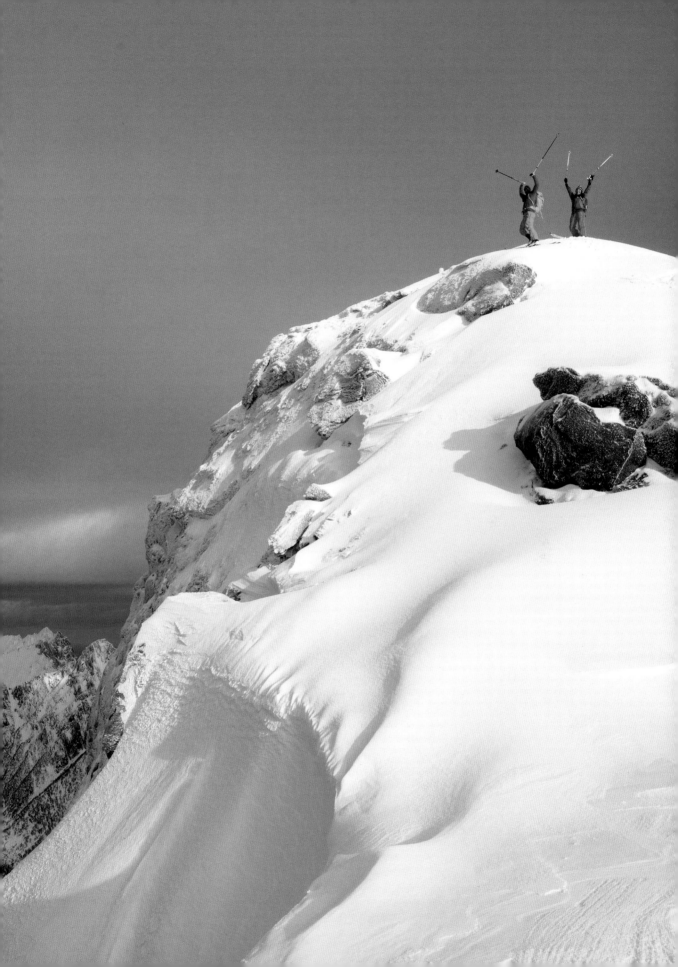

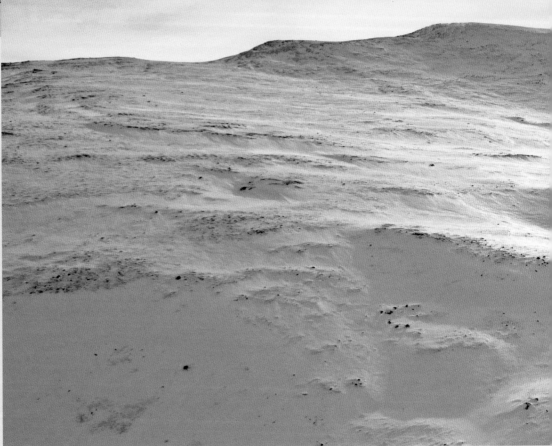

Access
Nearest airport:
Kiruna (132km)
Mainline station in
town

Ability Level
Beginner – expert

Season
Feb – Jun

Other Local Activities
Heli-skiing, cross-
country skiing,
dog-sledding,
snowmobiling

Resort Stats
Top: 1,350m
Bottom: 963m
Vertical: 387m
Lifts: 6
Pistes: 40km

www.riksgransen.se

RIKSGRANSEN, SWEDEN
A parallel universe

The website for Riksgransen ski resort keeps it short and sweet – when offering advice on how much off-piste the resort has it simply states 'A lot', which is just as well since you don't really travel 200km north of the Arctic Circle just to cruise around on pistes (of which there is a modest 40km, served by six lifts).

Nope, what you come here for is a hard-core ski culture, vast white swathes of open backcountry, 'affordable' heli-skiing and, depending on the time of year that you visit, the opportunity to ski beneath the midnight sun or the Northern Lights.

There's a parallel universe feel about Riksgransen, it's a place where you can forget about the faff and fuss of everyday life and immerse yourself in a mountain environment that literally sits on top of the world – this means, of course, that in mid-winter the lifts are closed due to perpetual darkness, but once the season gets underway in February the amount of daylight literally increases by several

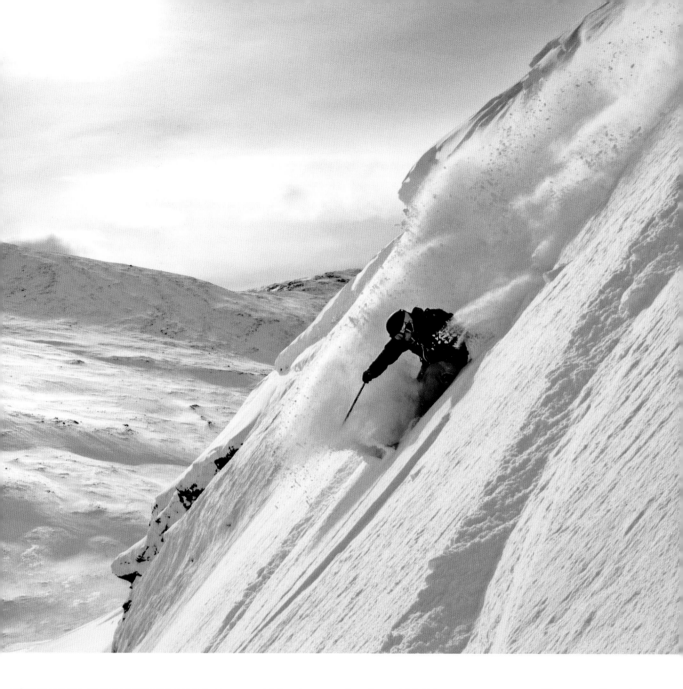

minutes per day, so that by season's end in June you can hit the slopes any time from midnight to – well – midnight.

You may think that it's a bit of a slog to get to Riksgransen but there wasn't even a road linking it with the 'outside world' until the 1980s. The Ofotenbanen rail link arrived here some eighty years before, in 1902, to service the vast iron ore mines at nearby Narvik in Norway (you can actually ski into Norway and back again as the border is so close), and this was followed by hotels and other infrastructure which eventually saw a ski lift being constructed in 1952.

On the slopes you'll encounter everyone from amped up freeriders and beardy, tweedy telemarkers to Swedish families having fun in the guaranteed snow and long hours of daylight. There's a decent range of generally easy pistes and some very amenable off-piste away to the side, but it's the expansive backcountry terrain that is the real draw.

It's good enough for the resort to have hosted the Scandinavian Big Mountain Championships every year since 1992 and to attract heli-ski operators who will whisk you to the top of one of numerous peaks rising up to around 1,300 metres for considerably less moolah than you'd shell out in North America, for instance, making Riksgransen a good place to try your first heli-ski experience.

You've just gotta get there in the first place...

Riksgransen offers epic backcountry skiing, accessible by ski lift, helicopter or on foot © riksgransen.se

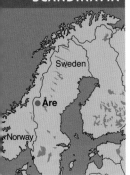

Access
Nearest airport:
Åre Östersund (87km)
Mainline station in
town

Ability Level
Beginner – expert

Season
Dec – May

Other Local Activities
Heli-skiing, cross-
country skiing,
tobogganing

Resort Stats
Top: 1,275m
Bottom: 380m
Vertical: 895m
Lifts: 42
Pistes: 100km

www.skistar.com

ÅRE, SWEDEN
Åre you up for it?

Åre (pronounced 'Oar-er') is Sweden's biggest resort – and whilst the local mountains are not Alpine in scale, the size, efficiency and modernity of the skiing infrastructure certainly is.

With almost 50 ski lifts, 192km of pistes and a very respectable 890 metres of vertical, not to mention a manic freeride scene, you won't get bored here whatever standard of skiing you enjoy, and the nightlife is pretty lively too as well as being cheaper than that in neighbouring Norway.

Åre is actually one of the world's oldest ski resorts, with the funicular railway that accesses the slopes dating way back to 1909; indeed, it was the arrival of the railway in the 1880s that saw the development of tourism, and many visitors still travel here by overnight train.

Back on the mountain the resort's wild, open upper slopes consist of two bowls which drop down to meet the treeline, where the runs continue down towards a frozen lake, providing a nice mix of terrain; the views from the top of the main lifts look out across a classic wild northern-latitude panorama of snow-plastered peaks, deep green forests and frozen lakes and, to add to the Scandinavian feel, you may encounter wild reindeer on the slopes.

Åre's terrain is ideal for beginners and intermediate skiers, but there's plenty of quality off-piste too, as well as heli-skiing for the deep of pocket, and Sweden's mountain culture is in plenty of evidence amongst the numerous freeriders and telemarkers you'll encounter on the slopes and lifts.

And, although Åre is a long way north, daylight hours are not so scarce that you can't ski right through the depths of winter, with the lifts open until 3.30pm in December and January, whilst extensive floodlit night skiing is also a signature of the resort; and as Spring approaches it becomes possible to ski well into the evening, with the lifts open until 8.30pm.

That said, 'After Ski', as it's called locally, begins as early as 3pm with everything from live music to singalongs; the charming old Diplomat Hotel in the centre of town is one of the most popular hangouts, and there are at least half-a-dozen nightclubs that stay open almost until the sun rises again by the end of the ski season.

Hooning downhill in Åre's long, twilight dusk © skistar.com

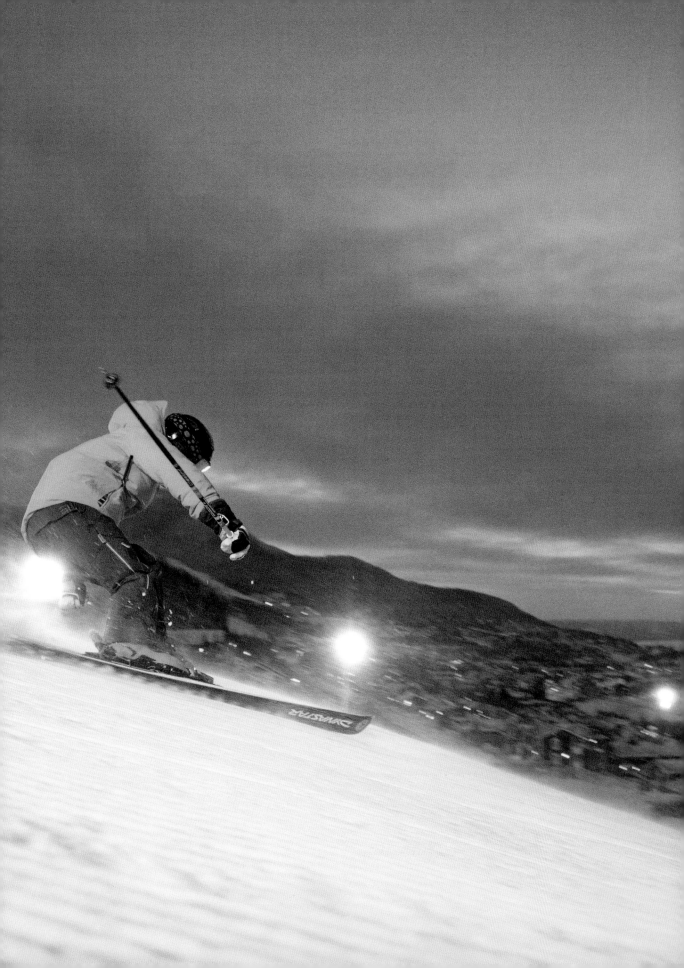

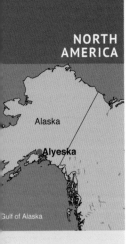

Alaska

Alyeska

Gulf of Alaska

Access
Nearest airport:
Anchorage (41 miles)

Ability Level
Beginner – expert, but
primarily advanced –
expert

Season
Nov – Apr

Other Local Activities
Heli-skiing, cat-
skiing, cross-country
skiing, dog-sledding,
whale watching,
polar bear watching,
snowmobiling

Resort Stats
Top: 3,939ft
Bottom: 250ft
Vertical: 2,500ft (lift
accessed)
Lifts: 29
Skiable acres: 1,610
acres

www.alyeskaresort.
com
www.chugachpow
derguides.com

ALYESKA, ALASKA
Why wouldn't you?

Mention Alaska and most skiers immediately think of heli-skiing in ridiculously deep snow on terrifyingly steep terrain – and that, is, of course, the big sell for America's most northerly state.

But ordinary mortals can enjoy skiing here too, and Alyeska is perhaps the best option if your idea of a great day on skis doesn't necessarily involve helicopters and slopes in excess of 55 degrees.

Located only an hour's drive from the state capital of Anchorage, it offers an eclectic mix of luxurious accommodation and groomed slopes set in the heart of true wilderness, and that wilderness is not short of the white stuff – a remarkable average of 56ft (16.5 metres) of snow falls on Alyeska most winters, which makes the 3-6 metres that resorts like Chamonix and St Anton receive look decidedly stingy.

So, one thing you're unlikely to have to worry about is lack of snow. And you needn't worry if chest-deep off-piste powder runs are not your thing either. Some ten percent of the terrain here is graded 'beginner', and over 50 percent is given over to intermediates, who will surely be tempted to give it a go in the powder beside the groomed pistes too – after all, who doesn't want to be able to say they've skied Alaskan pow?

But it is of course more accomplished skiers who are going to get the most out of what Alyeska has to offer, with seriously demanding trails such as North Face, alpine bowls, trees and terrain parks all accessible by ski lifts along with hike-to terrain including steep chutes and huge bowls above the lifts.

And then there's the heli-skiing... the local operator is the renowned Chugach Powder Guides who will fly you into the eponymous mountains to see and maybe even ski the kind of terrain that pops up regularly in extreme ski movies, but don't be unnecessarily alarmed at that thought since they also offer '... more terrain options than any other heli-ski operation in the world'. Which means you don't have to be on the Freeride World Tour to ski here; there are vast areas of gentler slopes and tamer terrain. And should the weather not play ball they also offer cat-skiing so you can still get into those powder-choked mountains.

It's possible to book a single day of heli-skiing with the company, and there are also 'stand-by' offers, so there's no need to commit to the huge expense of a multi-day heli-ski trip, although you'll still be shelling out a four-figure sum just for one day of heli-skiing.

Depending on when you visit Alyeska you may catch the Northern Lights (December to February being the best time) or, towards the end of the season, enjoy up to 14 hours of daylight, way more than that of resorts to the south.

Add to all this some of the most dramatic mountain scenery on the planet and rather than ask yourself why you should visit Alyeska the more sensible question would be 'why wouldn't you?'

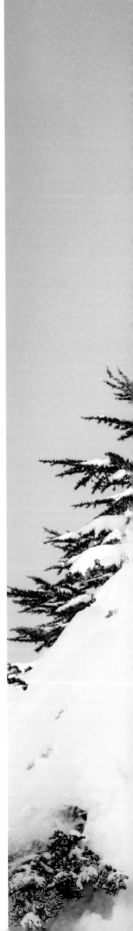

Enjoying the arboreal action in snow-sure Alyeska © Ralph Kristopher

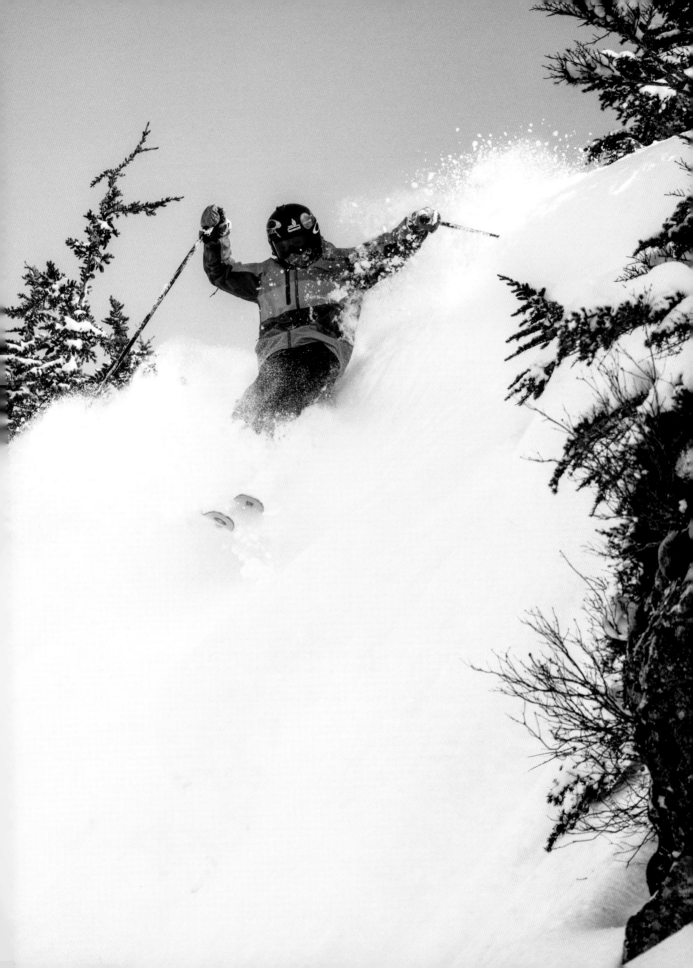

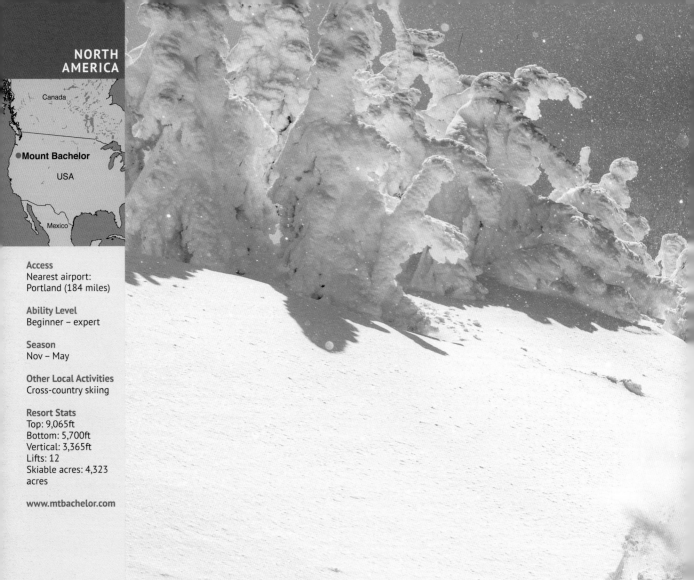

Canada

●Mount Bachelor

USA

Mexico

Access
Nearest airport:
Portland (184 miles)

Ability Level
Beginner – expert

Season
Nov – May

Other Local Activities
Cross-country skiing

Resort Stats
Top: 9,065ft
Bottom: 5,700ft
Vertical: 3,365ft
Lifts: 12
Skiable acres: 4,323
acres

www.mtbachelor.com

MOUNT BACHELOR, OREGON, USA
360 degrees of pure fun

Mount Bachelor is the town of Bend's local ski hill, and Bend is a settlement that is surely right at the top of the US Hipster Chart – few towns anywhere can have so many artisan breweries, funky barber shops and luxurious beards per head of population. God only knows what you do here if you're a bald teetotaller.

Perhaps you ski – which would be a very, very wise choice. For 9,065-foot Mount Bachelor is actually the sixth biggest ski area in the USA and has one of the country's longest seasons (mid-Nov to mid-May) and, best of all, you can ski every aspect of the mountain – 360 degrees of pure fun.

Even after a fresh dump in busy mid-February you can hit the slopes beneath the Northwest Express and Outback Express quads, for instance, to find an enticing mix of decently steep, wide open pistes and fun tree-skiing with barely a soul in sight, bearded or otherwise.

According to the resort's laid-back sales manager Reese Thedford "This is normal outside of holidays and busy weekends."

It's the same when skiing from the Summit Express lift at the top of the mountain – the double-black diamond slopes above the treeline soon see everyone fan out and head off in the direction that suits

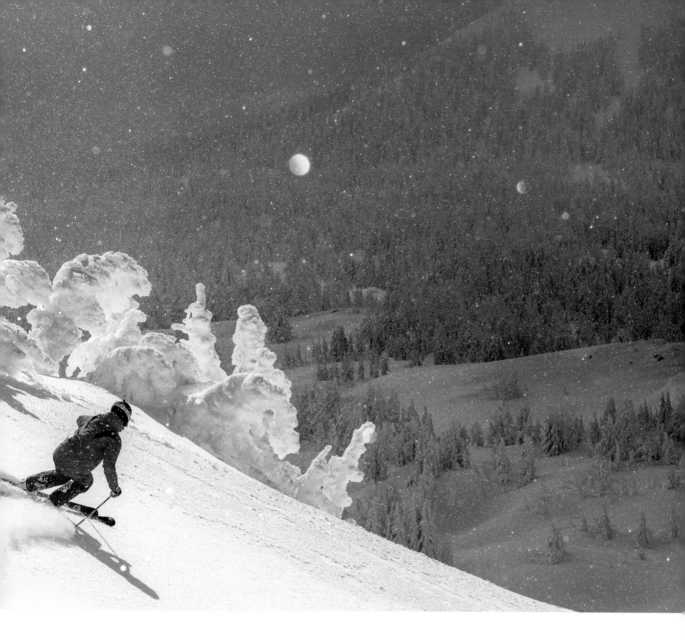

them best and, before you know it, you'll be sharing your chosen descent with just your mates and maybe one of two other interlopers.

Mount Bachelor is an extinct volcano, and it hides its light under a bushel – or to be more exact under 462 inches average annual snowfall, which is more than any of the better-known Colorado resorts. There's plenty of good, fun intermediate and beginner terrain on the lower slopes, whilst the south-facing slopes in particular have great steeps and tree-skiing for the more adventurous.

And there's the added attraction of skiing in the heart of Oregon's wild mountain country – once on the summit of Mount Bachelor you can see for huge distances in every direction and there's little if any sign of humanity, just other cone-shaped extinct or dormant volcanoes like Mount Jefferson and Mount Hood poking up above forests and high deserts – it's good for the soul to be amongst all this wilderness.

If 'regular' skiing isn't enough to entertain you it's also worth checking out the Woodward Mountain Park, a network of featured terrain zones spread across the mountain that, together, offer a balanced variety of exciting features of all sizes for all ages and abilities.

There's no accommodation at the base of the mountain, which some might see as a disadvantage; if you have a more positive outlook, you'll relish the opportunity this gives you to stay in the above-mentioned Bend; it's only 22 miles away and is one of the coolest outdoor towns in the Pacific Northwest – and lordy lord, you can even surf here on the Deschutes River in Bend Whitewater Park.

This place has it all...

Mount Bachelor -
something for everyone
© mtbachelor.com

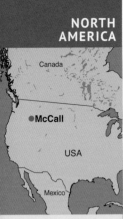

Canada

●McCall

USA

Mexico

Access
Nearest airport:
Boise (108 miles)

Ability Level
Beginner – expert

Season
Nov/Dec – May

Other Local Activities
Cross-country
skiing, snowshoeing,
snowmobiling, cat-
skiing (Brundage)

Resort Stats
Brundage
Top: 7,803ft
Bottom: 5,882ft
Vertical: 1,921ft
Lifts: 6
Skiable acres: 1,920
acres

Plus 420 acres
of unpatrolled
backcountry

Tamarack
Top: 7,660ft
Bottom: 4,900ft
Vertical: 2,760ft
Lifts: 7
Skiable acres: 1,100
acres

www.brundage.com
www.tamarackidaho.
com
www.visitidaho.org

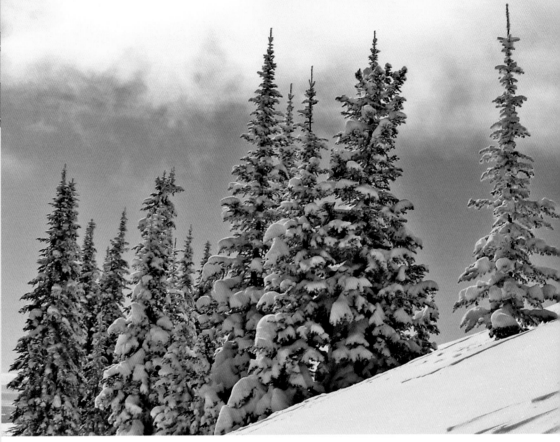

McCALL, IDAHO, USA
Escape the madding crowds

Deep powder; immense backcountry; immaculately groomed slopes; zero lift queues; great beer; great folks... that's McCall. You may just find you fall in love with the place.

Indeed, McCall may also be the coolest ski town you've never heard of. It's an attractive small settlement of 3,200 people beautifully located on the shores of Payette Lake in central Idaho, between two very modestly sized ski hills, Brundage Mountain nine miles to the north and Tamarack, 19 miles to the south.

Brundage dates back to 1961 and came about as an offshoot of the even older 'Little Ski Hill', set up as long ago as 1937; a single T-bar still operates here, and the local kids use it to learn to ski for free. As a resort, Brundage was 'designed' by legendary US skier Corey Engen and financed by money from the company that invented that culinary delight frozen French fries; and it regularly experiences masses of soft, floaty powder thanks to its location at the confluence of two major storm tracks.

Brundage markets itself rather rhythmically as having 'The Best Snow in Idaho' and it can certainly give Utah ('Greatest Snow on Earth') a run for its money.

Tamarack is the new kid on the block, having sprung up in the early noughties, then going on life-support following the financial crash in 2008 before bouncing back to life.

These two areas offer you the American West in all its glory. Head to the top of either of their high points and what you'll see in all directions are ridge after ridge of incredibly remote mountains with entrancing names such as the Sawtooths, the Gospel Hump Mountains, the Seven Devils and the

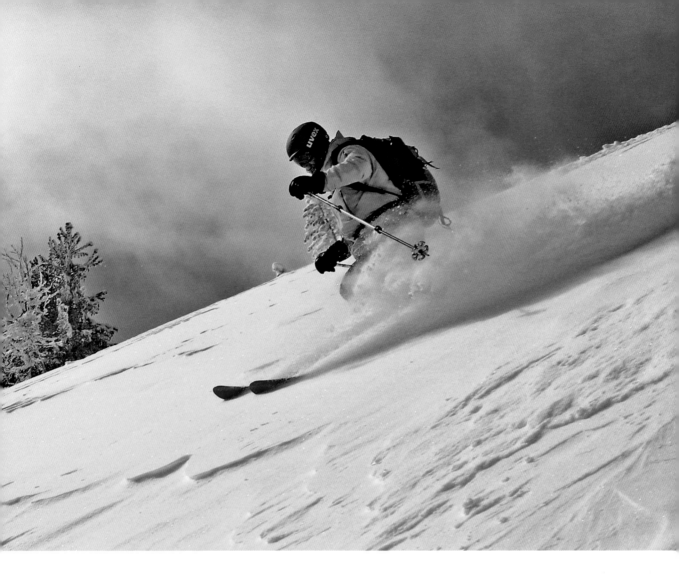

Wallowa Mountains; these are places with more bears, wolves, cougars and elk than humans, whilst close up the frozen surfaces of Payette and Little Payette Lake shimmer in the winter sunshine.

Neither Brundage nor Tamarack ever get really busy – hardly anyone lives here, and the nearest city of any size, Boise (population 243,000) is 108 miles away. If you're looking to escape the madding crowds this is the place to come.

Blasting around immaculately groomed runs at Brundage like Main Street, Engen and 45th Parallel you may begin to consider it busy if you see more than half a dozen people from top to bottom of the resort's 1,900 feet of vertical; head out to explore some of the sublime backcountry, such as the easily accessed 'Hidden Valley', and you'll discover deep pow and trees that Mother Nature, who clearly likes Idaho a lot, has serendipitously spaced to allow for maximum skier enjoyment and minimal arboreal arguments (in the course of which, as we all know, the tree always wins).

At day's end, grab a beer and spend time in Smoky's Bar getting into the local hobby of bullshitting and laughing, and wonder how Tamarack will compare tomorrow.

It puts up a good fight for a place that's so small – three chairs access the mountain, from the summit of which 2,800 feet of vertical encompasses everything from open powder fields to perfectly-spaced trees and the inevitably deserted groomers.

Even during the busiest weeks of the US ski season you can do lap after lap and see no more than the occasional skier or snowboarder, and no one at all if you venture into the trees; sure, Tamarack is tiny with just 1,100 acres of terrain, but there's masses of hike-to skiing and by using McCall as a base you could easily ski here and at Brundage for a week or more and never get bored – and never stand in a lift queue either.

Yes, it's a bit of a schlep to get to McCall, but for a taste of real, hometown America and superb, crowd-free skiing, it's most definitely worth it.

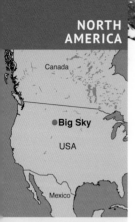

Canada

● Big Sky

USA

Mexico

Access
Nearest airport:
Bozeman (45 miles)

Ability Level
Beginner – expert

Season
Nov – Apr

Other Local Activities
Cross-country
skiing, snowshoeing,
snowmobiling, dog-
sledding, sleigh rides,
zip lines

Resort Stats
Top: 11,165ft
Bottom: 6,800ft
Vertical: 4,365ft
Lifts: 38
Skiable acres: 5,850
acres

www.bigskyresort.
com

BIG SKY, MONTANA, USA
Big in every sense of the word

Big Sky, big mountain, big landscape – everything about this resort revels in its situation in the heart of Montana's wild west. For committed skiers Big Sky is a resort that has to be ticked off at some point in their ski career – with empty slopes, the most consistent snowfall in the North American Rockies and some extremely exciting expert terrain (along with plenty for the rest of us) it has a magnetic attraction despite its relatively isolated location.

The ski area totals 5,850 acres and as such Big Sky is one of the few ski resorts in North America that can match the big European resorts in terms of size – but with the huge advantage of not having European numbers on the mountain. The resort claims that on most days you can ski with about two acres of snow per person as opposed to about two centimetres per person in a busy French resort during the holiday season.

At 11,166ft Big Sky's high point of Lone Mountain stands proud and mighty above the surrounding peaks, and is only accessible via a 15-person 'tram' so you can be pretty sure that the slopes it accesses are never going to suffer from overcrowding (although the queue for the tram will be busy on a powder day).

The most challenging runs on Lone Mountain are those off the Big Couloir and the North Summit Snowfield but, before you do them, stop to check out the tremendous views over three of the USA's

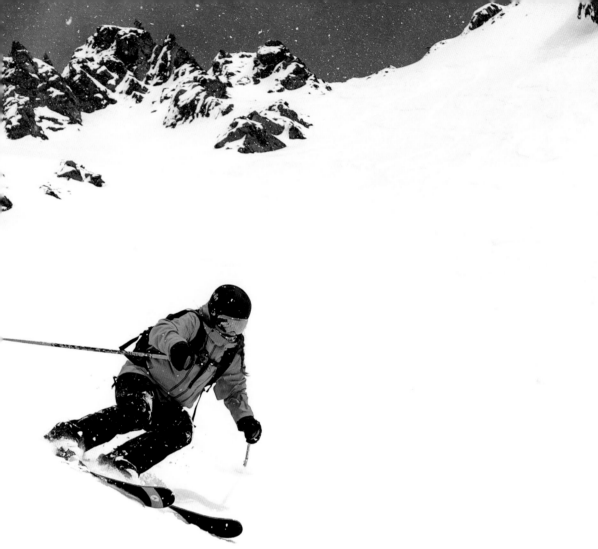

Big sometimes is best
© Jon Resnick

wildest and most beautiful states – Montana, Idaho and Wyoming, along with nearby Yellowstone National Park.

Now, back to Lone Mountain – if you don't like skiing black-, double- or triple-black diamonds you simply don't want to be up here. The majority of the runs are steep, challenging and often exposed, and an absolute blast if that's your thing; if you find you've bitten off more than you can chew, head for Liberty Bowl, which is the easiest way down.

You'll also find some lovely gladed runs lower down the resort on Andesite Peak, whilst Headwaters, in the Moonlight Basin sector of the resort, offers an enticing mix of increasingly steep couloirs as you hike and good tree-skiing lower down.

All this makes it sound like you're wasting your time skiing at Big Sky unless you're a ski pro, but that's most definitely not the case. In fact the majority of the terrain is actually intermediate, so if this is you, you'll love the place given the vast amount of space in which to hoon around on a huge number of blue runs served by fast chairs, whilst there are a number of gently angled bowls where you can practise your off-piste technique in comfort and safety. Even beginners are well catered for, with their own area at the base of the Explorer chair and a separate Explorer pass. And there are a number of terrain parks too.

Next door to the Big Sky is the exclusive Yellowstone Club, which can be seen from Big Sky's slopes, although the only way to get to ski these is to be invited by a member (which includes the likes of Bill and Melinda Gates, Google's Eric Schmidt, Justin Timberlake and Jessica Biel), or if you're considering building a property on site – and if you have to ask how much it costs, you can't afford it...

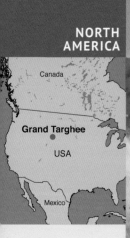

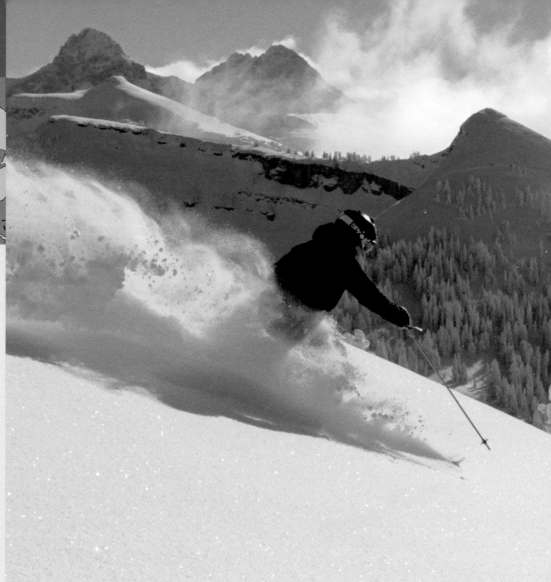

Access
Nearest airports:
Jackson Hole (45
miles), Idaho Falls (83
miles), Salt Lake City
(296 miles)

Ability Level
Beginner – expert

Season
Nov – Apr

Other Local Activities
Cat-skiing, cross-
country skiing,
snowshoeing,
snowmobiling, avy
dog demos, tubing, fat
biking trails

Resort Stats
Top: 9,862ft
Bottom: 7,851ft
Vertical: 2,011ft
Lifts: 5
Skiable acres: 2,602
acres plus 600 acres
cat-skiing

www.grandtarghee.
com

GRAND TARGHEE, WYOMING, USA
Skiing the other side

As the crow flies, Grand Targhee is just a few miles from Jackson Hole. But as the skier skis, the two resorts are a million miles apart. Everyone has heard of Jackson Hole, yet whilst Grand Targhee's profile has been elevated somewhat in recent years it's nowhere near as well-known as its bigger neighbour, despite the fact that it has the perfect mix of great snow (an average of 500 inches per year), stupendous panoramas and relatively empty slopes.

This may be in part because Grand Targhee is less easily reached than Jackson Hole – it suffers the curious anomaly of being inaccessible by road from within its home state – the only road here arrives via the neighbouring state of Idaho.

Tucked in the shadow of 13,770ft Grand Teton this is serious alpine terrain, and few mountains in the Rockies compare to the Tetons when the last rays of the sun bathe their craggy flanks at the end of a sunny winter day. You're skiing in the shadow of these grand peaks, whilst if you gaze in the opposite direction, several thousand feet below the huge, wide plain of the Teton Valley greets your view, mirror flat and dotted with cattle ranches.

That same location is also responsible for the relative lack of crowds; there are no population centres of any consequence within hundreds of miles of Grand Targhee, and few out-of-state visitors (unless you

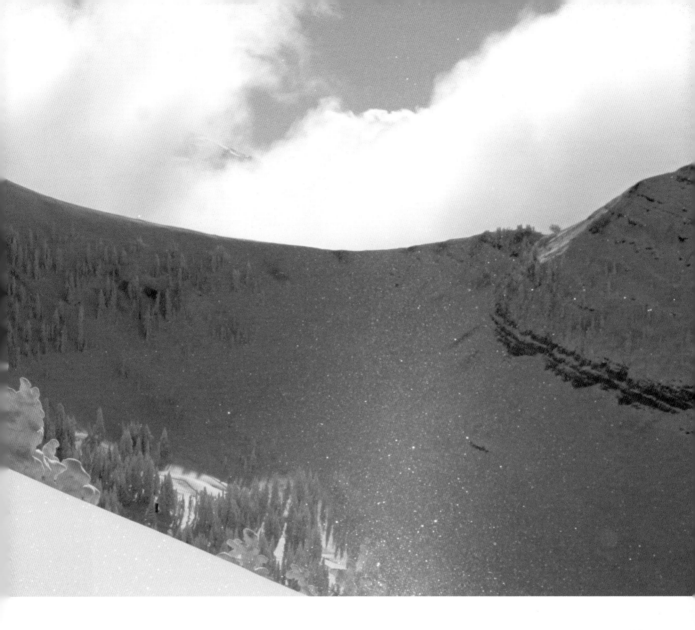

Grand in every sense of the word © grandtarghee.com

call Idaho, about five miles away, out-of-state) other than during holiday periods; consequently there are less people around to crowd out the slopes.

Targhee consists of three peaks, 10,000ft Fred's Mountain, 9,700ft Peaked ('Peak-ed') Mountain and the in-bounds, hike-only terrain of 9,920ft Mary's Nipple, plus a 600-acre cat-skiing area beside Peaked which is excellent value and well worth checking out.

Intermediate skiers invariably love the place, since the majority of the terrain is graded blue to black and there's lots of easily-accessed side country where you can practise your off-piste skills.

And more experienced skiers who are into backcountry adventures may just find the place they've been searching for at Grand Targhee. Clues as to the seriousness with which locals take their skiing can be seen easily enough in the lift lines – telemark gear, fat skis, avy bags and beards are de rigeur. And that's just the ladies.

The locals like to refer to Targhee as 'The Other Side', referring to both their geographical position and their attitude and outlook on life in comparison with Jackson Hole. It's not that the skiing here is necessarily any harder than at Jackson, it's just that the folks hereabouts have a more downhome approach to things than their higher profile neighbour to the east.

If you think you're up for it, join them as they hike from the top of the Dreamcatcher Lift for some serious action on the back of Mary's Nipple (oo,er missis…), or go the whole hog and get a guide to show you the famed backcountry terrain off nearby Teton Pass. Small and isolated it may be, but if you want a challenge – whatever standard of skier or boarder you may be – Grand Targhee will provide it.

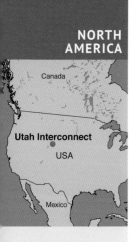

Canada

Utah Interconnect

USA

Mexico

Access
Nearest airport:
Salt Lake City (29
miles to Alta)

Ability Level
Strong intermediate
– expert

Season
Nov/Dec – Apr/May

Other Local Activities
Cross-country
skiing, snowshoeing,
snowmobiling,
zip line, tubing,
bobsleighing, dog-
sledding, sleigh rides,
ballooning depending
on base resort

www.skiutah.com

UTAH INTERCONNECT, UTAH, USA
Get connected

The 'Utah Interconnect' is one of the USA's great days out on skis, a 25-mile-long guided adventure that uses a combination of ski lifts and easy backcountry skiing to take you between what are arguably the best resorts in Utah.

Anelise Bergin, Director of Communications for Ski Utah, sums up the appeal nicely: "You don't need to have any backcountry experience or even any backcountry gear. It is safely guided by our expert tour guides, and no skinning or backcountry touring expertise is required... you simply need to be comfortable skiing ungroomed black diamond level terrain."

If this is you, read on...

Over the course of some six hours you'll take in Deer Valley, Park City, Solitude, Brighton, Alta and Snowbird, providing everything from the glitzy (Deer Valley and Park City) to the hard core (all the rest), at the end of which you're whisked back to the start point in a minibus.

These iconic US resorts are not linked by ski lifts – if they were, they'd easily make up the largest linked ski area in North America. It would require little more than a couple of lifts to create this giant powder paradise, but there's ferocious opposition to the idea from the large local contingent of backcountry aficionados who are keen to keep 'their' mountains unsullied by machines and metalwork.

If you're lucky you'll get to do the Interconnect in the famous Wasatch Mountain powder, marketed and trademarked somewhat bombastically as 'The Greatest Snow on Earth', but it's not guaranteed so don't take on the adventure assuming you'll float your way around it – you may just end up with the kind of 'ordinary' snow the rest of the skiing world has to endure.

It all starts start easily enough with a couple of whoop-it-up runs on the freshly groomed 'corduroy' beneath Deer Valley's Sterling Express lift, after which you duck under the boundary ropes for a short hike, skis on shoulders, into the neighbouring Park City ski area, to hit some more groomers before heading into relatively wild terrain where some very mixed backcountry skiing is on offer. Trees, open meadows, one or two steep pitches and a long, flat run out take you into Big Cottonwood Canyon and the resort of Solitude.

Solitude is aptly named – at times it seems so empty you wonder how they can afford to run the lifts. No one complains about this state of affairs though as it means you get to blast down wide, empty pistes at full bore.

From here it's an easy hop into Brighton for a little more piste skiing before retracing your tracks back to Solitude. This is for the eminently sensible reason that the onward journey to Little Cottonwood Canyon and the final two Interconnect resorts of Alta and Snowbird can only be completed from Brighton by lots of hiking, and who wants that? From Solitude it's easy – you just have to do the 'Highway to Heaven', a twenty-minute traverse to access the highlights of the Interconnect, the linked resorts of Alta and Snowbird.

Both offer lots of steep, challenging off-piste terrain, plenty of fast and furious groomers and a friendly, old-school feel that make it hard for any skier not to fall in love with them – Alta perhaps more so since, as at Deer Valley, snowboarding is banned.

'The Greatest Snow on Earth' – it can be all yours on the Utah Interconnect
© Chris Pearson, Ski Utah

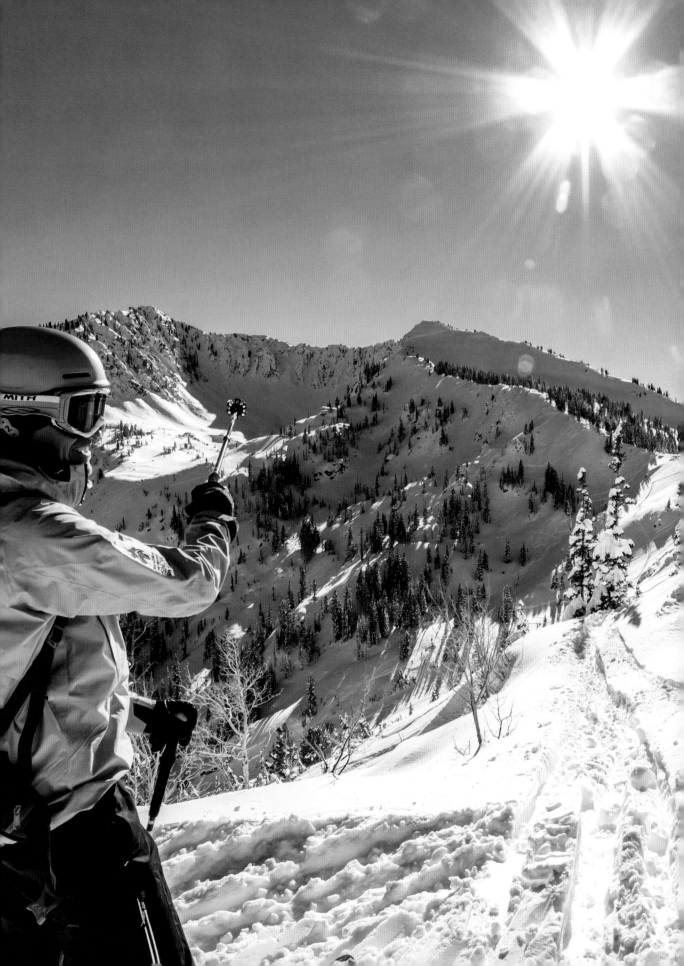

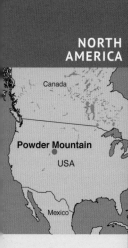

Canada

Powder Mountain •

USA

Mexico

Access
Nearest airport:
Salt Lake City (54 miles)

Ability Level
Beginner – expert

Season
Nov – Apr

Other Local Activities
Heli-skiing, cat-skiing

Resort Stats
Top: 8,900ft lift-served; 9,422ft via snowcat
Bottom: 6,890ft
Vertical: 2,010ft
Lifts: 5
Skiable acres: 8,500 acres including cat- and heli-ski terrain

www.
powdermountain.com

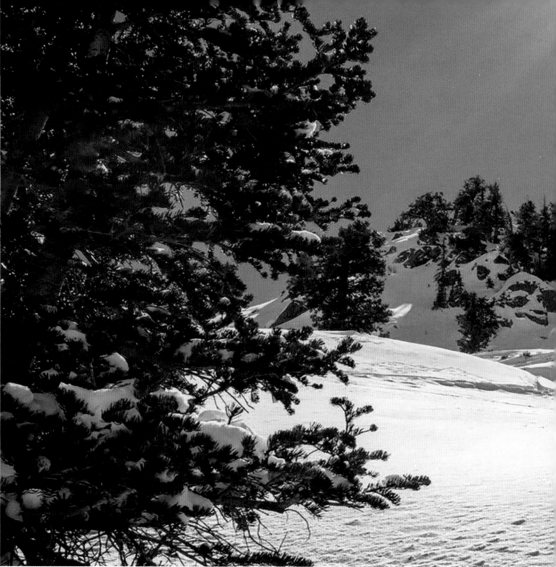

POWDER MOUNTAIN, UTAH, USA
Enough to make a strong man cry

There's an urban myth that the Inuit have around a hundred words for snow (although a recent article in the Washington Post claims the figure is actually 50), but North American marketing men seem intent on pushing the number of English words for the white stuff even higher.

Steamboat Springs has its 'champagne powder' (trade-marked too, so don't try using it without permission; which I just have); BC skiers float through 'white smoke'; and, of course, if you're in Utah you'll be skiing the 'Greatest Snow on Earth'.

Or will you? Well, that's for the individual to decide, but there is some credible science behind the claim. It's based upon Utah having a combination of snow with a low moisture content – typically 8.5 percent compared to over 10 percent in the Alps – along with enough 'body' to allow you to float through it; this is the gift of storms passing over the Great Salt Lake to the west, in a phenomenon known as the 'Lake Effect'.

That said, many Colorado and Wyoming resorts get snow with a moisture content as low as 6 percent, and in New Mexico it can be even lower; however, Utah tends to enjoy more deep powder days and higher amounts of snowfall than resorts in these other states – an average of 547 inches a year at Alta, for example.

"Scientifically, we can't show anywhere has the greatest snow on Earth," Jim Steenburgh, chairman of the University of Utah department of meteorology told the *Salt Lake City Tribune*. "But the combination

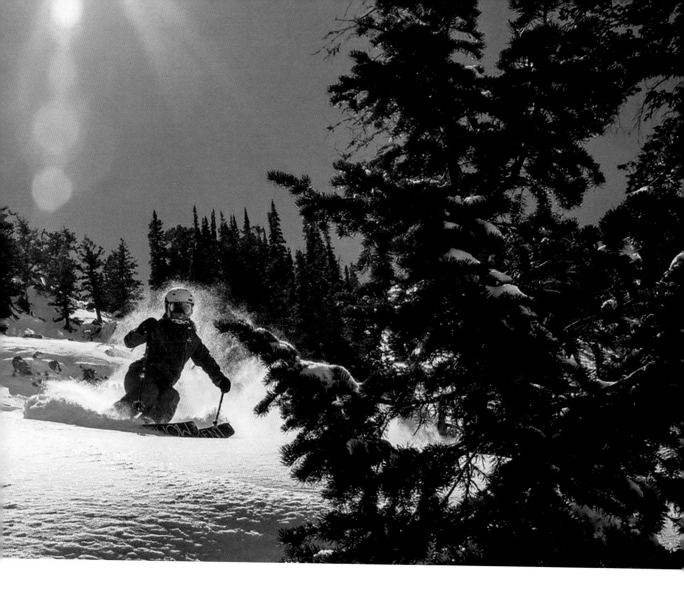

of the amount of snow we get [in Utah], the quality and how it falls during storms is particularly special here. We get a lot of snow and it's good snow. Other places get drier snow, but not as much. Other places in the world get more snow, but it's wetter snow than we see here."

But it still means that, as with any ski area, it's really all about hitting the place at the right time if you want to score that 'greatest' snow.

Which is where we finally come to Powder Mountain. Located just north-east of Ogden, 'Pow Mow' has the largest skiable acreage in the USA, yet despite this immense amount of terrain the number of lift tickets sold each day is restricted to 1,500.

Skiers here have the options of piste, side country, backcountry and cat-skiing (single ride tickets available) and much of the time it's in that famous 'Greatest Snow on Earth', of which an annual average of more than 500 inches descends upon the place.

Because of the enlightened decision to restrict lift ticket sales it can often feel like you and your buddies are the only people on the mountain; groomed pistes remain in perfect condition all day long and when you head off-piste you can find untracked lines days after a snowfall.

It's a million miles away from the city-like hubbub and chaos of so many the big European ski resorts in the holiday periods, where you get the distinct feeling that it's all about cramming in the punters and to hell with the ski experience, and as a business model it seems unlikely that it'll catch on. Which is a shame.

But there is one slight catch – imagine you arrive at Powder Mountain on a bluebird day after a huge dump, only to discover you are customer 1,501 at the lift ticket office – jeez, it would make a strong man cry...

Powder Mountain – restricted
access in a good way
© Ski Utah

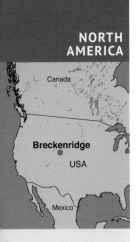

Canada

Breckenridge
●
USA

Mexico

Access
Nearest airport:
Denver (102 miles)

Ability Level
Beginner – expert

Season
Nov – Apr/May

Other Local Activities
Cross-country skiing,
snowshoeing, alpine
coaster

Resort Stats
Top: 12,840ft
Bottom: 9,600ft
Vertical: 3,240ft
Lifts: 34
Skiable acres: 3,308
acres

www.breckenridge.
com

BRECKENRIDGE, COLORADO, USA

The man who starts avalanches

Breckenridge, aka 'Breck', boasts the highest ski lift in North America in the form of the Imperial Express four-person chair which tops out at 12,840ft, so you can guarantee that it's not just the great ski terrain and spectacular views which will leave you feeling breathless when you ski here.

One person who is well-acclimatised to the altitude is Hunter Mortensen, the man who starts avalanches. That is, of course, a facetious way to describe the head of the Breckenridge Ski Patrol who, with his avalanche dog Tali, does all he can to make the slopes safe – but this does mean setting off avalanches on a regular basis.

"We try to make avalanches happen," says Hunter. "By initiating controlled avalanches after heavy snowfalls we're able to make the resort's slopes safe for the thousands of skiers who use them daily throughout the winter."

This is, of course, common practice throughout the world's ski resorts, and there are various techniques that are used to initiate controlled avalanches at Breckenridge, such as firing explosive shells from one of four cannons or ski patrollers simply putting their own weight on the top of a slope in order to make it give way. As Hunter points out, the biggest attribute of his team members is trust; "I can grab any patroller and trust them to do the job safely and vice versa."

Of course, when you put yourself in the line of fire, the chances are you'll eventually get hit. "Yes, many of us have been caught in slides," says Hunter with a wry smile. "But none of us have been buried, fortunately."

Hunter also puts equal trust in his dog Tali. The border collie-cross is one of a team of dogs who have undergone a two-year training course to become 'avy dogs', capable of locating and digging out an avalanche victim up to twenty times faster than a team of humans.

Hunter and Tali make their way to work on the mountain every day via snowmobile, sometimes as early as 4am, rolling up to the Ski Patrol Hut on Breckenridge Resort's 'Peak 8' where Hunter will check out weather forecasts and the results of snow stability tests in order to decide if and where avalanche control work needs to be done. Tali meanwhile snoozes beneath a table.

"Tali is a great ambassador for the mountain," says Hunter. "The public love interacting with her, but it's great to know that she's available in an emergency – as with my fellow patrollers, I know I can trust her implicitly should the worst happen."

And, as with Hunter's relationship with Tali, it's also reassuring for those of us who ski at one of Colorado's best ski resorts to know that we too can place our trust in the sterling and invaluable work of Hunter, Tali and the rest of the Breckenridge Ski Patrol team.

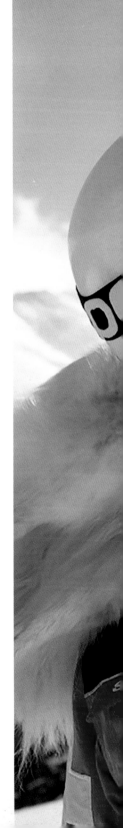

Hunter and Tali make avalanches happen in a good way
© Breckenridge Ski Patrol

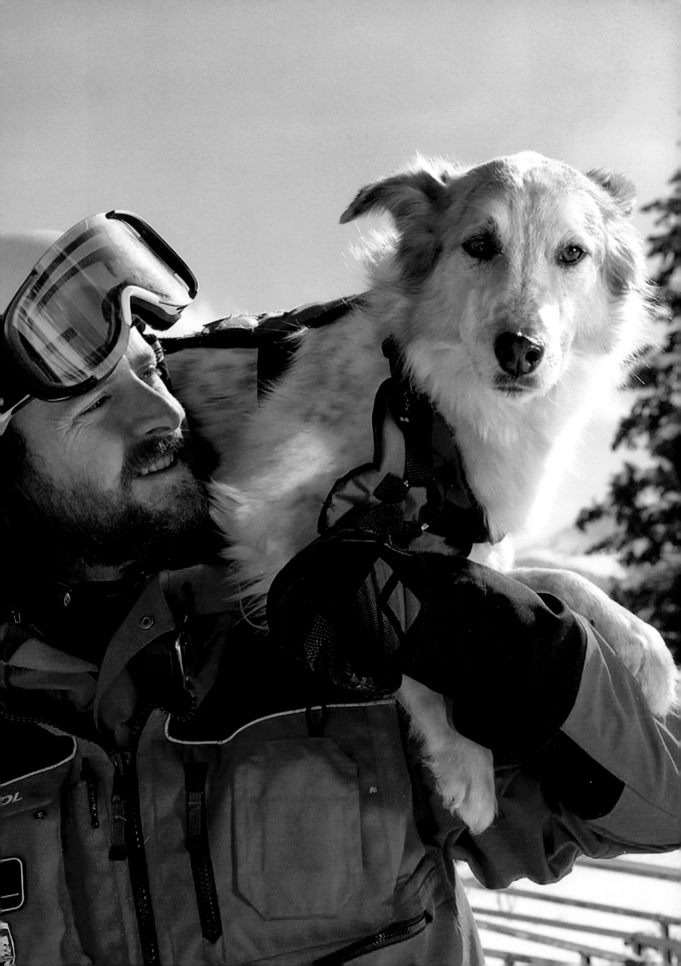

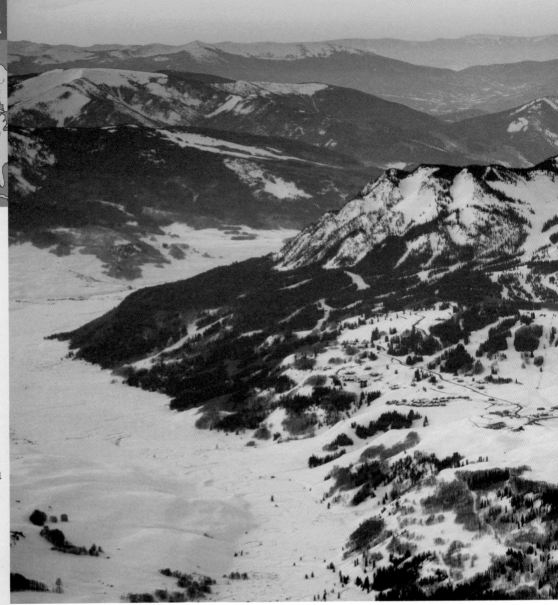

Canada

USA
●Crested Butte

Mexico

Access
Nearest airports:
Gunnison (27 miles),
Denver (230 miles)

Ability Level
Beginner – expert

Season
Nov – Apr

Other Local Activities
Cross-country
skiing, uphill skiing,
adventure park and
ziplines, sleigh rides

Resort Stats
Top: 12,162ft
Bottom: 9,375ft
Vertical: 2,775ft (lift
accessed)
Overall: 3,062 vertical
ft (access requires
short hike)
Lifts: 15
Skiable acres: 1,547
acres

www.skicb.com

CRESTED BUTTE, COLORADO , USA
Skiing in outlaw country

Kochevar's Bar in the colourfully painted downtown Crested Butte has an unusual claim to fame – it's
where Butch Cassidy left his handgun on the bar when being chased by bounty hunters.

The famous outlaw hit the town after robbing the San Miguel Valley Bank in Telluride in 1889, high-
tailin' it with $21,000 (around $500,000 in today's money). Apparently, shots were fired in Kochevar's
as Cassidy and his gang were pursued, and the bullet holes are still there – as is the pistol he forgot to
take with him.

As we all know Cassidy escaped to go on and enjoy a career in Hollywood, and Crested Butte
retired from the limelight for several decades until it re-emerged as one of the great outdoor towns of
Colorado.

Unlike some ski resorts this is a place where you really should spend a good proportion of your visit
negotiating the streets as well as the steeps. Crested Butte's downtown is a trip back in time – remove
the cars, pick-up trucks and fat bikes and you could pretty much be back in the 1890s. The town has

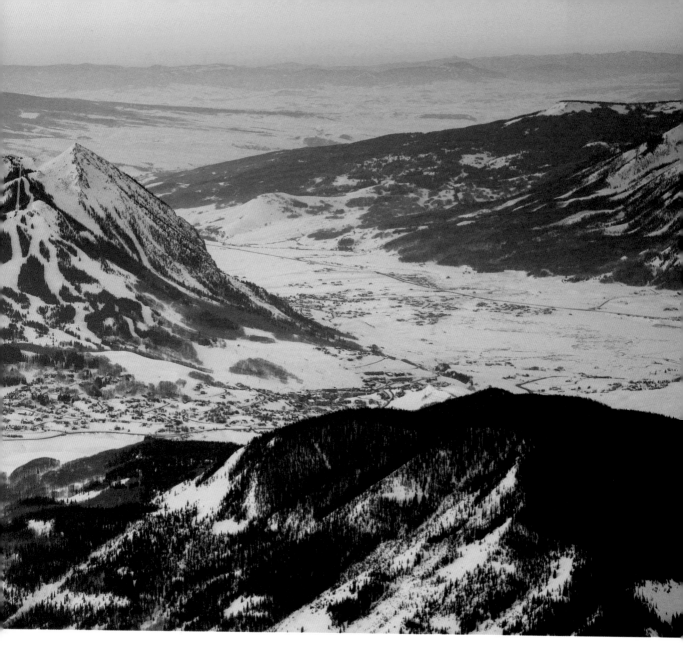

a wealth of classic cowboy town architecture, such as the Masonic Building, the Grubstake and the Company Store, and anyone who has ever enjoyed a Western movie will love the authenticity of it all.

Although the ski hill, located five-minutes uphill from the town, is small by European standards, there's still enough to keep anyone of any ability more than happy for several days; and the harder you want to push it, the happier Crested Butte will be, for however big the gauntlet you lay down, the resort is more than a match for it.

Before you start it's worth remembering that Crested Butte's base area stands at 9,375ft (2,857m), and it tops out at 12,162ft (3,706m) on the hike-to Elevation Peak, so most skiers other than locals will already be gasping for breath just getting on to the chairlift.

Head across to the resort's renowned extreme terrain such as 'Extreme Limits' and you'll be suffering serious oxygen debt. Not only do you have to hike in, but this is true double-black diamond terrain as serious and demanding as you'll find in-bounds at any ski area in North America.

That said Crested Butte isn't all so wild and woolly. The wide, easy groomers that snake between the trees above the base station and off East River, Paradise and Teocalli chairs are perfect for skiers looking for something less serious.

And novice or expert, when the skiing is over, you'll love the old western town and its fine array of bars and restaurants.

149

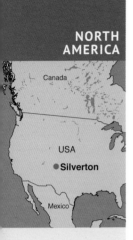

Canada

USA

●Silverton

Mexico

Access
Nearest airports:
Durango (52 miles),
Montrose (50 miles),
Telluride (110 miles),
Grand Junction (100
miles), Denver (355
miles)

Ability Level
Advanced – expert

Season
Nov – Apr

Other Local Activities
Heli-skiing

Resort Stats
Top: 12,300ft (chair);
13,487 (hike to)
Bottom: 1,000ft
Lift serviced vertical
drop: 1,900ft
Hike-to & helicopter
accessible vertical
drop: 3,887ft
Lifts: 1
Skiable acres: 26,819
acres

www.
silvertonmountain.
com

SILVERTON, COLORADO, USA
No easy way down

Any normal skier – especially one visiting from Europe – would surely question whether it's worth travelling several thousand miles to visit a ski resort (and I use the word 'resort' in its loosest possible sense) with just one ski lift – and even that is no more than a rickety old two-person chair that most modern resorts wouldn't tolerate as part of their high-tech lift system.

The answer to that question is short and simple, however.

'Yes'.

Professional freeskier Chris Davenport sums it up nicely: "Silverton Mountain is pretty close to the purest skiing experience one can find today – an epic mountain, bountiful snowfall (the deep and light Colorado kind), and none of the distractions of other ski areas [such as] crowds – Silverton is like heli-skiing [but] with a chairlift!"

That ticks most of the boxes then. However, there are a few things you need to bear in mind before you book your flight and pack your fat skis. This is the highest and purportedly the steepest lift-accessed mountain in North America (the most gently angled slope is 30 degrees); it tops out at a lung-busting 13,487ft and, as the Silverton website almost gleefully points out, 'There are loads of bowls, chutes, cliffs and wonderful natural terrain features to be discovered everywhere you look... and no easy way down.'

This is not hyperbole either – last time I skied there I found myself using a rope to descend a small cliff band on one run, and since the single chairlift only takes you up to 12,300ft there's a certain amount of hiking involved if you want to make the most of the vertical that's on offer, so like pretty much everyone else I also found myself gasping for air most of the time.

Other than avalanche control, none of the terrain is treated in any way, so what you ski is what Nature provides, pure and simple. Another huge bonus is that lift ticket sales are restricted to a maximum of 475 per day although there are usually far fewer skiers than that on the mountain – especially mid-week – so scoring fresh tracks, even days after a snowfall, is par for the course on pretty much every descent.

The idiosyncratic nature of skiing at Silverton doesn't end when you get to the bottom of your chosen run, since you'll be picked up by an old bus and taken back to the base to head up and do it all again.

Catch this place after a fresh dump and on a bluebird day and, without a doubt, it's one of the most remarkable skiing experiences in North America; and make sure you spend at least one night in the nearby town of Silverton too, since if you're looking for a taste of the old Wild West you'll definitely find it here.

Silverton – steep enough for ya? © Scott DW Smith / Imagesmith Photo

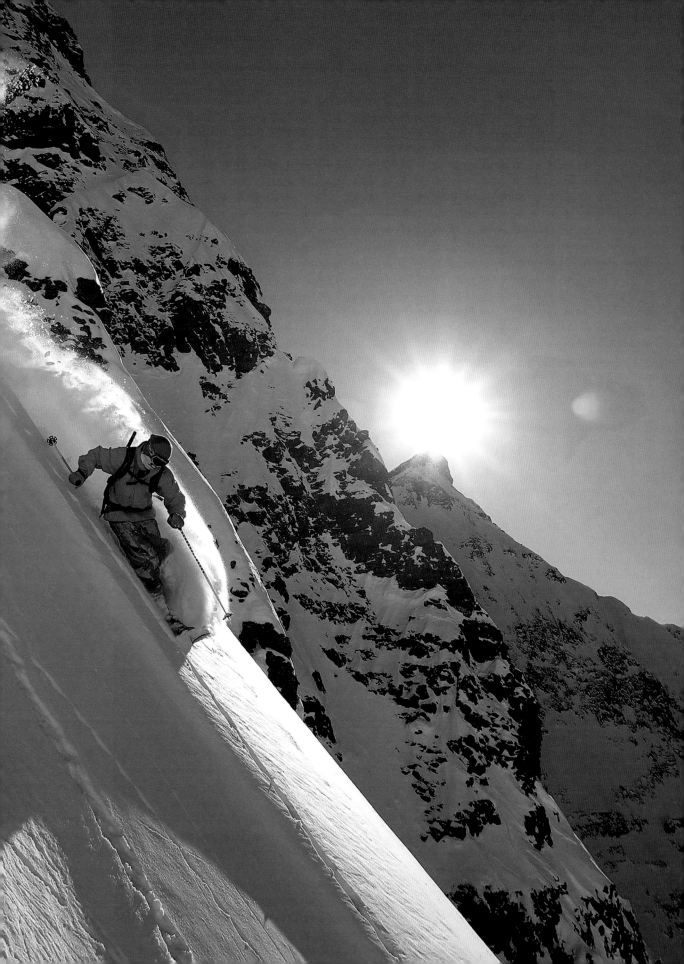

ON THE ROAD, USA
Hit the road, Jack...

Nowhere lends itself to a ski road trip like North America – here are a few suggestions that almost guarantee world-class skiing, great scenery and the ultimate driving adventure.

Fernie – Kimberley – Panorama – Kicking Horse (aka 'Powder Highway')

The legendary Powder Highway doesn't get its name for nothing. Starting with Fernie's (page 164) bowls of fluff (and the option of cat-skiing at Island Lake Lodge, which is next door), you can then head west to Kimberley, which is a slightly bizarre ski town – Bavaria / Olde England meets the Canadian Rockies – before driving north up Highway 95 to Panorama (page 180), which boasts some of the biggest vert in North America along with some tidy skiing for everyone from families to freeriders. The scenery is never less than awe-inspiring as you continue north to Kicking Horse (page 172) and some of the steepest and most challenging terrain in BC.

Bogus Basin – Sun Valley – Lost Trail Powder Mountain – Silver Mountain – Schweitzer Mountain

Other than Sun Valley you may not have heard of these Idaho ski hills; reason enough to go and check them out. Bogus Basin sits just outside the state capital Boise and is great value as it's a not-for-profit operation.

Sun Valley is the opposite, glitz and glamour with some of the finest piste grooming in the USA. From here drive through classic Rocky Mountain scenery – look out for elk, moose and bald eagles en-route – to tiny Lost Trail Powder Mountain (there's a clue in the name as to what you'll find there), then Silver Mountain, home to the world's longest gondola and some testing tree-skiing, before finishing up amongst the 'snow ghosts' at Schweitzer Mountain (page 156) close to the Canadian border.

On the road approaching Castle Mountain, Alberta © Alf Alderson

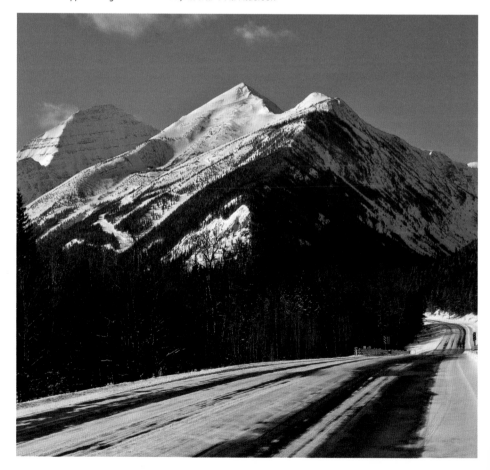

Alta – Jackson Hole – Grand Targhee – Big Sky

Alta remains one of the few ski hills left to ban snowboarders, a big appeal for many skiers, whilst neighbouring Snowbird has equally good snow and terrain (and boarders).

From here head up to Jackson Hole via Interstate 80 for its legendary steep terrain. The landscape becomes truly spectacular as you drive north-west over the Teton Pass to powder-choked Grand Targhee (page 140). Last stop is Big Sky (page 138); the USA's biggest linked ski area has eerily deserted slopes and is just a 45-minute drive away from Yellowstone National Park if you fancy a side trip, although access is limited in winter.

Silverton – Telluride – Beaver Creek – Breckenridge

It's a long old drive to Silverton (page 150) from anywhere, but the pay-off for the hours behind the wheel is steep, deep, high-altitude, powder-sure skiing. The relatively close town of Telluride (page 154) also has challenging high-level skiing along with superb groomers, and the latter is the selling point at Beaver Creek, a day's drive to the north. If the über-expensive slopes here are too much for your budget, the short hop along Interstate 70 to Breckenridge (page 146) will provide better value and great skiing for all abilities.

Mammoth Mountain – Kirkwood – Heavenly

Fly into LA, rent a SUV, enjoy a quick surf then hit the road and six hours later you could be driving into Mammoth. Famed for its mighty snowfalls, Mammoth also has an appealing mix of alpine bowls and great wooded terrain that isn't too common in North America, not to mention a total of ten terrain parks and a very long ski season extending well into summer some years. From there it's on to remote, quiet Kirkwood, then north to Heavenly, above the deep blue waters of Lake Tahoe.

Parked up in Whitewater, British Columbia © Alf Alderson

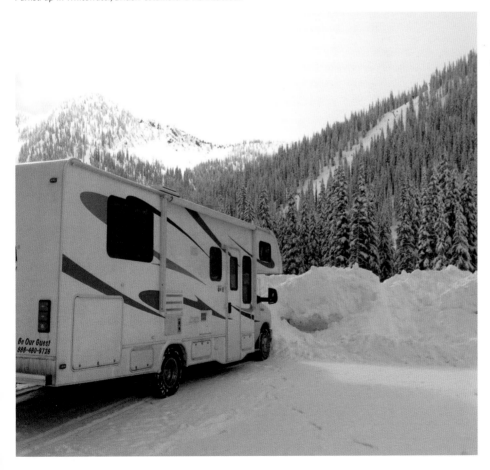

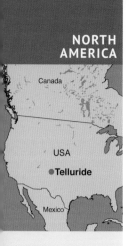

Canada

USA

●Telluride

Mexico

Access
Nearest airport:
Denver (330 miles)

Ability Level
Beginner – expert

Season
Nov – Apr

Other Local Activities
Heli-skiing, cross-country skiing, snow-biking, snowshoeing, snowmobiling, ice climbing

Resort Stats
Top: 13,150ft
Bottom: 8,725ft
Vertical: 4,425ft
Lifts: 17
Skiable acres: 2,000 acres

www.telluride
skiresort.com

TELLURIDE, COLORADO, USA
Where the west is still wild

Driving down Telluride's wide main strip, aka Colorado Avenue, is quite an experience; authentic western-style hotels, bars and restaurants line the street, the snow-draped ridges and peaks of the San Juan Mountains line the horizon and the steep ski runs of the town's high altitude ski resort snake down to the edge of town – throw in a Hollywood star lounging about on the corner of Colorado and Aspen and it all becomes slightly surreal.

And that notion is not as peculiar as it may sound; Tom Cruise had a gaff here until recently (sold for a snip at $59 million), Oprah Winfrey also has a place in Telluride and, had you been in town a few years ago, you may have seen the likes of Samuel L. Jackson and Quentin Tarantino sauntering around town during the shooting of *The Hateful Eight*.

The big names go back even further – Butch Cassidy was once to be seen high tailin' it out of town with $21,000 (around $500,000 in today's money) in his saddle bags after holding up the San Miguel Valley Bank on Colorado Avenue.

And the skiing here is even more exciting than the street life, for Telluride's real trademark is steep terrain. So steep that you have to access some of it by stairs and a steel bridge...

The resort's now infamous 'Stairway to Heaven' is a combination of steel staircases and a bridge that allows access to Gold Hill Chutes for skiers who like their riding to encompass a touch of sheer terror.

Gold Hill Chutes sit below the resort's high point, 13,150ft Palmyra Peak, and the scenery does its best to compete with the skiing in an effort to impress. Telluride itself lies in a big, bold and rugged Rocky Mountain landscape similar to that of the Alps; where many Rocky Mountain resorts lie beneath the tree line so that forests are a prime feature of the scenery, Telluride has the altitude to ensure that its higher peaks stand above the trees.

There's a feeling of true wilderness as you look out across the San Juan Mountains, and in this sense it's very different from the Alps – there are no neighbouring ski resorts and associated infrastructure, no mountain villages, alpages or roads to be seen – were you to venture off into the backcountry you'd be seeing the area much as it appears in *The Hateful Eight*, which is set around 150 years ago.

The fact that the higher slopes lie above the tree line has its advantages if your tree-skiing tends to be more of an accident avoidance exercise than a graceful dance between the firs, since you can find plenty of open bowls in which to lay down wide, easy turns – or you can simply head to the wide array of exciting pisted terrain above town.

Telluride also boasts the highest restaurant in the USA, 'Alpino Vino', where the cuisine is inspired by that of the Dolomites (which is perhaps no bad thing in the land of burgers and fries).

All the above skiing machismo is not to say there are not plenty of superbly maintained groomers for those skiers who prefer to keep things a little more sedate/safe/less suicidal, but it's more adventurous skiers who will get the most from what Telluride has to offer.

This, along with the genuine rootin' tootin' Wild West past that's so evident when you wander downtown, is what makes Telluride so special, and it seems that the unconstrained behaviour of this former mining town hasn't been lost so much as just migrated up into the mountains where, on your skis, you can push it as hard as you want.

If Butch had skied instead of robbed banks, he'd have loved it...

Cool town, huge mountains, great skiing – Telluride has the perfect mix
© telluride.com

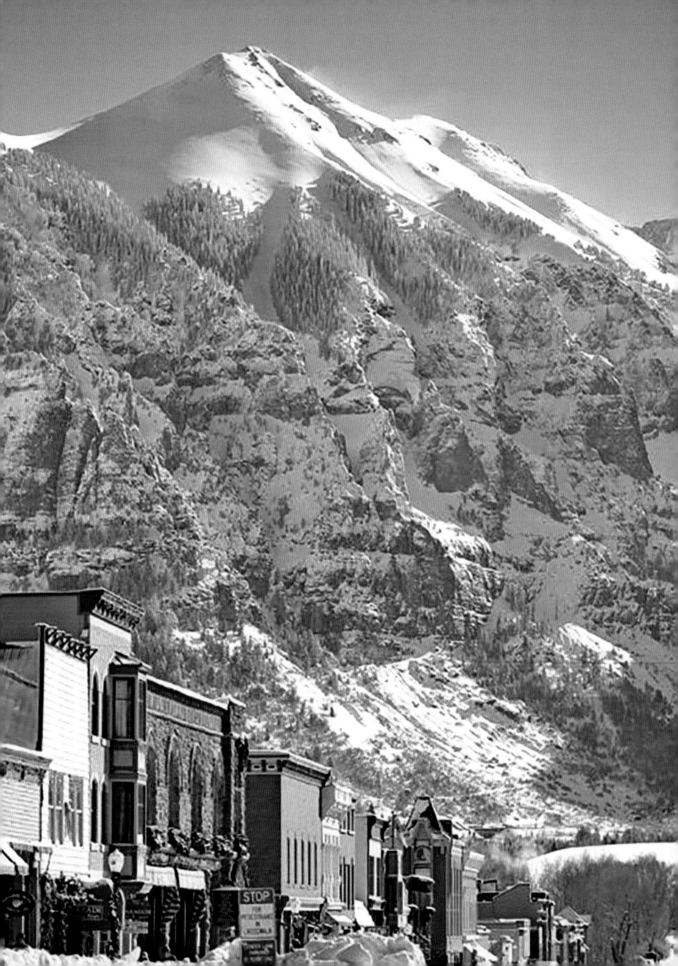

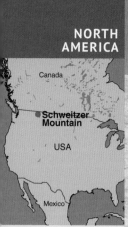

Canada

Schweitzer
Mountain

USA

Mexico

Access
Nearest airport:
Spokane (84 miles)
Mainline station in
town

Ability Level
Beginner – expert

Season
Nov – Apr

Other Local Activities
Cat-skiing, cross-
country skiing, snow-
biking, snowshoeing,
snow-mobiling,
tubing

Resort Stats
Top: 6,400ft
Bottom: 3,960ft
Vertical: 2,440ft
Lifts: 10
Skiable acres: 2,900
acres

www.schweitzer.com

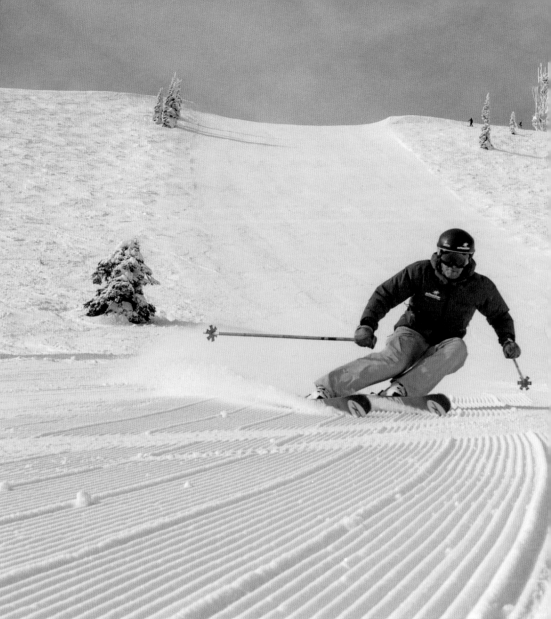

SCHWEITZER MOUNTAIN, IDAHO, USA
Skiing amongst the snow ghosts in Idaho's far north

Located at the top end of the Idaho Panhandle, there's a definite Canadian feel about Schweitzer Mountain – not surprising really as it's only a few miles as the bald eagle flies to the Canadian border.

Voted 'The Best Kept Secret in North America' by *Ski* magazine, it lies at the southern end of the Purcell Mountains above the eclectic lakeside town of Sandpoint, where you'll find hipsters and craftspeople wandering the streets alongside ranch hands and cowboys.

The deep-blue waters of Lake Pend Oreille lie below the resort, and snow-encrusted pine trees, otherwise known as 'snow ghosts', stand tall and solid on the upper slopes of peaks which rise to almost 6,500 feet.

Despite the modest altitude Schweitzer still offers almost 2,500 feet of vertical on what is often uncrowded powder – it is in fact the biggest ski area in Idaho, and should it become busy you can go cat-skiing amongst the trees on the north side of the resort. Lift queues are a rarity, especially if you head over to Outback Bowl which offers terrain that will quite literally bring a smile to the face of everyone from novice to expert.

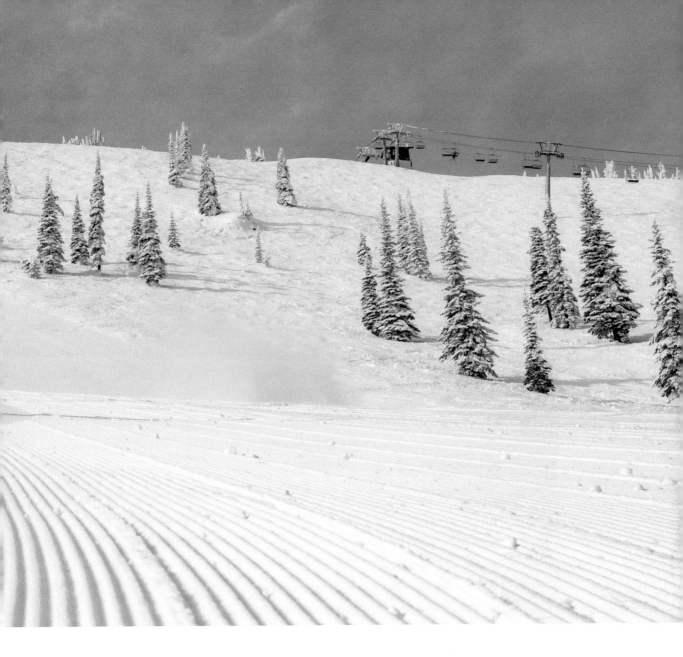

Schweitzer as a whole has a very enticing mix of inviting beginner terrain close to the village centre, wide, swooping blues and steeper, more demanding black and double-black diamonds, more tree-skiing and bowls than you can shake a ski stick at and three terrain parks – in flat light the trees enable you to enjoy a full day of action, broken perhaps by a lunch stop to refuel at the excellent Sky House summit restaurant.

Under-populated slopes are a feature of Schweitzer Mountain © Schweitzer Mountain Resort

There's perfectly adequate ski in / ski out accommodation on the mountain, which means you don't really need to leave the resort, but it's worth taking a trip down the hill to Sandpoint for its alluring mix of bars, restaurants and music venues, and there's also a wistful melancholy about watching a locomotive slowly making its way across the Long Bridge over the wide waters of Pend Oreille River and into Sandpoint Station, the only operating Amtrak station in Idaho and the oldest remaining active passenger depot of the former Northern Pacific Railway (so you can actually travel to Schweitzer by train).

For most skiers Schweitzer Mountain, like Brundage and Tamarack further south in Idaho, are somewhat off-the-beaten track and, given their size, it may not seem worth the effort of travelling there, especially if you're used to the bigger resorts of Europe; but why not relish the adventure, head to Idaho's northern reaches and you'll discover some great skiing, super-friendly locals and sublime landscapes that provide a sense of freedom and adventure that's not always easily found in more accessible, commercialised ski areas.

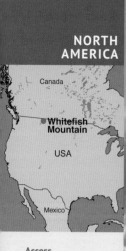

Canada

Whitefish Mountain

USA

Mexico

Access
Nearest airport:
Kalispell (19 miles)
Mainline station in
town

Ability Level
Beginner – expert

Season
Dec – Apr

Other Local Activities
Night skiing, cross-
country skiing (based
in town)

Resort Stats
Top: 6,817ft
Bottom: 4,464ft
Vertical: 2,353ft
Lifts: 15
Skiable acres: 3,000
acres

www.skiwhitefish.
com

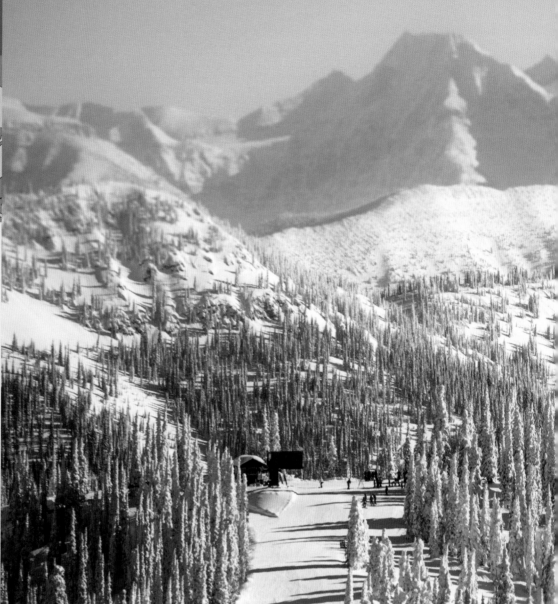

WHITEFISH MOUNTAIN, MONTANA, USA
Ski the fish

It's not often that you come across a ski resort named after a fish and indeed, Whitefish was once known as 'Big Mountain', which isn't exactly original nor inspiring. It's current moniker does at least relate to one of the area's natural features – Whitefish Lake, alongside which sits the eponymous town, an eclectic little spot which is well worth checking out if you have a down day.

Whitefish essentially has a south side and a north side, which generally helps to ensure decent snow conditions throughout the season. You'll access the skiing from the south side (aka Front Side), and would be well advised to hop aboard Chair 1, the Big Mountain Express quad, which will take you to the resort's high point, 6,817ft Summit House.

The reason for this will become apparent as you rise up into the heights. Looking back down the hill you'll enjoy ever better views (if at the risk of neck ache) of Whitefish Lake and Whitefish town close to hand, and the flatlands leading south towards Flathead Lake.

This all seems pretty spectacular until you come over the final rise to Summit House and encounter to the north-east a truly mesmerising view of Glacier National Park and its mighty walls, crags and

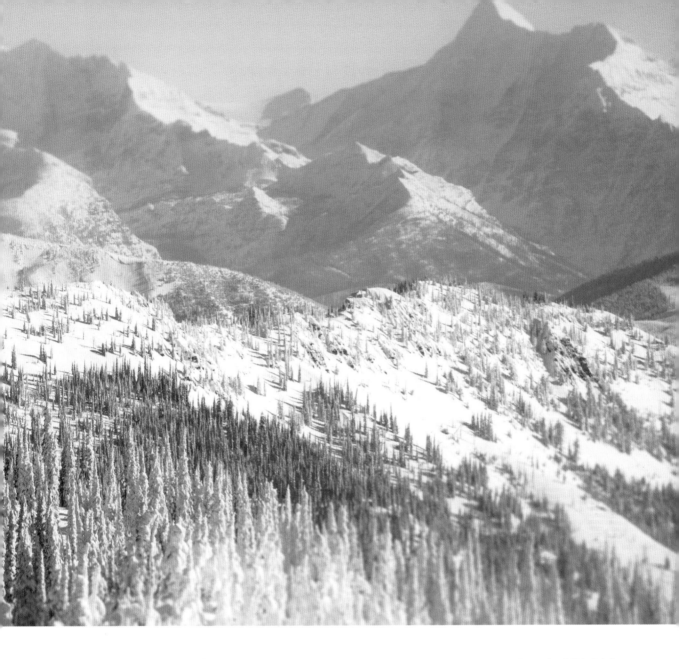

peaks, including the pointy Mount St Nicholas (9,381ft), reminiscent of the Matterhorn, and Mount Stimson (10,147ft), the second highest peak in Glacier National Park.

You're close to the Canadian border and there's a palpable sense of being on the edge of true wilderness country which is the home of grizzlies, black bears, wolves, cougars and other spectacular wildlife.

Some of the terrain at Whitefish is as wild as some of the local fauna – the double-black diamond of Bighorn on the North Side is more cliff than ski run, and there are plenty of equally challenging glades along with, for instance, the Picture Chutes in Hellroaring Basin to provide all the challenges anyone is likely to want.

If, on the other hand, you'd prefer to cruise down something less demanding, try Inspiration, a sublime blue ridge run which starts off from Summit House with those glorious views of Glacier before winding its way south to reward you with yet more marvellous views towards Flathead Lake. Or get orientated with a free tour of the mountain with one of the resort's 'Mountain Ambassadors', easily recognised in their bright yellow ski jackets.

This being northern Montana, where people are few in number, crowds and lift queues are rarely an issue so, once you've found your favourite runs, it's no problem to do lap after lap at a good old lick on lifts that generally also ascend at a decent speed too, so you'll soon rack up the vertical – which is just how it should be.

What a view! Whitefish lies on the edge of the spectacular Glacier National Park
© skiwhitefish.com

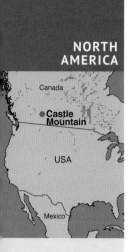

Access
Nearest airport:
Calgary (255km)

Ability Level
Advanced – expert
will get most out of
Castle Mountain

Season
Nov/Dec – Apr

Other Local Activities
Cat-skiing

Resort Stats
Top: 2,274m
Bottom: 1,410m
Vertical: 864m
Lifts: 7
Skiable acres: 1,454
hectares

www.skicastle.ca

CASTLE MOUNTAIN, ALBERTA, CANADA
A diamond in the rough

It's only a few years ago that the road to Castle Mountain was
paved, taking you into the heart of wild mountains that rise up
from Alberta's mirror-flat prairies like a gigantic wall.

Take the Tamarack Chair to the upper shoulders of
2,391-metre Gravenstal Mountain and you can see essential
Canada in all its glory, with nothing but mountain and forests
to the west and little other than flatland to the east.

And then take a look below at what Castle Mountain offers
the more adventurous skier – an average of 900cm of annual
snowfall that is rarely anything less than blower pow, a mix of
steeps and glades with varying densities of timber, and a cat-
ski operation if you want to escape the crowds.

But crowds? What crowds? Castle Mountain is so far
removed from the frenetic lift queues and busy slopes of
bigger resorts that there is simply no such thing as a 'crowd'
here (except maybe in the T-Bar pub at the base of the
mountain when the day's skiing is over).

This very welcome low density of skiers means that when
skiing here mid-week you can feel like you're the only skier on
the mountain, and there are no plans to change that – indeed,
one of the resort directors, Dean Parkinson, says that Castle
Mountain is committed to maintaining "... a low density of
skiers and moderate prices so the ski experience isn't ruined"
(there are a few French mega-resorts that could learn a lesson
from that enlightened approach).

The skiing can be challenging here and Castle Mountain
has a wild, outback sort of feel about it as well as being very
personable – everyone chats to each other on the lifts and in
the ski shop, cafés and bar at the base and you'll soon feel like
a local when you ski here (although you probably won't ski like
a local).

Head to The Chutes, for instance, where virtually every run
is a double-black diamond, or venture into the ample supply
of glades and it soon becomes obvious that this is a ski hill for
serious skiers.

Sure, the elevation is relatively modest, topping out at 2,274
metres and the 'vert' is less than a thousand metres, whilst the
lifts are old and slow, but when you get to ski fresh tracks in
featherlight powder virtually all day, so what? And the slow
lifts will seem like a boon by mid-afternoon when your quads
are desperate for a rest.

And yes, Castle Mountain is well off the beaten track, and
pretty much at the end of the road to nowhere, but sometimes
a trip to nowhere can reveal all sorts of surprises...

Revelling in the solitude at the end of the road to nowhere
© Nick Thornton

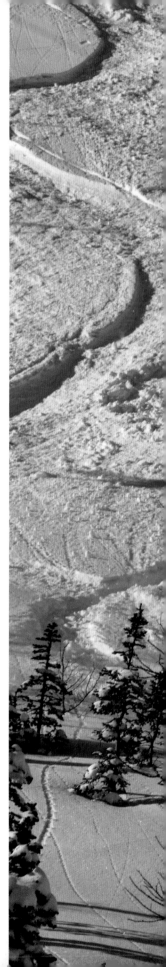

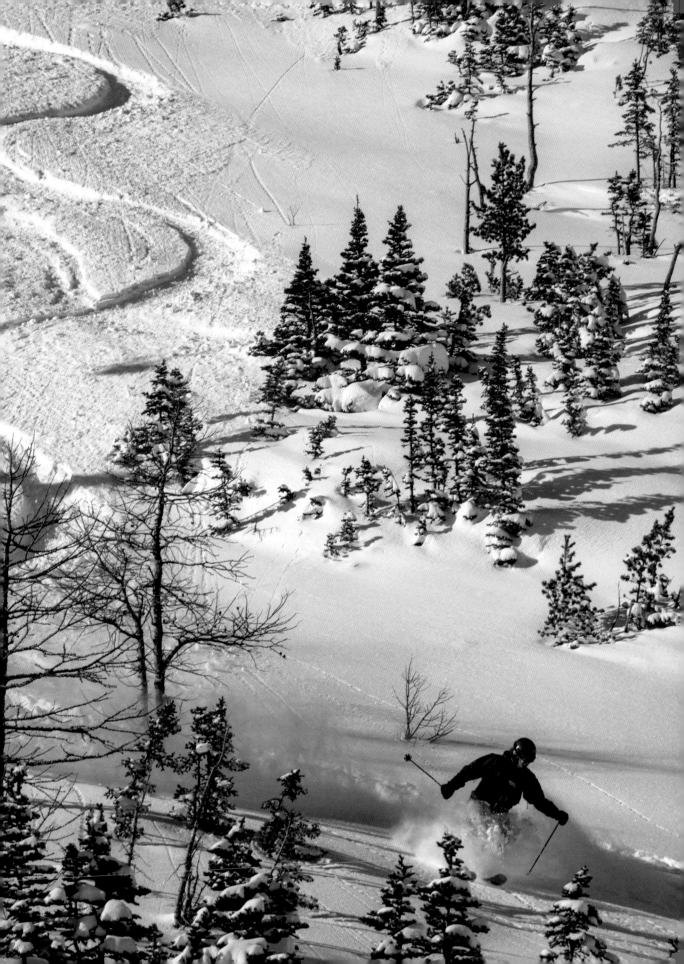

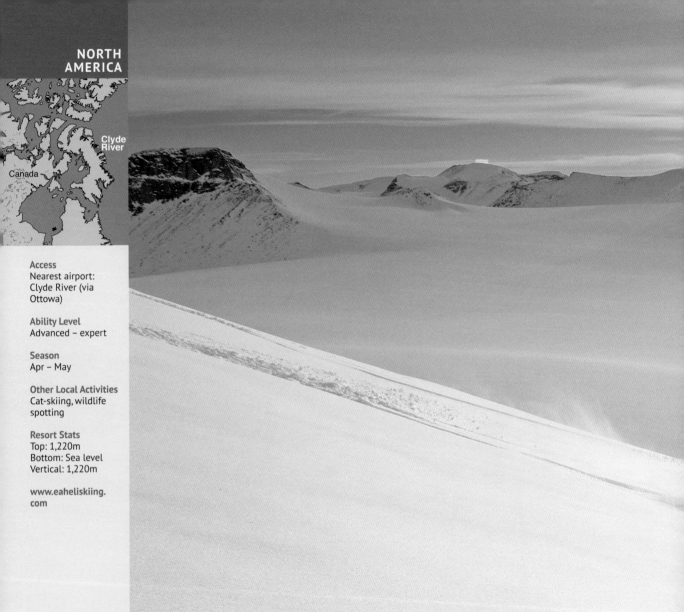

Clyde River

Canada

Access
Nearest airport:
Clyde River (via
Ottowa)

Ability Level
Advanced – expert

Season
Apr – May

Other Local Activities
Cat-skiing, wildlife
spotting

Resort Stats
Top: 1,220m
Bottom: Sea level
Vertical: 1,220m

www.eaheliskiing.
com

CLYDE RIVER, BAFFIN ISLAND (QIKIQTAALUK), CANADA
Pretty good skiing...

Baffin Island is a place of superlatives – it's the largest island in Canada, fifth largest island in the world, the heli-ski base at the small Inuit settlement of Clyde River has two-and-a-half months of continuous sunlight in summer (whilst in winter the sun sets on November 22 and doesn't rise again until January 19 of the following year) and the heli-ski operation here is the most northerly in the world.

And the skiing is pretty good...

The island (it seems strange to call it a mere 'island' when Baffin Island is bigger than most countries) lies in the path of a generally northerly airflow all year round, creating a very cold climate and perfect snow conditions, with spring arriving much later than other areas which straddle the Arctic Circle as does Baffin Island. Consequently, heavy snow can occur all year round, although the ski season only runs from April to early May (should you get socked in by bad weather there's cat-skiing as a back-up).

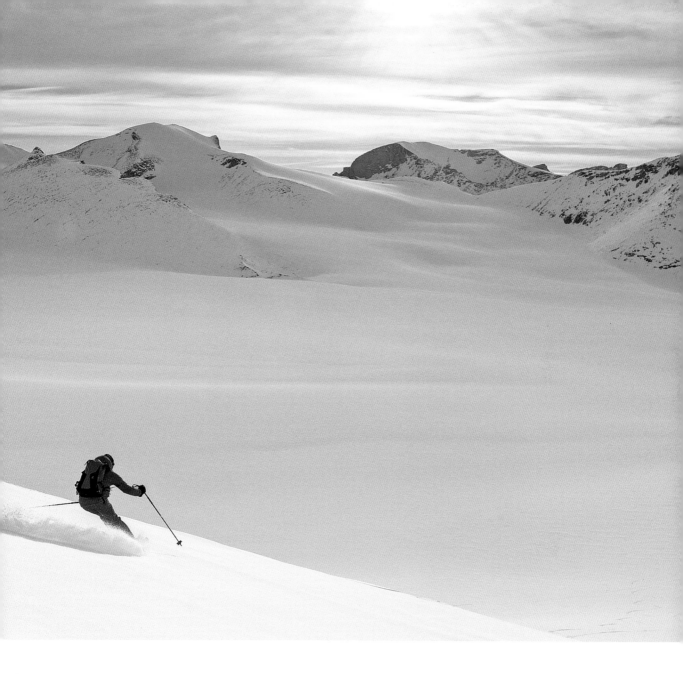

For most of this period the nearest you'll get to night is a brief spell of twilight, so it's possible to ski almost 24-hours a day.

You'll be whisked up by helicopter into a phenomenal landscape which is quite literally a vast mountain wilderness that's devoid of humans and home to wildlife such as barren-ground caribou, polar bear, Arctic fox, Arctic hare, lemming, Arctic wolf and snowy owl.

Huge glaciers descend to frozen fjords, home to harp seals, walrus, Beluga whales and narwhals, and incredible ski terrain stretches as far as the eye can see, allowing you to enjoy superb powder descents like the four-kilometre run from the summit of Mount Wordie all the way down to the sea.

The unique nature of the skiing here also applies to the accommodation, an unusual and unique heli-ski 'lodge' – or to be more accurate an upmarket 'expedition camp' – consisting of six individual 'igloos' that have been shipped by boat to the Arctic and allow you to stay on the snow and ice right in the heart of this spectacular destination.

You'll also get to experience the local culture – Clyde River is a small Inuit village (despite the name) where traditional activities such as dog-sledding, drum dancing and throat singing are still practised.

Clearly heli-skiing on Baffin Island is not for everyone (there's the small matter of cost for a start), but if you really are searching for a very different skiing adventure, this could well be it, 70 degrees north in the Arctic Circle.

The world's most northerly heli-ski operation © eaheliskiing.com

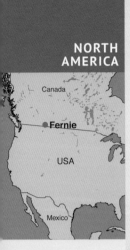

Canada

Fernie

USA

Mexico

Access
Nearest airport:
Calgary (300km)

Ability Level
Beginner – expert

Season
Dec – Apr

Other Local Activities
Snowshoeing, fat
biking, cross-country
skiing, cat-skiing,
sleigh rides

Resort Stats
Top: 2,134m
Bottom: 1,052m
Vertical: 1,082m
Skiable acres: 2,500+
acres

www.skifernie.com

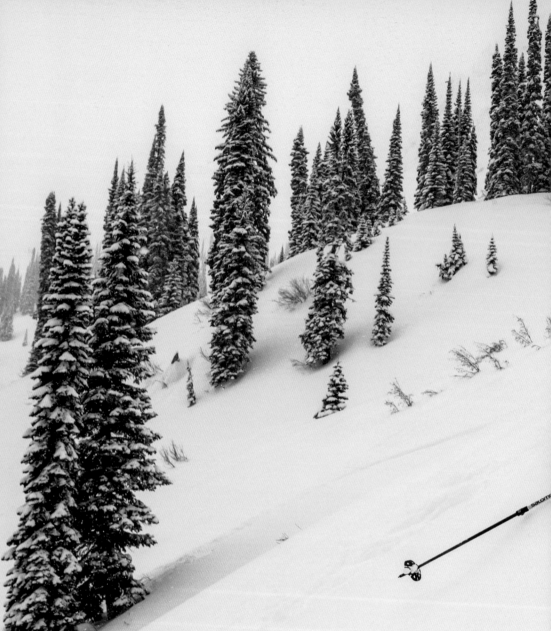

FERNIE, BRITISH COLUMBIA, CANADA
Where patience is a virtue

They like their bowls at Fernie, so much so that all five (Siberia, Timber, Currie, Lizard and Cedar) are picked out individually on the trail map, and they're usually choked with powder – the resort receives over 900cm of featherlight white stuff each winter on average.

Above these bowls is a huge Rocky Mountain headwall, which in a roundabout way has resulted in Fernie becoming one of the best avalanche-controlled ski hills in North America. The thing is, over 70 percent of the skiing on offer at Fernie is in avalanche terrain, which means that the ski patrollers here have their work cut out in making it safe after each of the resort's frequent powder dumps.

Each patroller has to be qualified / have experience of avalanche control and forecasting along with qualifications in first aid, toboggan, rope, lift and avalanche rescue (and there are also avy dog teams too), and as a result the Fernie Ski Patrol is one of the best around – patrollers from other resorts often come here to brush up on their technique.

This all makes for an interesting patroller / skier relationship – whilst skiers are obviously chomping

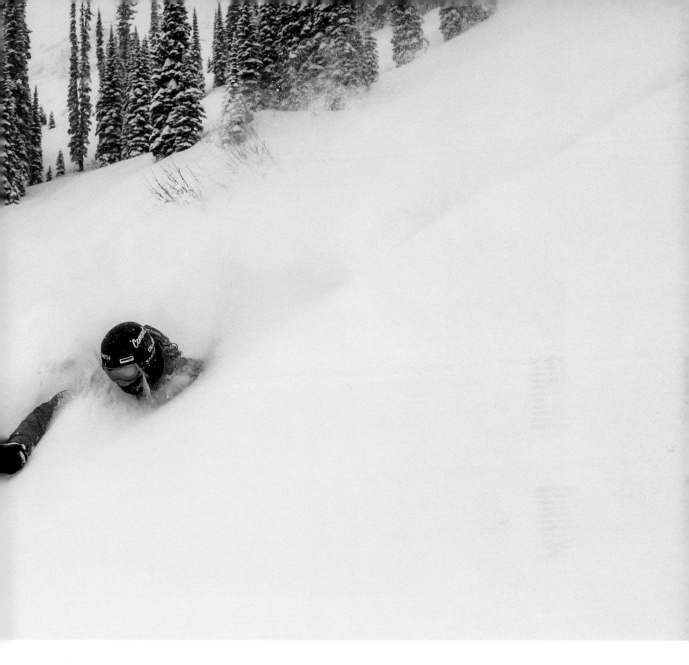

Fernie's bowls will bowl you over
© Nick Nault

at the bit to get on to the mountain after a dump, ski patrol is working systematically to ensure that the terrain you'll be riding is safe, including firing their two 'avalauncher' cannons early in the morning to start the whole risk-limitation exercise off with controlled slides and then, in teams, moving into different areas of the mountain to throw hand chargers and ski-cut smaller avalanche features to gradually open up the various bowls.

What this means, if you're amping to hit Fernie's excellent array of steeps, glades and cruisers after a heavy snowfall, is that you may have to master the art of patience, as not all the bowls will be accessible immediately after the lifts open; it also means it's well worth getting to know a few locals who are likely to have a good idea of what will open when, and in what sequence.

If you do, and you follow their lead, you could find yourself getting fresh tracks – or close to – for much of the day as the resort gradually opens up to reveal some of the best tree and steep skiing in Canada.

And when you've exhausted yourself in the bowls, you'll need to hope you have a little energy left to check out Fernie the town, just a few kilometres down the road. It's one of the most laid back, bohemian ski towns in Canada, with a fine selection of bars, restaurants, ski shops and coffee houses, the kind of place where it's easy to meet the locals – and maybe pick their brains about where the best skiing will be tomorrow.

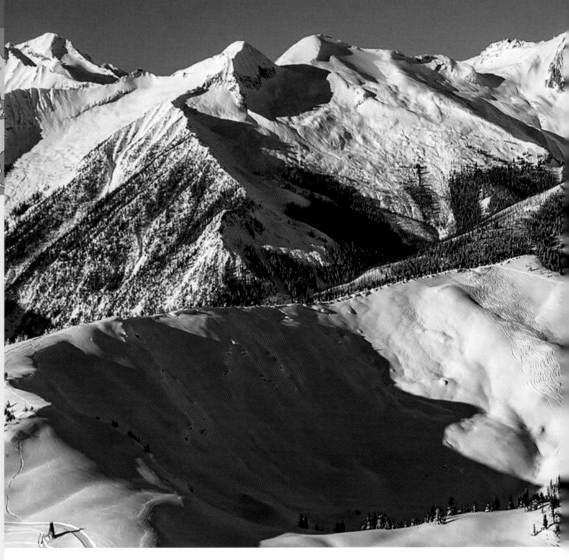

Canada

● Selkirk

USA

Mexico

Access
Nearest airports:
Castlegar (152km),
Trail (184km)

Ability Level
Advanced – expert

Season
Dec – Apr

Other Local Activities
Yoga, sauna, hot tub,
massage

Resort Stats
Top: 8,300m
Bottom: 4,200m
Vertical: 4,100m
Skiable acres: 12,000
acres

www.
selkirksnowcatskiing.
com

SELKIRK SNOWCAT SKIING, BRITISH COLUMBIA, CANADA
Cool for cats – the author heads into the wild

It was about as wild as it gets. The Purcell Mountains' Macbeth Icefield to the east, the Selkirk Mountains' Purcell Glacier to the west and a set of cougar tracks right in front of us. This was a whole new take on cat-skiing.

Our guide Joe had pointed out these hand-sized paw prints before telling us a little story about his friend who had been skiing in the same area and came across similar tracks, so decided to follow them. Eventually he ended up right back where he'd started from, and it occurred to him that, having described a large circle, was it he who was following the cougar, or the cougar that had been following him?

Time to make a quick exit...

An 'average' quick exit at Selkirk Snowcat Skiing may start with a big open bowl, then descend into a tighter gully before hitting the tree line, where the firs and pines are invariably spaced just so – not too tight, not too open – and on the steeper and deeper runs you'll experience snow cascading past your thighs, your waist, even over your shoulders.

This marvellous crystalline perfection is not reached easily, of course – it's quite a hike from

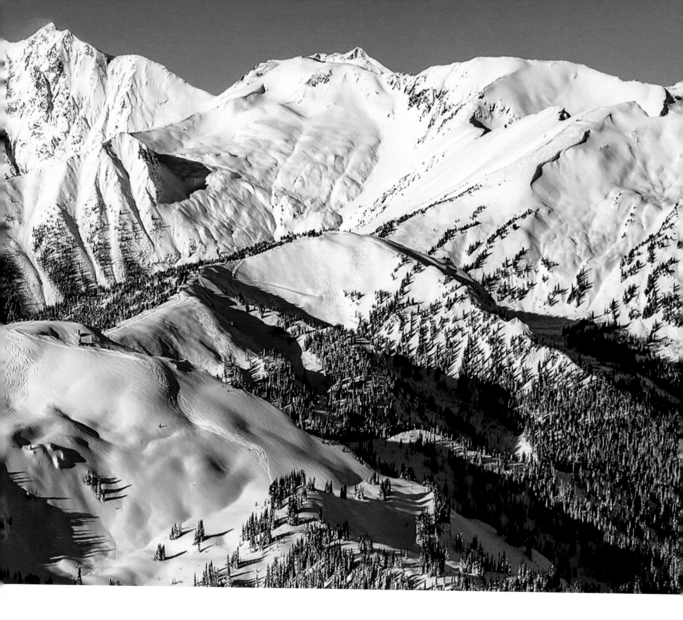

whichever airport you fly into, but then getting there through gorgeous British Columbian landscapes is part of the fun.

And nor was this inspirational ski terrain found easily in the first place, as the company's affable owner Allan Drury – alas no longer with us – told me over a beer after my tiring but immensely satisfying second day of riding 'his' mountain.

Allan used to work as a ski instructor and a geologist in the Canadian Rockies and as such had seen a whole heap of mountains and snow when, in the mid-1970s, he decided to look for an alternative to the increasingly crowded resorts he'd been teaching in and the expensive wilderness skiing option of heli-skiing.

"I thought that cat-skiing would be a good bet since snowcats are cheaper to buy and require less maintenance than helicopters and they can take you into the same terrain as a helicopter – so I got hold of topographic maps of the regions I considered suitable and spent months researching until we finally settled for our location here in the Selkirk Mountains."

The magnificent, wild Selkirk Mountains are high enough and the snowfall light and consistent enough (400 inches a year) to all but guarantee world-class skiing throughout a season that stretches from early December to April (although it's quite possible to ski for months either side of that) and in 1975 Allan's operation was born, the first snowcat skiing of its kind in the world.

There's enough terrain here to provide guests with fresh tracks for literally weeks after a snowfall, and, almost fifty years after it was born, just one visit to this incredible mountain playground will show you why Selkirk Snowcat Skiing was not only the first but is still one of the best.

As wild as it gets – cat-skiing in the Selkirk Mountains © selkirksnowcatskiing.com

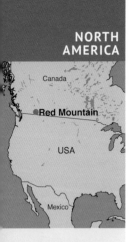

Access
Nearest airport:
Spokane (198km)

Ability Level
Beginner – expert

Season
Dec – Apr

Other Local Activities
Cross-country skiing,
cat-skiing, heli-skiing,
snowshoeing, ice
skating

Resort Stats
Top: 2,075m
Bottom: 1,185m
Vertical: 890m
Lifts: 8
Skiable acres: 3,850
acres

www.redresort.com

RED MOUNTAIN, BRITISH COLUMBIA, CANADA
Good gets gooder

This is clearly a book based to an extent on personal experience, and Red Mountain is the most personal entry of all since it was a prolonged visit here in 1999/2000 that set me on course for a career in ski journalism.

Basically, I fell for Red and its funky satellite town of Rossland thanks to a marvellous mix of great skiing, fantastic personalities, friendly vibe and the fact that it's exactly what I expected a small Canadian ski hill to be like (although it's no longer so small, now ranking amongst the top ten ski resorts in North America in terms of acreage).

So, dear reader, allow me the self-indulgence of describing an 'average' day at Red Mountain...

It's 9.10am on a snowy Sunday morning and I'm sitting on the Silverlode chair with my mate Roly. I arrived later than many of the locals to join the lift queue for first tracks, but Roly, a long-time local and former Red Mountain ski patroller, was close to the front and invited me to join him.

I've skied with Roly many times since we first met at Red in 1999, and he always makes it his job to introduce me to the best terrain on the mountain. After hopping off Silverlode and on to Motherlode Chair we reach the top of the resort, from where we ski across to Grey Mountain, which opened a few years ago to add an extra thousand acres of the eminently skiable terrain for which Red is so renowned (or as Roly jokingly remarked "It was good before – now it's gooder").

In falling snow and poor vis, we hike for five minutes from the top of Grey Mountain Chair along a gently angled ridge above the Chute Show glades. Here we drop into pow that is light, deep and virtually untracked.

We skim through shin-deep snow between trees that – for me at least – are just right; not too tight, so you can relax a little, but certainly close enough to make you concentrate.

By late morning we decide to ski across to Kirkup Mountain, the next peak on from Grey, where you can go cat-skiing for just 10 Canadian dollars – it's a great way of trying it for the first time, and if you get hooked, as you will, you'll struggle to get through more than $CAN100 before collapsing in an exhausted heap.

We enjoy one run here in that legendary BC 'cold smoke' before heading for lunch at the Paradise Lodge on Granite Mountain, where everybody seems to know everybody else, then we hit the fun, open pistes of Paradise Bowl before heading back up Grey Mountain.

Everywhere we go there's the option of well-groomed and sparsely populated pistes or even less sparsely populated glades and steeps of varying degrees of verticality, along with spectacular views of the Columbia River Valley way down below.

Venturing down EZRyder, a steep black that offers opportunities to snake between trees we holler and hoot to keep track of each other's whereabouts before eventually riding back up Granite on the Motherlode Chair, when I hear someone say today has been "... one of the busiest days EVER" at Red (it's a holiday weekend).

In Europe, this would be a quiet day – which is why, along with the terrain, the snow, the locals and the après-ski in Rafters Lounge at the base you should visit Red Mountain. And I may well see you there...

Red Mountain – the classic Canadian ski experience © redresort.com

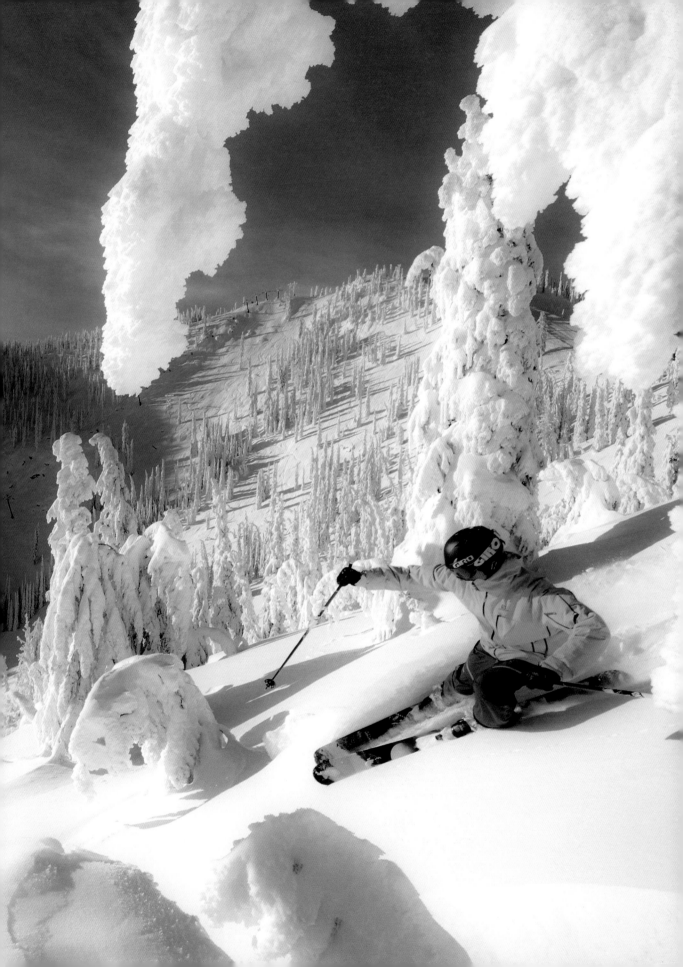

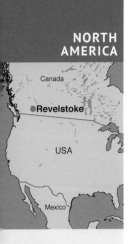

Canada

●Revelstoke

USA

Mexico

Access
Nearest airport:
Calgary (425km)

Ability Level
Beginner – expert

Season
Nov/Dec – Apr

Other Local Activities
Cat-skiing, heli-skiing, cross-country skiing, snowshoeing, fat biking, hiking, snowmobiling, dog-sledding

Resort Stats
Top: 2,225m
Bottom: 512m
Vertical: 1,713m
Lifts: 5
Skiable acres: 3,121 acres

www. revelstoke
mountainresort.com

REVELSTOKE, BRITISH COLUMBIA, CANADA
Something for everyone

Revelstoke's various claims to fame are all likely to put a broad smile on the face of any keen skier; it has the biggest 'vert' in North America at 5,620ft, easily comparable with major European resorts, it offers lift, cat- and heli-ski-accessed skiing (apparently the only ski resort in the world to do so) and it has a very impressive annual average snowfall of 10.5 metres – although the record annual snowfall figure here is a mighty 24 metres.

So not much more you need to know really, is there? Other than what the skiing is like, of course.

In a nutshell, it's superbly varied – especially if you take into account that, should funds allow, you can also head by cat or helicopter to ski the remoter reaches of the local mountains – indeed, what is now Revelstoke Mountain Resort was originally a heli-ski tenure, so even if you don't get to go heli-skiing you'll get some idea of what the terrain might be like if you did.

Also worth bearing in mind is that both the cat and heli operations can be – and in the case of most skier usually are – booked for a single day, so you don't have to make the kind of financial commitment required of a multi-day trip to a lodge.

Revelstoke resort has a wide range of alpine bowls and glades, the latter of which come in very useful on the frequent snowy days when visibility is limited – glades such as Tally Ho and Powder Monkey allow you to shred when the high alpine bowls are completely socked in; and when the sun bursts forth, follow the rays to spots such as South Bowl and enjoy classic runs like Jalapeño or Hot Sauce, which keep the sunlight through the afternoon.

And if you don't mind a bit of hiking look out for the footsteps leading off the top of Stoke Chair up to Subpeak, where you can drop into either North Bowl or South Bowl.

If all this sounds a bit serious, not a bit of it – yes, tree-skiing can be daunting, especially if you're more used to the generally treeless alpine terrain of the Alps, but Revelstoke's runs have been designed so there's plenty of fun to be had in the glades whatever your level of ability – there are even green runs that snake gently down the mountain between the firs.

Which makes it entirely reasonable to say there really is something for everyone at Revelstoke.

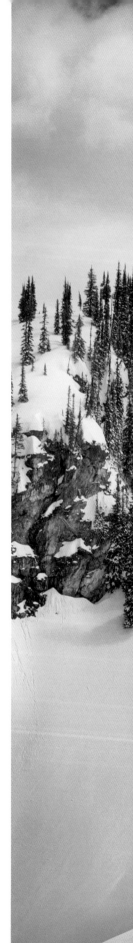

The biggest 'vert' in North America is just one of Revelstoke's many attractions © Ian Houghton

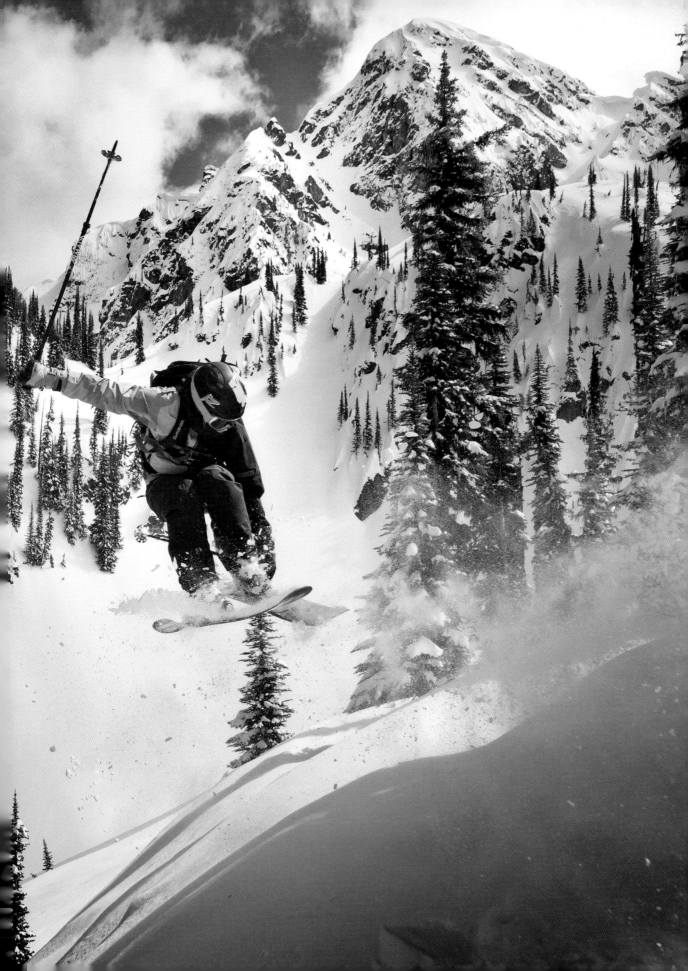

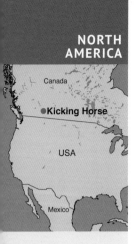

Canada

● **Kicking Horse**

USA

Mexico

Access
Nearest airport:
Calgary (212km)

Ability Level
Beginner – expert

Season
Dec – Apr

Other Local Activities
Heli-skiing, cross-country skiing, tubing, snowshoeing, ice skating, snowmobiling

Resort Stats
Top: 8,033m
Bottom: 3,900m
Vertical: 4,133m
Lifts: 5
Skiable acres: 3,486 acres

www.
kickinghorseresort.
com

KICKING HORSE, BRITISH COLUMBIA, CANADA
Food (and champagne) for the soul

The Golden Eagle Express gondola is the only means of accessing the steep bowls and fluffy powder for which Kicking Horse is rightly renowned, so everyone here is, like you, going to be doing laps if they intend to ski top to bottom of the hill.

This is a good thing. It means that you pretty much get to know the collection of mainly Aussie and Canuck lifties personally, and like everyone else in this corner of British Columbia – 14km outside the blue collar logging and railroad town of Golden – they're a friendly bunch. On the lift you'll encounter dudes and dudesses from Canada, the States, Scandinavia, Australasia, and Europe, and a bit of subtle questioning may well reveal where the best lines are to be found.

That said, there's no real need to be sniffing around for secret stashes at Kicking Horse, because you can see much of what the mountain has to offer as you cruise up on the gondola to the summit station in front of the chi-chi Golden Eagle Restaurant (North America's highest, apparently).

As you ascend, you'll find yourself looking down upon some seriously steep, gladed terrain off CPR Ridge, while off to your left are two of the resort's four bowls, Bowl Over and, beyond this, Super Bowl. These are split by the 'hike-to' T1 North Ridge and T2 South Ridge (it takes about 20 minutes to reach the skiing depending on how fit you are) from which a series of double-black diamond runs plummet down through alpine and then treed terrain.

Avert your gaze to the right as your ride up the mountain continues and two more big white bowls reveal themselves, Crystal and Feuz, separated by thrillingly steep ridges. You can only access the furthest of these, Redemption Ridge, via the creakingly slow Stairway to Heaven chair, from which there's another huge selection of chutes of ever increasing steepness that drop you a-whoopin' and a-hollerin' into Feuz Bowl – and the slowness of the Stairway to Heaven chair can have its advantages – it gives your legs a rest...

But back to the much more swanky Golden Eagle Express. Hop off and, if you have the patience, stop for a moment to check out the magnificent view – down below the resort basking in winter sunshine; lower still is Golden nestled in the vast Rocky Mountain Trench at the confluence of the Columbia and Kicking Horse rivers, surrounded by mountains so innocent of humans that many are yet to be named. It's food for the soul.

Try warming up with one of the gentler chutes off CPR Ridge – you'll drop in to what is invariably a pretty narrow entrance, plumes of powder billowing around your knees (all being well; the resort averages 256 inches of the white stuff each year and has trademarked itself as 'The Champagne Powder Capital of Canada') and your turns necessarily tight and focussed, before things open up lower down and you can let rip with some serious speed as you hoon down into Crystal Bowl.

You'll now hit some outrageously fun groomers – black Bubbly drops you into blue Wiley Coyote where you can weave around like a man or woman possessed on what are wide, open and, usually, far from overpopulated slopes.

Similar options await off every ridge at Kicking Horse but, whichever descent you take, by the time you reach the base station your quads will certainly know you've just ridden the 'Horse'.

And that was just the first of many laps of one of the finest ski hills in North America...

Guaranteed fun coming up – who's first? © Cali Burk

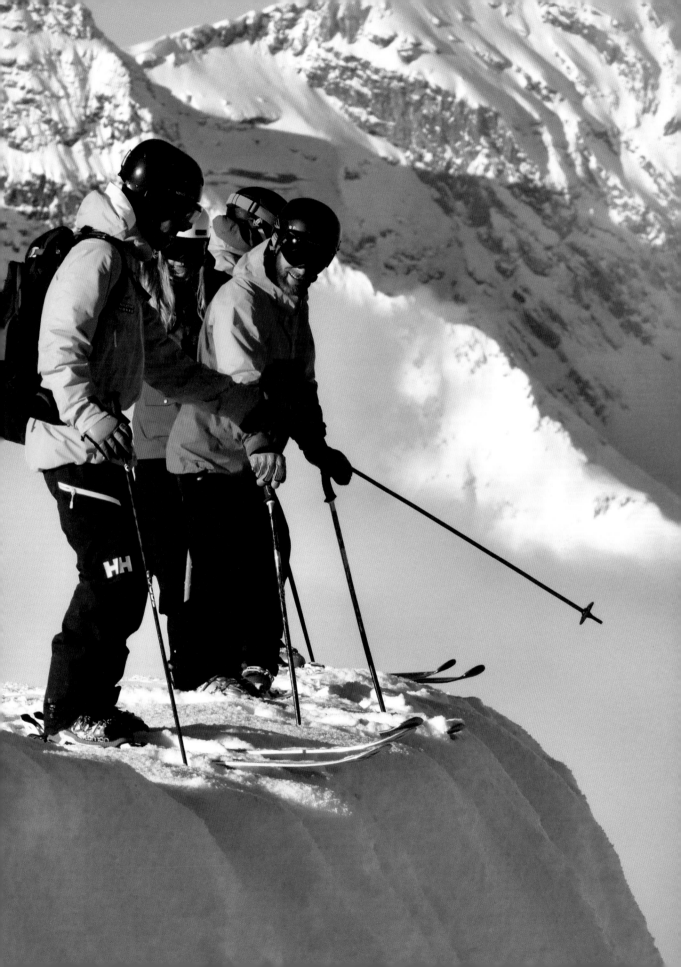

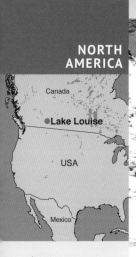

Canada

Lake Louise

USA

Mexico

Access
Nearest airport:
Calgary (196km)

Ability Level
Beginner – expert

Season
Nov – May

Other Local Activities
Heli-skiing, cross-country skiing, snowshoeing, ice skating, dog-sledding

Resort Stats
Top: 2,637m
Bottom: 1,645m
Vertical: 992m
Lifts: 10
Skiable acres: 1,619 hectares

www.skilouise.com

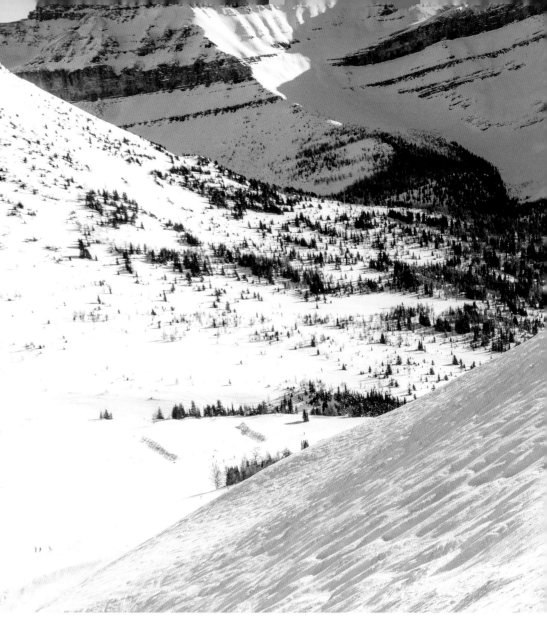

LAKE LOUISE, ALBERTA, CANADA
A room with a view

Go on, spoil yourself. If and when you decide to ski Lake Louise, stay – for one night at least – at the magnificent Chateau Lake Louise. And endeavour to arrive at night. For when you arise from your slumbers the following morning it won't just be the grandeur and opulence of the hotel that impresses you, but the truly staggering vistas that are revealed when you draw back the curtains.

Huge mountain walls rising to knife-edged ridges; peaks draped by gleaming ice-blue glaciers; the snow-frosted, frozen waters of Lake Louise surrounded by dense, green pine forests – it's the Canadian Rocky Mountains exactly as you'd expect them to be.

And lost in the middle of all this is Lake Louise ski resort, the biggest ski hill in the Canadian Rockies, from where the views are even more impressive – whichever of the resort's main lifts you choose to take, the higher you get, the more magnificent the panoramas – check out 11,622ft Mount Temple, for example, its glacier seeming to defy gravity as it appears to hang from the summit.

It was this jaw-dropping scenery that led to the creation of the Banff National Park in 1883, 2,500 square miles of some of the most beautiful mountain scenery in North America that is also a UNESCO World Heritage Site. The wildlife here plays a part in that designation, and although you're unlikely to

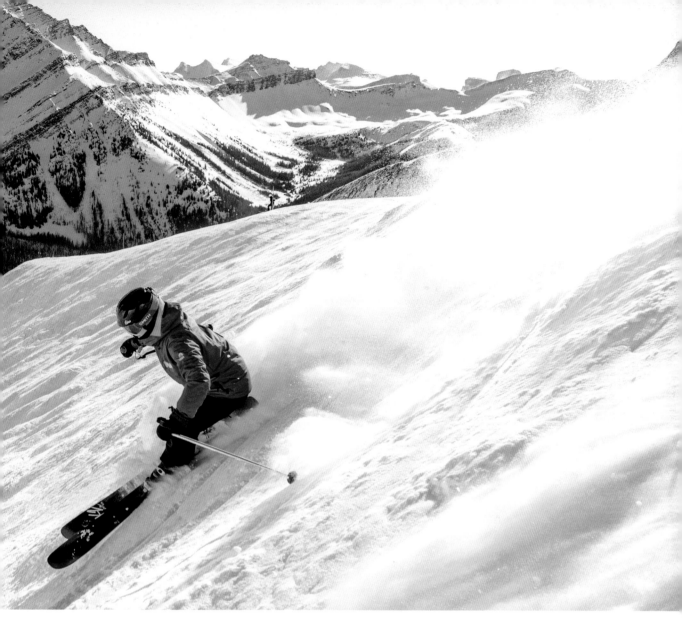

see such exotic species as grizzlies and black bears in winter, you may well spot moose and elk.

You don't have to be a great skier to get high up for the best views either, since Lake Louise has plenty of skiing for every level of ability. There's a green run off every lift except the steep Summit Platter button lift, and while some may present a challenge to weaker skiers, greens such as Wiwaxy on the Front Side allow you to ski the mountain with ease.

Intermediate skiers can cruise down the wide, open runs on Front Side and the Larch area, many of which start above the tree line, while advanced skiers can launch themselves into some superb steep, deep runs including the exciting Men's and Ladies' Downhill courses.

Experts will find steep, challenging lines all over the place – Back Side has lots of variety, there are some great chutes on Ultimate Steeps and the gladed terrain off the Ptarmigan Chair is often very quiet.

Indeed, the slopes are usually pretty quiet throughout the resort during weekdays, although it can get busy at weekends when locals from nearby Calgary arrive – which makes a good excuse to take a day away from skiing and visit nearby Banff, surely one of the most spectacularly-sited mountain towns in the world – with huge rock walls and towering ridges blocking out the skyline, it's Canada's answer to Chamonix and Zermatt.

It can get very cold at Lake Louise, so it's well worth arming yourself with your best thermals, but of course that frigidity keeps the snow in good condition, and the season here is long, often extending from early November to early May, when the bears may even be waking up...

Skiing in the heart of some of the most spectacular scenery in Canada at Lake Louise
© Sarah Magyar

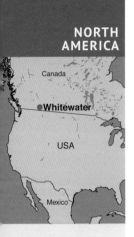

Access
Nearest airport:
Castlegar (45km)

Ability Level
Beginner – expert

Season
Dec – Apr

Other Local Activities
Cross-country skiing,
snowshoeing, snow-
biking

Resort Stats
Top: 2,045m
Bottom: 1,422m
Vertical: 623m
Lifts: 4
Skiable acres:
479 hectares (lift
accessible)

www.skiwhitewater.
com

WHITEWATER, BRITISH COLUMBIA, CANADA
Small can definitely be better

Whitewater is tiny by European standards, and it has a very modest vertical drop of 623m from a high point of only 2,045m. But don't turn away just yet... for Whitewater also has an annual average snowfall of 1,200cm, or 40 feet. Yes, you read correctly – 40 feet.

This is one reason why ski photographers and film makers flock here to get their action shots; in fact the chances are that when you pick up a ski mag some wild action from Whitewater will feature in amongst the most spectacular shots (they like leaping off cliffs in these parts).

So, I'm standing with my friend and local ski patroller Andrew Voigt at the top of Whitewater's Glory Ridge Chair and we're about to take on one of the resort's gladed runs, but stop first to admire the views, which are classic British Columbia; forested mountains draped in snow as far as we can see, little sign of human activity other than in the resort, and towering over it all to our right the craggy face of 7,867-foot Ymir Peak which culminates in a perfect triangular summit (the name, pronounced 'Why-Meer', comes from the fact that many of the region's early European settlers were Nordic, Ymir being the name of the Norse frost giant).

Andrew and I have known each other for a few years, so I can ask him without too much embarrassment not to take me down anything too terrifying, for Whitewater thrives on its reputation as the haunt of skiers who consider cliffs, 45-degree-plus slopes, waist deep powder and trees as tight as two coats of paint all part of a good day in the mountains.

And 'hike-to' is also a very big thing here – in fact for a large proportion of local skiers the lifts are merely the start of the journey to find the best 'cold smoke'.

So, we begin by dropping into the easy blue of Ramble On, where the pines are widely spaced, the angle is easy and the snow is soft and forgiving. We descend diagonally onto a black called Jack Leg Glades, where the trees begin to crowd in a little more and the slope gets steeper, but it's still fun and the snow is still soft and light, then suddenly we're under the lift line and heading for the base station.

It's all over pretty quickly compared to the average descent in the Alps, but the concentration involved in skiing trees – which let's face it are not a big part of European skiing – pretty much make the concept of time meaningless. We're living in and for the moment and enjoying every second of it.

As we ascend again on the two-person Glory Ridge chair I ask Andrew what it is that's kept him skiing here for so many years. "It's the consistent quality of the snowfall – that simple. And the way the friendly 'small-town' vibe of Nelson carries up onto the ski hill."

Ah yes, Nelson. I forgot about that. Nelson is Whitewater's satellite town, about 15-minute's drive away; there's no accommodation at the hill, just a great restaurant and bar plus a small souvenir shop, so Nelson is where visiting skiers lay their heads.

This bohemian lakeside settlement regularly wins awards for 'best ski town', 'best outdoor town' and the like and Andrew is right about that small-town vibe also being present on the hill. Everyone seems to know each other, and they will soon start chatting to the stranger in town (you) on the lifts and in the base lodge.

They'll enthuse about the local skiing in a way that may seem just a little over the top when you consider how small Whitewater is; but there again, if your favourite ski hill enjoyed 40ft of snowfall every winter, wouldn't you get a bit excited too?

Trace Cooke flies through the timber at Whitewater © Ryan Flett

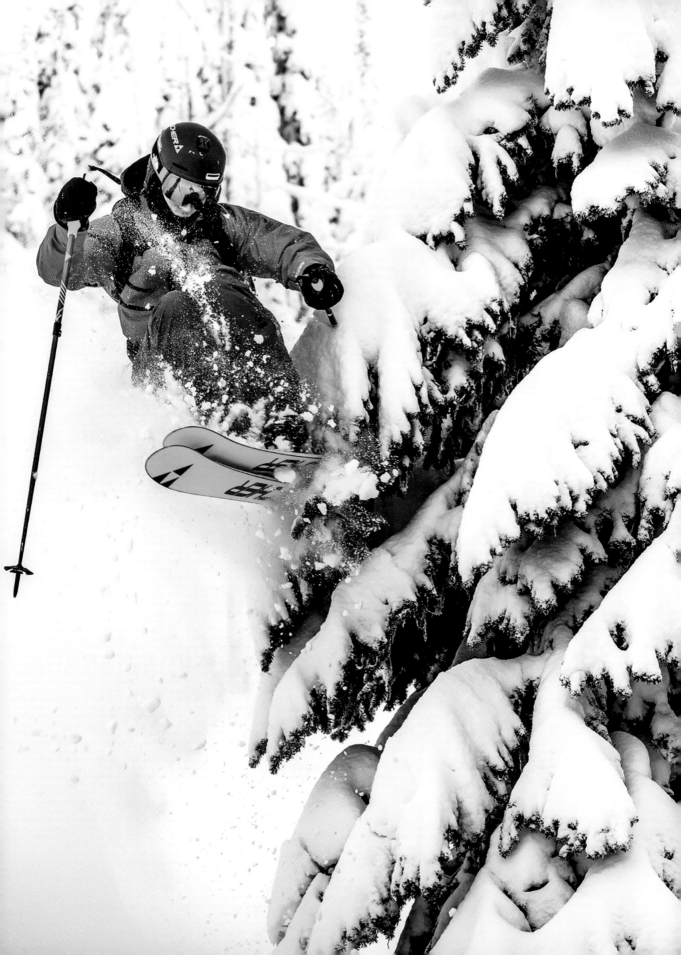

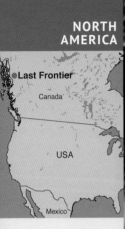

● Last Frontier

Canada

USA

Mexico

Access
Nearest airports:
Terrace (342km),
Smithers (359km)

Ability Level
Advanced
intermediate –
expert

Season
Dec – Apr

Other Local Activities
Cross-country skiing,
snowshoeing, skeet
shooting, ski touring,
archery, target
shooting, fat biking

Resort Stats
Highest drop-off:
2,600m
Average run length:
900m
Longest run length:
2,000m
Skiable area:
10,100sq.km

www.lastfrontierheli.
com

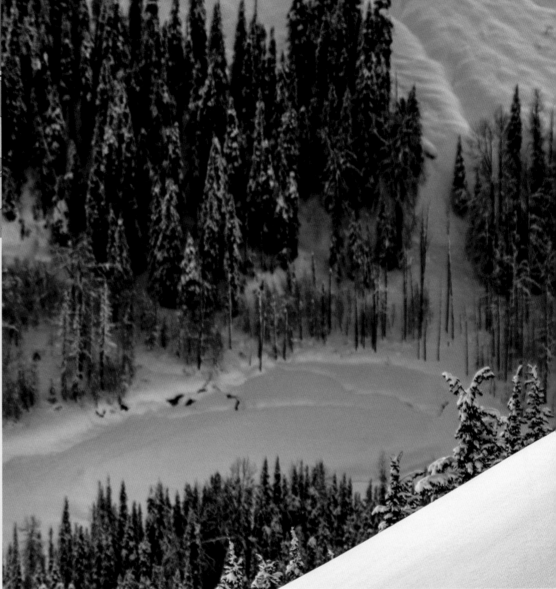

LAST FRONTIER HELISKIING, BELL 2 LODGE, BRITISH COLUMBIA, CANADA
A parallel universe

Everything here on Canada's border with Alaska is out of the ordinary – the remote, wild, snow-plastered Skeena Mountains are so unexplored that many of the peaks are yet to be named, and some of the people who know them best – the guides and pilots at Last Frontier Heliskiing – have access to an extraordinary 10,100sq.km of ski terrain and over a thousand named runs, making it the largest such operation in the world.

This, of course, gives you an extraordinary amount of choice in terms of terrain – high alpine, massive glaciers, sprawling tree runs, and everything in between (Last Frontier also run an operation out of Ripley Creek in the Coast Mountains to the south, but this tends to be a little more challenging – nothing to stop you checking that out too, mind).

The A-Star B2/B3 helicopters that Last Frontier use are the fastest and most exciting ski lift there are, and can have you on the slopes – which literally lie in every direction from the lodge – in only five minutes.

Once there you'll be standing on a snowbase of up to 330cm (or more) of superlight powder ready to

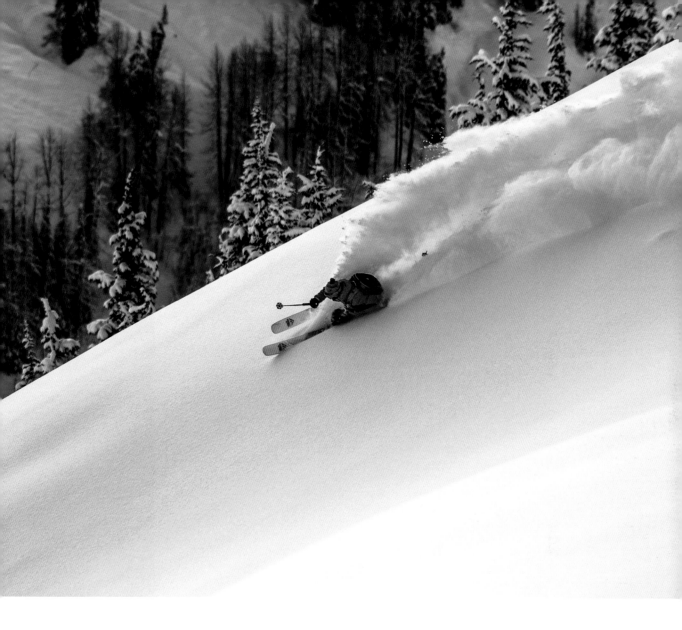

take on runs that may offer over 2,000 metres of 'vert', with a maximum of four guests plus guide, so unlike heli-skiing in bigger groups you spend more time skiing and less time faffing about.

When you experience the sheer and absolute joy of scything through untracked snow on a vast, sunny powder field in the middle of nowhere on a mid-week morning in March – when normal life would have most of us sitting behind a desk tapping at a keyboard or some other such dull drudgery – well, you can't help thinking you may have inadvertently slipped through a 'wormhole' into a parallel universe.

Snow like this allows you to ski like a hero in terrain that makes you feel like a hero and you even have 'hero transport' awaiting you at the end of the run. After all, is there any more macho, adrenaline-rush-inducing kind of journey than a helicopter ride through wild mountains?

The snow is rarely less than perfect and you feel and hear the hiss of a million glittering, dust-dry snow flakes against your thighs as you descend, whilst the terrain varies from easy cruising to steep, tight turns where the snow sloughs excitingly behind you as the landscape moves from high alpine glaciers surrounded by purple-walled mountains to fir-bedecked valleys where the aroma of pine hangs in the cold, blue air.

Indeed, the snow is so light that the skiing is not even that tiring – well not until you arrive back at the lodge where, beer in hand and body in hot tub, you're well aware that you've had a hell of a day's skiing.

Of course, none of this comes cheap, but sometimes the finer things in life justify the price tag...

One of the finer things in life – heli-skiing in BC's Skeena Mountains
© Reuben Crabbe

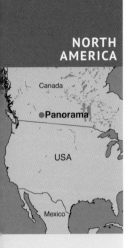

Canada

● Panorama

USA

Mexico

Access
Nearest airport:
Calgary (311km)

Ability Level
Beginner – expert

Season
Nov/Dec – Apr

Other Local Activities
Cross-country skiing,
cat-skiing, heli-
skiing, snowshoeing,
night skiing, ice
skating, paragliding,
snowmobiling, fat
biking

Resort Stats
Top: 2,450m
Bottom: 1,150m
Vertical: 1,300m
Lifts: 10
Skiable acres: 2,975
acres

www.
panoramaresort.com

PANORAMA, BRITISH COLUMBIA, CANADA
Plenty of everything

For one reason or another – and it certainly isn't for want of self-promotion – Panorama continues to remain somewhat below the radar for many skiers, despite the fact that it's one of Canada's biggest ski hills in terms of both area and vertical, is renowned for the quality of its snow (although the amounts are not as high as many of the other resorts of western Canada), can offer great skiing for all levels of ability and has a very mellow and friendly vibe.

Located as it is in the Purcell Mountains, Panorama is also pretty centrally located for skiers taking on the resorts of the Powder Highway, as well as being a relatively short drive from the international airport at Calgary – add all these factors together and it actually makes it a great place to visit whether for a day or two or a week or more.

With a good selection of ski in / ski out accommodation you can be on and off the hill in a trice from either of the two different levels of the resort and there's even the centrally located Panorama Hot Springs Complex in the 'upper village' where you can wind down after a hard day on the slopes. All starting to sound pretty good, hey?

Once on the hill you'll find things get even better, especially for more advanced skiers – the slopes are all below the tree line, with glades of varying degrees of tightness, making Panorama a great destination if tree-skiing is your thing – or if you want to improve your technique of dodging around our arboreal friends.

Those in the know will head for the Extreme Dream Zone where the skiing matches the name, or Taynton Bowl, which was originally heli-ski terrain and has some exciting chutes which descend with some degree of verticality into treed terrain.

That said there's some great terrain for adventurous intermediates – Sun Bowl, where you can practise your off-piste and tree-skiing, comes to mind, whilst there's plenty of fun if you love to blast down long cruisers – bear in mind that Panorama has the fourth longest 'vert' in Canada so your legs will know all about it after a lap or two.

There's also well-developed beginner and family / kids' terrain, terrain parks and an absolute stack of other snowy options (see opposite) if you decide to take a break from skiing, and given Panorama's relatively low profile you won't find yourself standing in long lift queues or searching for your own bit of space on the slopes.

Two's company, three would be a crowd in Panorama
© panoramaresort.com

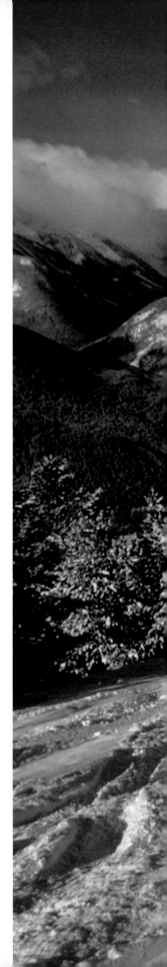

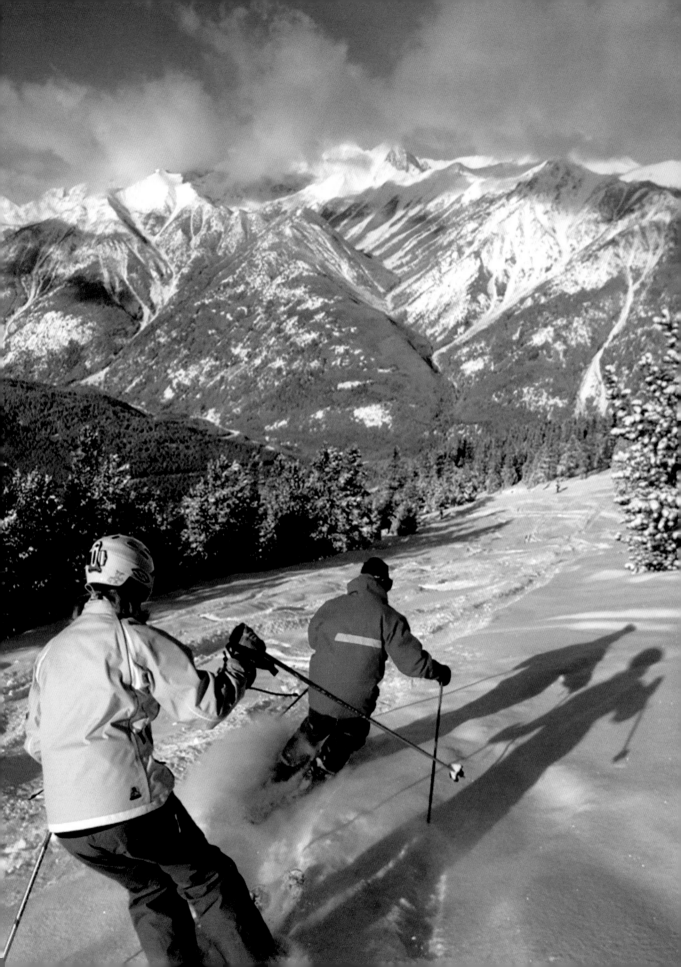

Russia

●Kamchatka

Pacific ocean

Access
Nearest airport:
Petropavolvsk-
Kamchatsky

Ability Level
Advanced – expert

Season
Dec – Apr

Other Local Activities
Skiing at
Petropavolvsk's two
small ski hills, dog-
sledding, sightseeing

Resort Stats
Top: 3,456m
Bottom: Sea level
Vertical: 3,456m
Lifts: 1
Pistes: None

www.eaheliskiing.
com

KAMCHATKA, RUSSIA
Skiing in the land of ice and fire

Kamchatka is one of the most active volcanic regions on Earth, an integral link in the infamous Pacific Ring of Fire. It's not a place you'd immediately think of for a ski trip, and indeed you need a helicopter to make the most of the slopes here but, if you do have access to one, you'll encounter some of the most spectacular skiing on Earth.

The helicopter most commonly used for accessing Kamchatka's truly spectacular mountains from your base in the city of Petropavlovsk-Kamchatsky is the ex-Russian military Mi8. There are no seat belts to the hard bench seats, and the fuselage is big enough that you can get up and wander around during the flight and even open the porthole-like windows to stick your head out for a better view.

And the views through those portholes are awe inspiring – to the east the cobalt-blue waters of the Pacific lap against a snowbound shoreline, whilst in every other direction range upon range of snow shrouded mountains lay in a powder-blue haze beneath clear sunny skies (if you're lucky), banners of smoke and steam rising here and there where cracks in their flanks extend all the way down to the Earth's core.

A ski descent in Kamchatka is a tad different to that of your average ski resort. It starts with skiers tumbling out of the helicopter and cowering close to the ground in a blizzard of rotor-whipped snow until the machine has clattered away to meet the group later in a valley some 2,000 metres below.

Once the snow has settled and silence returned to the mountains it would be quite easy to stand and stare all day at the awesome panoramas on view, were it not for the magnificent sight directly below – an untracked powder field the size and length of which no ski resort in the world can match.

On the best days each run will consist of a thousand metres or more of floating through shin deep powder, soft, light and deep and quite clearly the very elixir of life – how else to explain the wide grins and whoops of joy from every skier in the group? But it's not just the snow that brings this feeling of utter exhilaration – it's also the vastness of the landscape, the absolute wilderness in which you're immersed and the knowledge that there probably isn't another skier for a thousand miles in any direction.

Depending on the descent, the bright orange Mi-8 may be waiting silently for you in a valley where a small stream meanders aimlessly across a wide snowy flood plain and the solitude and silence are palpable; it could be tucked beside steaming hot springs where you can strip off and slide into the hot water to ease tired muscles; or it may be standing on a pebbly beach which gives you the unique opportunity to ski to the sea and go skinny dipping in 4°C water.

This isn't the kind of skiing that will suit everyone – James Morland of Elemental Adventure organises ski trips to Kamchatka and advises clients that: "This is adventure skiing rather than powder skiing. You should be prepared for any conditions – if you are it will be the ski adventure of a lifetime."

And when you're not skiing? "Well", says James. "There's the Cosmic nightclub in Petropavlovsk – that always seems to be popular with our clients. One of the guys on our first Kamchatka trip almost got himself married off to a local girl he met there!"

Volcanic vents and powder slopes, Kamchatka © Alf Alderson

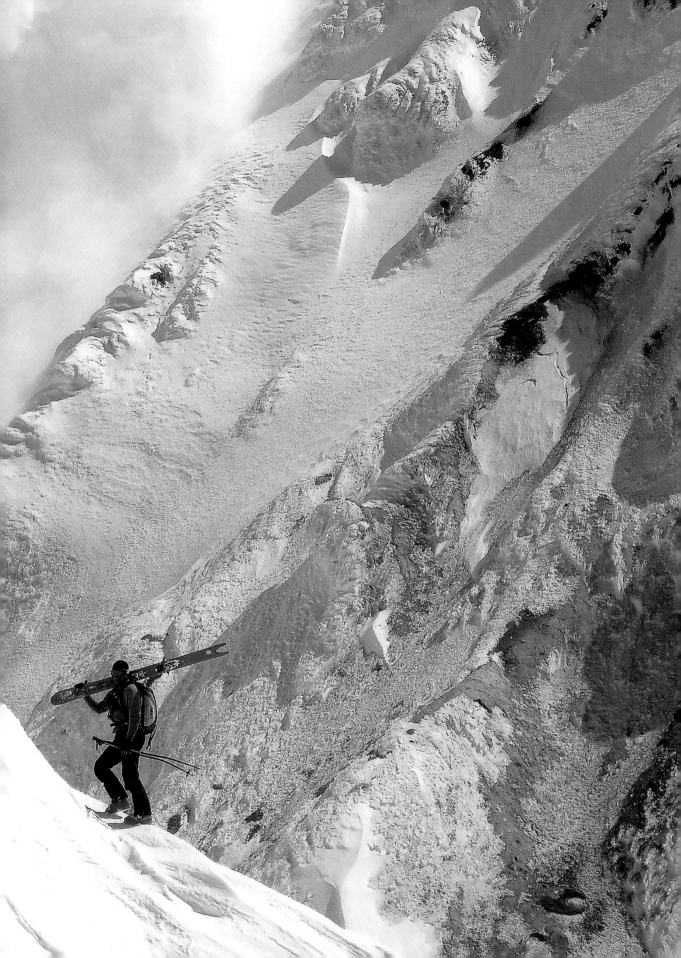

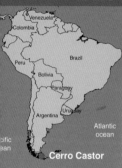

Cerro Castor

Access
Nearest airport:
Ushuaia (26km)

Ability Level
Beginner – expert

Season
Jun – Oct

Other Local Activities
Heli-skiing

Resort Stats
Top: 1,057m
Bottom: 195m
Vertical: 862m
Lifts: 12
Skiable acres: 650
hectares

www.cerrocastor.com

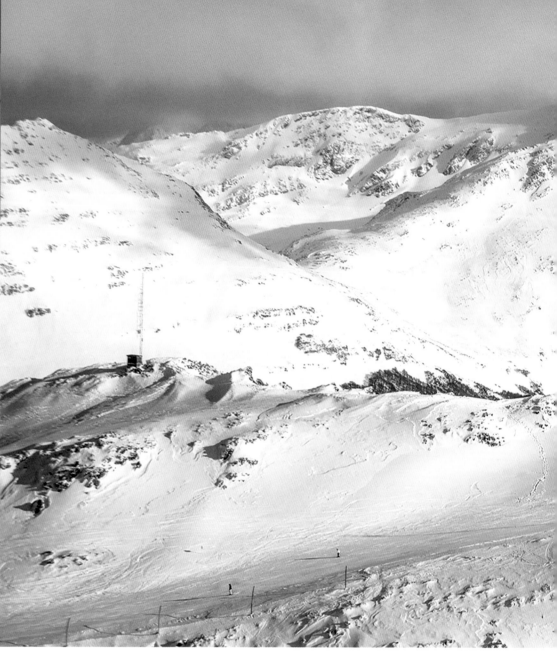

CERRO CASTOR, ARGENTINA
Skiing at the end of the world

'Skiing at the end of the world' may sound like the usual advertising hokum, but in the case of Cerro Castor it's no hype – this is the world's most southerly ski resort, which opened in 1999, and from its high points you can see west into neighbouring Chile, south-west to the town of Ushuaia (needless to say the most southerly town in the world) and south across the Beagle Channel beyond which lie wild, windswept islands and islets, storm-battered Cape Horn and – somewhere out there – Antarctica.

Thanks to the remote location at the very end of South America and the relatively small population of nearby Ushuaia (150,000) it rarely gets too busy on Cerro Castor's decent array of slopes, particularly during weekdays, and the very southerly location (54.72 degrees south; close to the equivalent northerly latitude of Lake Baikal, see page 202) means the snow is reasonably consistent, although it tends to fall in short but regular low-volume storms rather than big dumps. Either way, the snow and

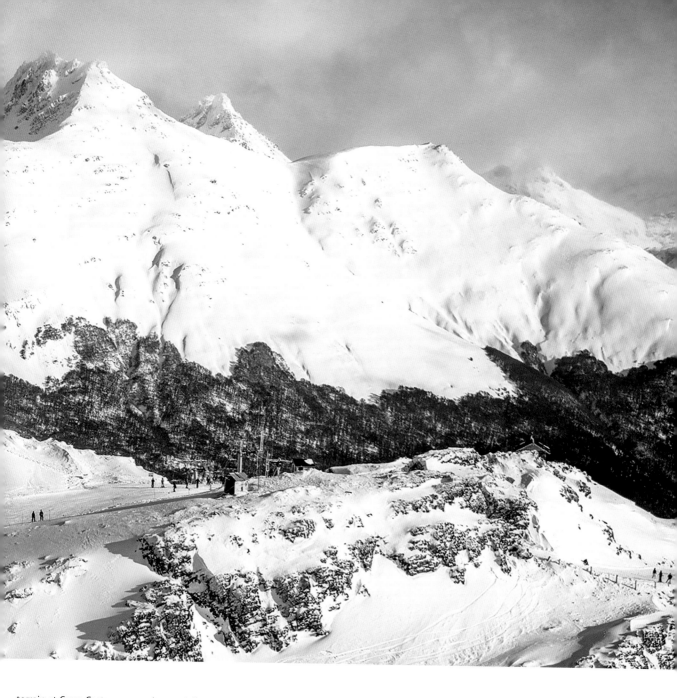

terrain at Cerro Castor are good enough for several European ski teams to use it as a northern summer training base and provides the longest ski season in South America.

The upper half of the ski slopes is above the tree line, with a few steep bowls and the occasional chute along with some open groomers, then you drop into the trees – not so much the thick, deep green firs and pines of, say, Canada, but lower and less intimidating beech and Southern Hemisphere conifers; fun intermediate runs snake between them and there are opportunities to ski various glades as well – useful on stormy, low vis days.

There's also some very good lift-accessed backcountry which can be relatively quiet, especially when compared to the better-known ski resorts of the Northern Hemisphere.

Chances are you'll end up staying in Ushuaia if you ski Cerro Castor since resort accommodation is very limited; whilst this means a 26km schlep up to the hill each morning it does give you a chance to see the capital of Tierra del Fuego, which is surprisingly lively, has accommodation to suit all budgets and an interesting history despite only dating back to 1884.

But then pretty much everything about this distant outlier of the ski world is interesting...

Next stop Antarctica – Cerro Castor is the most southerly ski resort in the world © Aggy Ferrari y Thomas Finstebsch

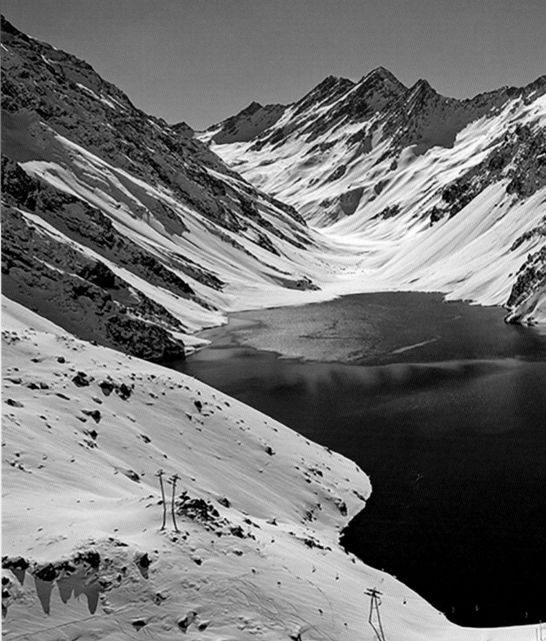

Access
Nearest airport:
Santiago (160km)

Ability Level
Beginner – expert

Season
Jun – Sep

Other Local Activities
Heli-skiing

Resort Stats
Top: 10,860ft
Bottom: 8,360ft
Vertical: 2,500ft
Lifts: 13
Skiable acres: 500
hectares

www.skiportillo.com

PORTILLO, CHILE
Ride the slingshot

Portillo is renowned for three things in particular – the bright yellow Hotel Portillo at the foot of the slopes beside the turquoise water of Laguna del Inca, the infamous 'va et vient' lifts (aka slingshots – four- or five-person drag lifts which go uphill at speeds of up to 27kph and have a tendency to hurl those who are less adept at using them into the snow), and its steep skiing and high quality side and backcountry terrain.

And we shouldn't forget the spectacular location in the Andes of course – Portillo is close to Aconcagua, which at 22,837ft (6,962 metres) is the highest mountain in the world outside of Asia.

So, for intrepid skiers looking to sample some Southern Hemisphere skiing Portillo makes a good choice. You'll also find that lift queues and crowded slopes are almost unknown here due to the limited amount of resort accommodation along with the fact that lift ticket sales are also limited.

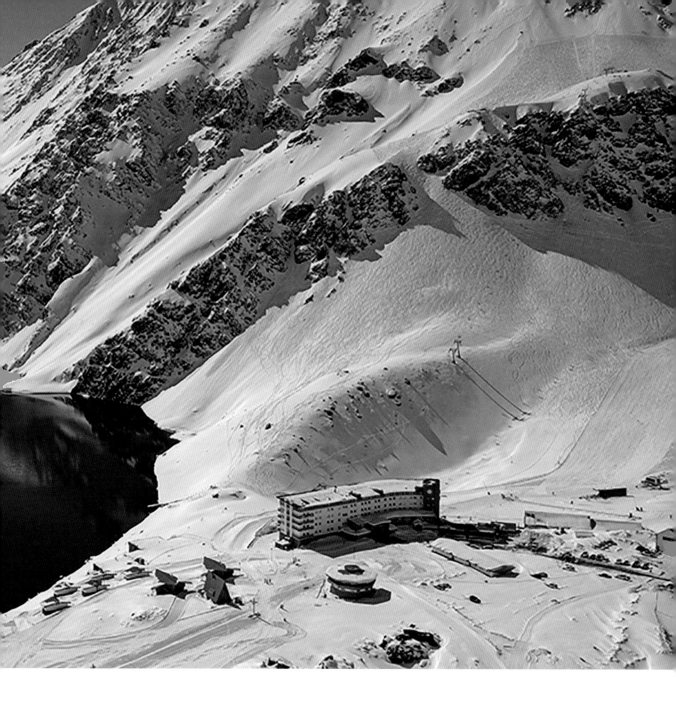

That said, you'll need to acclimatise – the resort's base sits at an altitude of almost 9,500ft and the highest lift takes you to 10, 680ft, so it's not just the scenery that will leave you breathless in Portillo.

The quality of the pistes and the snow here is perhaps best summed up by the fact that several international ski teams, including the USA, Canada, Austria and Norway use Portillo for their summer training camps, and it's worth noting that since Portillo is American-owned the piste grading system is the same as in North America, unlike other Chilean resorts which use the European system.

Due to the layout of the resort this is also a particularly sociable place to ski – there are only 450 beds within Portillo in total, located in either the Hotel Portillo, the Octagon Lodge or the Inca Backpackers Lodge and all the resort services, from dining to bars and an outdoor pool are within the grounds of the hotel, so it's pretty easy to get to know your fellow guests.

Portillo is, of course, a long way to travel for European skiers – a little less so for those from North America – which makes it difficult to go at the drop of the hat on the basis of a good snow forecast, and it can mean forsaking your summer holiday to return to winter, but there are plenty of skiers around who much prefer snowy mountains to sunny beaches, and if that's you then you'll find Portillo a very different ski experience and a great place to get your snow fix.

Portillo – ideal for getting your summer snow fix
© skiportillo.com

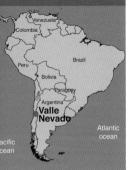

Venezuela
Colombia
Peru
Brazil
Bolivia
Paraguay
Argentina
Valle Nevado
Pacific ocean
Atlantic ocean

Access
Nearest airport:
Santiago (79km)

Ability Level
Beginner – expert

Season
Jun – Sep

Other Local Activities
Heli-skiing

Resort Stats
Top: 12,041ft
Bottom: 9,843ft
Vertical: 2,198ft
Lifts: 14
Skiable acres: 900
hectares

www.vallenevado.
com

VALLE NEVADO, CHILE
Sunshine and snow in the 'Snowy Valley'

Valle Nevado ('Snowy Valley') gives you exactly what it says on the tin – it's snowy, with an annual average of seven metres of snow, and the resort sits in a valley. That said, this particular valley is well over 3,600 metres high, and is surrounded by peaks of over 6,000 metres in height, so things are pretty spectacular visually.

Given the altitude – the resort tops out at a very impressive 12,041ft – you'll need to acclimatise before you make the most of Valle Nevado, which is popular with prosperous locals from nearby Santiago.

Although regarded as an intermediate ski area, there's huge scope for exploring the off-piste terrain between the well spread out and efficient lift system, and you can also access the neighbouring resorts of La Parva, El Colorado and Farellones (which are less upmarket than Valle Nevado).

Unfortunately, a multi-resort pass isn't available – a bit of an oversight as far as skiers looking to explore the area as conveniently as possible are concerned – but the close proximity to Santiago and its international airport is a definite boon for international travellers, or for any skier who finds themselves based in the city for a few days and wants a break in the mountains at what is probably the best-organised ski resort in Chile (along with the efficient lift system and good quality ski in / ski out accommodation readily available in Valle Nevado).

It's worth bearing in mind, however, that being close to Santiago means Valle Nevado can be busy at weekends, so try to time your skiing for weekdays if possible.

Like other Chilean ski resorts Valle Nevado gets lots of sunshine in between snow storms – the resort claims that it is sunny 80 percent of the time, which can result in some amazing skiing after a storm, with the perfect combination of fresh powder providing great skiing and clear skies and low humidity providing spectacular views over the Andes (the downside of course is that the high levels of sunshine don't always treat the snow too kindly, although the high altitude helps to ameliorate this).

In terms of the skiing there's actually a decent mix of terrain to suit all abilities – Valle Nevado is particularly popular with intermediate skiers who will enjoy the wide groomers, but more advanced riders will appreciate the mix of steeper bowls and chutes along with some easily accessible side country and masses of backcountry options, which are best tackled with a guide. And there's also heli-skiing if you don't mind shelling out your hard-earned.

All of which makes Valle Nevado a great introduction to Southern Hemisphere skiing...

A great intro to Southern Hemisphere skiing © vallenevado.com

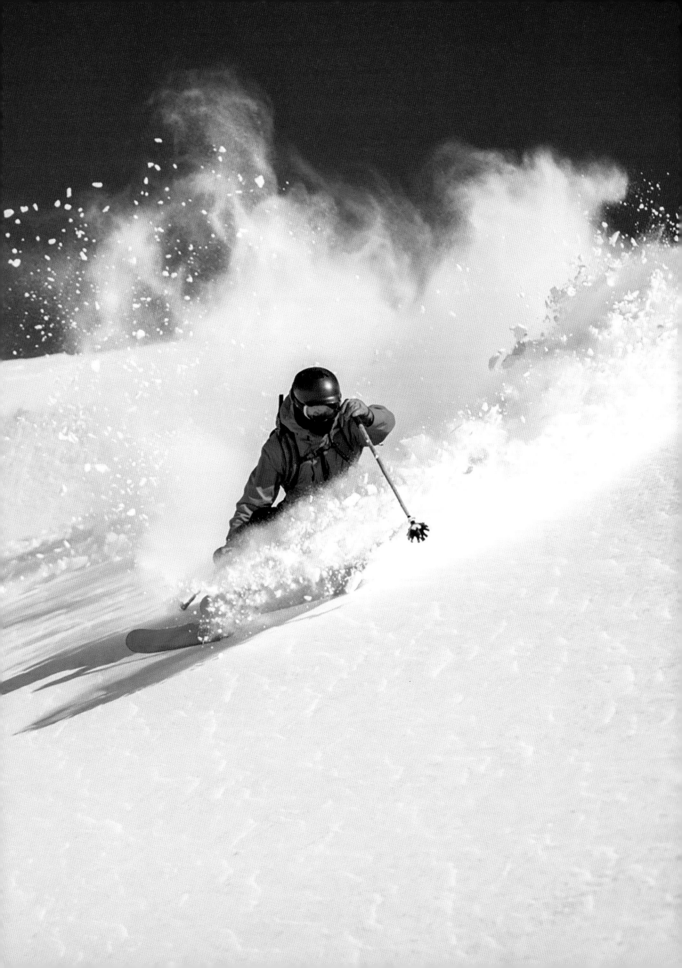

Greenland

Iceland

Access
Nearest airport:
depends on ski
location

Ability Level
Advanced – expert

Season
Apr – May

Other Local Activities
Sightseeing, wildlife
spotting

Resort Stats
Top: 1,500m
Bottom: Sea level
Vertical: 1,500m

www.eaheliskiing.
com

GREENLAND
Fresh tracks every run

Just as most of us are thinking about putting away our skis and getting out our summer toys, those skiers who are fortunate enough are looking to go heli-skiing in Greenland.

As the days grow longer from April onwards the sea ice surrounding Greenland starts to melt, providing a spectacular scene of gigantic, turquoise-blue glaciers and calving icebergs as you descend on your skis towards the sea, but this northerly land is still cold enough to provide super-light powder through which to enjoy runs which may be around 1,500 vertical metres from summit to sea.

As spring progresses the snow conditions tend to change from powder to a powder / corn snow mix in early May and then mainly corn snow later in the month – and given the long hours of daylight you can pretty much pick your lines at any time of day that suits you and your fellow skiers, guides and pilot.

You may find yourself skiing down from the Greenland icecap to spectacular fjords, or on one of the islands that dot the Greenland coast, but wherever your skis take you it's certain that you'll be amongst some of the most dramatic terrain on Earth.

However, you won't be living in the lap of luxury as in most North American heli-ski operations – no fancy lodges here, this is expedition-style heli-skiing in a wild Arctic environment, and with that comes more complicated logistics and uncontrollable variables so you need to be both adaptable and adventurous.

Besides the skiing you'll also have the chance to discover and experience Inuit culture and the way these remarkable people live in such an extreme environment, and you may even come across the King of the Arctic – a polar bear (do not get too close...!).

Ironically, despite the true wilderness experience of heli-skiing in Greenland, it is remarkably easy to access since the country is located midway between Europe and North America. So, if cost isn't an issue (or you're prepared to really tough it out and go ski touring here, which really is an adventure of epic proportions), Greenland offers the opportunity to ski some of the wildest, least populated terrain on Earth; expect fresh tracks every run.

Beware of polar bears – heli-skiing in Greenland © eaheliskiing.com

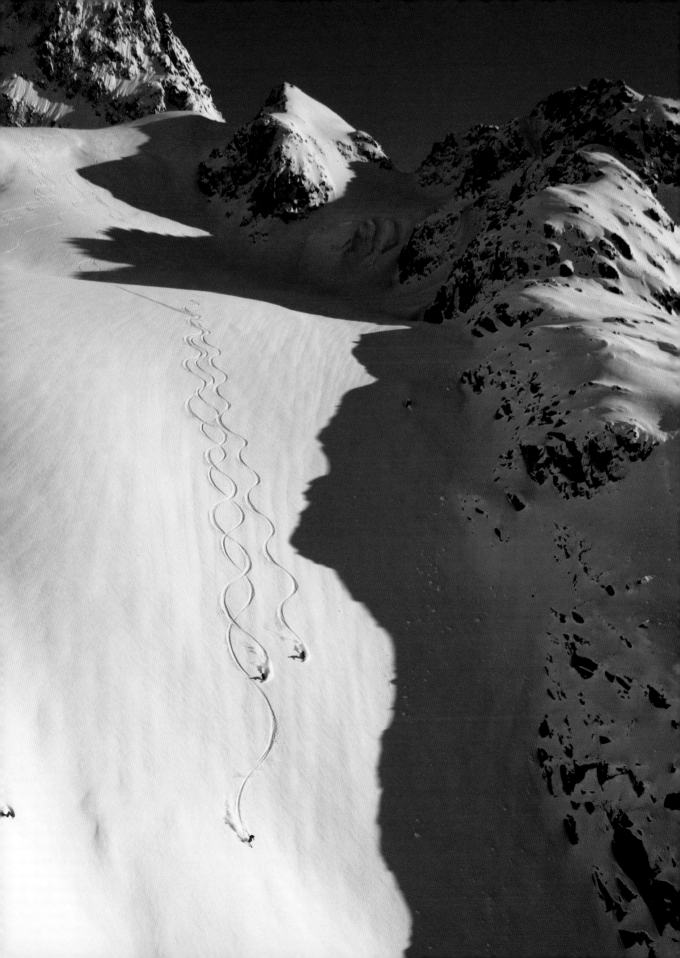

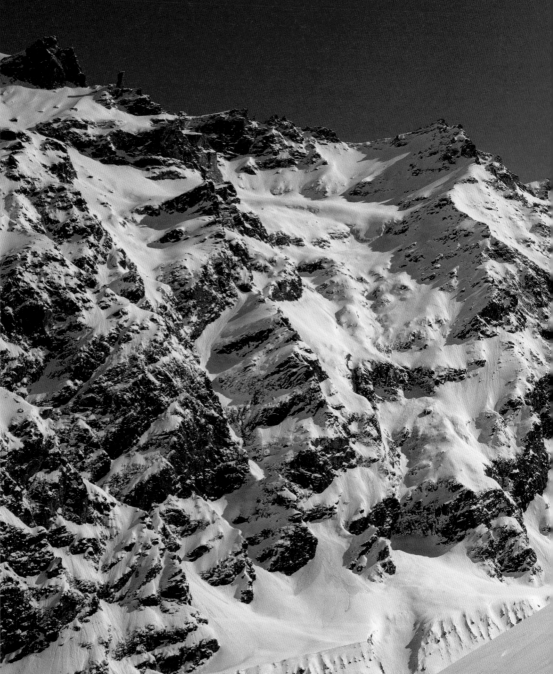

China

● Manali

India

abian sea

Bay of Bengal

Indian ocean

Access
Nearest airport:
Kullu (31 miles) via
New Delhi

Ability Level
Advanced – expert

Season
Feb – Apr

Other Local Activities
Resort skiing in
Solang Valley,
snowmobiling,
paragliding

Resort Stats
Top: 5,000m
Bottom: 1,950m
Vertical: 3,050m

www.eaheliskiing.
com

MANALI, HIMACHAL PRADESH, INDIA
Some of the highest skiing in the world

Yes, you could ski here using the single ski lift that operates in Manali's Solang Valley; you could do it the hard way and skin up the region's gigantic peaks, rising as high as 6,500 metres; or you could splash out and opt for the easy but most exciting way to ski the region – by helicopter.

And if you do, what incredible skiing you'll discover. Of course, the mountains of the Himachal Pradesh are somewhat lower than the 8,000-metre giants of neighbouring Nepal and Pakistan, but they're way higher than anything you'll ski in the established ski resorts of Europe and North America, and perfect, untracked powder is the norm here.

The length and diversity of the runs is exceptional – starting high in the alpine with drop-offs up to 5,000 metres above sea level amongst some of the most beautiful mountain panoramas on Earth, you

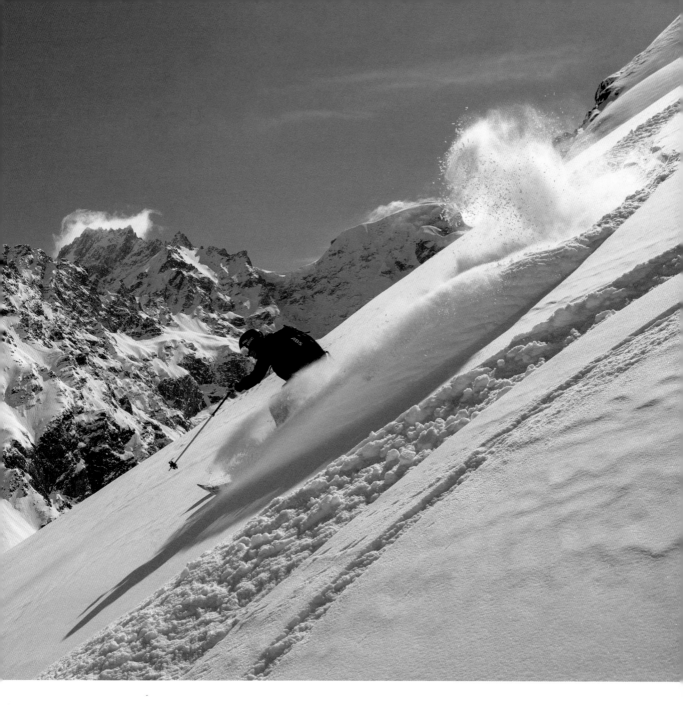

Piling up the vertical in Manali
© eaheliskiing.com

ski down steep bowls and long rolling ridge lines, through glades of perfectly spaced birch and oak trees and finish in towering forests of cedar.

Everything runs with impeccable expertise and efficiency since guides, pilots and helicopters all come from Switzerland and in some cases have thirty years or more experience of heli-skiing in the Himalayas.

Skiing in the Manali region is about more than just scything through pristine powder, of course – the vibrant culture of the Kullu Valley, often referred to as the 'Valley of the Gods', makes it something of a tourist hub, and Manali itself was once the beginning of an ancient trade route to Ladakh and from there over the Karakoram Pass on to Yarkand and Khotan in the Tarim Basin of north-west China. Apple, pear and plum orchards dot the valley today in a landscape far removed from the towering alpine terrain above.

You may want to set aside some time to see the region in leisurely fashion after your heli-ski adventures, since with an average of ten runs per day of 1,000 metres vertical or more your legs are going to be needing a rest at some point.

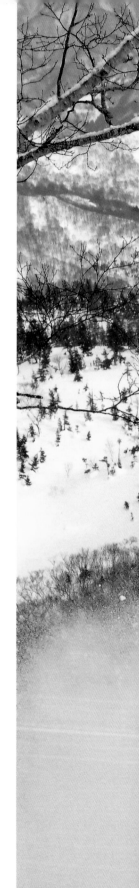

Access
Nearest airport:
Tokyo Haneda
(300km)

Ability Level
Beginner – expert

Season
Nov – May depending
on resort

Other Local Activities
Snowshoeing,
snowmobiling, hot
springs

Resort Stats
Depends on resort – 9
resorts, 200 lifts

www.hakubatourism.
jp

HONSHU ISLAND, JAPAN
Peace, tranquillity and powder

Think of skiing in Japan, and most people think of Hokkaido and its legendary powder. But Honshu, to the south, actually has more ski areas, a great mix of terrain and is easier to reach than Hokkaido – it's no more than four hours from Tokyo airport to one of the main ski areas, Hakuba, using the bullet train (which you simply must as part of the Japanese travel experience).

Here you can enjoy the full Japanese ski experience – take Hakuba Happo-One, for instance, one of nine resorts in the Hakuba Valley. The piste map is not the easiest to follow with its combination of Japanese and English characters, tinny J-pop blasts from speakers on the lift towers, a mix of Japanese and predominantly Aussie skiers and boarders slide haphazardly around the slopes and, looking beyond all this, the classic Japanese mountain landscape of snow-shrouded slopes decorated with delicate silver birches informs you that, yes, you are very definitely in Japan.

The side country can be easily reached from the lifts but, if you want to see the 'real' alpine Japan, get your skins out and start walking (ideally with a guide). For instance, ride to the top of the Tsugaike-Kogen ski area of the Hakuba Valley and then skin upwards to discover a steep north-facing bowl where you may just find some great powder skiing among the trees.

The high, craggy peaks of Mount Hakuba-Yare-Ga-Take, Mount Sakushi-Dake and Mount Shirouma-Dake, all just under 3,000 metres and located in the Chubu Sangaku Kokuritsu Koen National Park, are ever present over your left shoulder as you climb; beneath their jagged faces is a panorama of snow-laden deciduous and evergreen slopes, famed for holding some of the best powder in the world.

Alaskan mountain guide Bill Glude has guided in Hakuba for over a decade, so what's persuaded him to spend so many seasons here when Alaska is not exactly short of great snow and great ski touring?

"I like the fact that you've got a very good chance of scoring good powder here – not so much as in the past, due to climate change, but it's still pretty consistent. I also appreciate the way local skiers respect the mountain environment; for instance, there were proposals recently to install a ski lift that would have impinged on a quiet part of the mountain that's popular for ski touring, and they ended up being dropped so as to maintain that natural environment for those who appreciate it."

This is something you'll notice about Japan – the mountains are an intrinsic part of Japanese life – after all, some 73 percent of the country is alpine in nature. Get off the beaten track at a tiny resort like Manza Onsen (four small chairlifts offering a very modest vertical of a little over 200 metres) and just being in the mountains is what it's all about for Japanese guests, who will likely spend as much time relaxing in the local hot springs as skiing.

The sense of peace and tranquillity is almost palpable at times, and it's very easy to see why mountains play such a big role in Japanese culture and history.

The author drops into the Tsugaike-Kogen backcountry © Pete Coombs

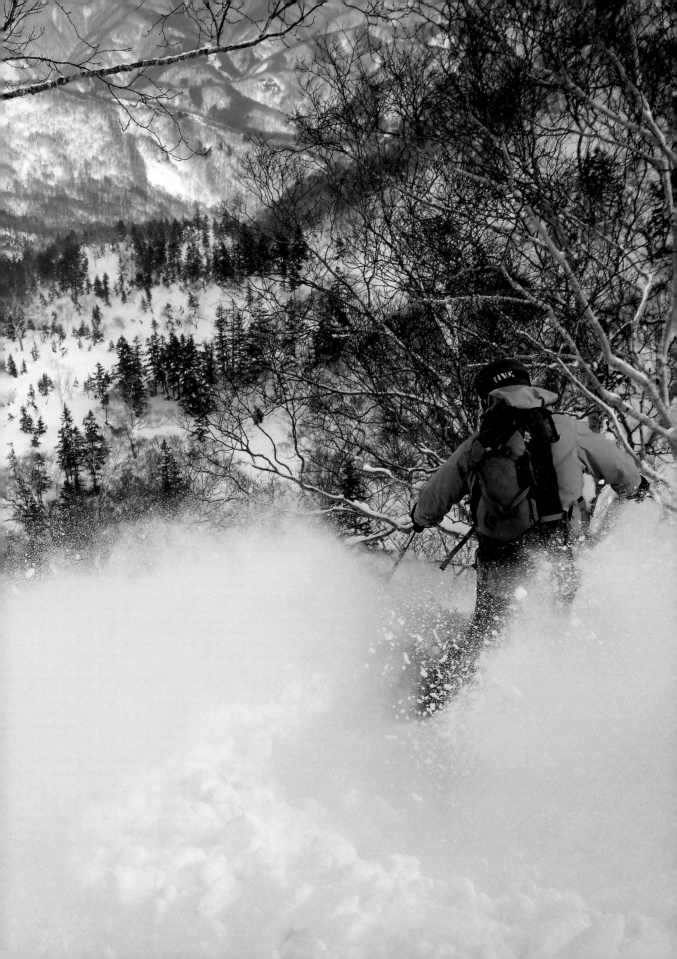

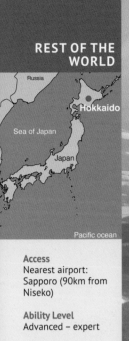

REST OF THE
WORLD

Russia

Hokkaido

Sea of Japan

Japan

Pacific ocean

Access
Nearest airport:
Sapporo (90km from
Niseko)

Ability Level
Advanced – expert

Season
Nov/Dec – Apr/May
depending on resort

Other Local Activities
Vary depending on
resort

Resort Stats
Depends on resort

www.jnto.go.jp/eng/

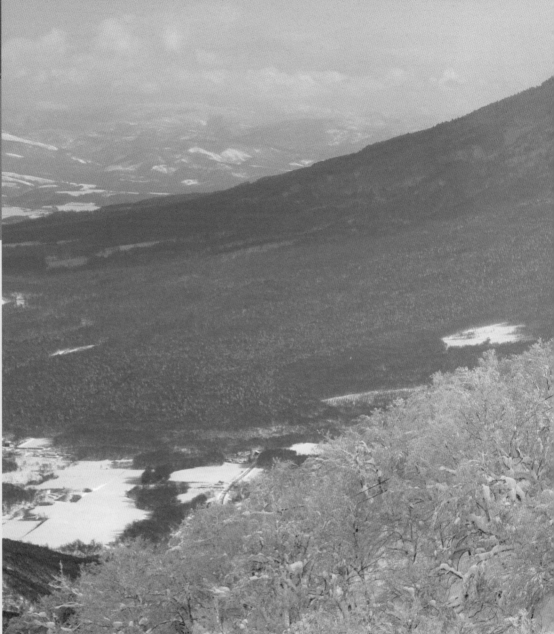

HOKKAIDO, JAPAN
Pow, pow, pow!

These days everyone knows that Hokkaido is the place to go if you're in search of deep, light, consistent powder snow. Most skiers head for Niseko, Rusutsu or Furano, and it's not difficult to organise a trip that takes in all three resorts (Niseko and Rusutsu are half-an-hour apart, whilst Furano is around four hours from Niseko).

However, there are around 120 other ski areas on the island of Hokkaido, so there's absolutely no reason to restrict yourself to the three best-known ski areas – indeed, for adventurous travellers lesser-known albeit smaller resorts such as Asahidake, Kurodake, Kamui or Pippu will provide a more authentic Japanese experience since they're not so westernised.

But what is it that gives Hokkaido the pretty well-deserved reputation for having some of the best and most consistent powder on Earth?

As with Utah's famous 'Greatest Snow on Earth' (which the Japanese may well dispute) it's all about geography. Local weather systems invariably move from west to east, with intensely cold air from

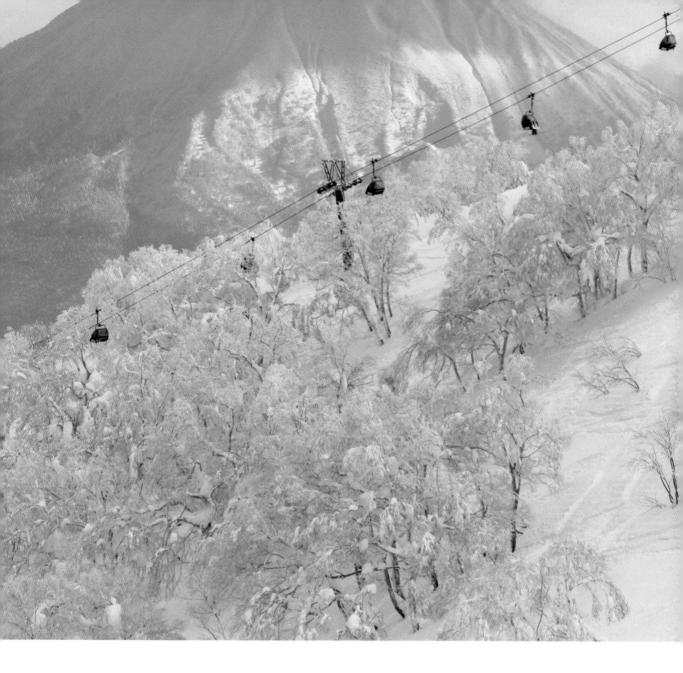

Hokkaido, where the snow can fall for 'weeks and weeks' at a time © into.go.jp

Russia and China passing over the Sea of Japan, where it picks up moisture since the sea never freezes (if it did snowfall would be much reduced), then rising over the Japanese mountains, where all that moisture is dumped in very heavy snowfalls.

What's more these weather systems pass consistently over the mountains so that between December and February in particular it's quite common to go for day after day with the snow falling relentlessly – one reason tree-skiing is so popular in Japan (the venerable old *Where to Ski & Snowboard* guide used to regard it as a negative factor of skiing on Hokkaido that 'Snowfall can go on for weeks and weeks' – I'm not sure how many of us would agree with that!).

Hokkaido tends to get more snow than the neighbouring island of Honshu to the south (although this isn't always the case), with average figures of between 7 and 15 metres being common at the base of ski stations, although the amounts falling towards the resorts' high points can be close on double this.

All of which means that if you're looking for deep, fluffy pow (and you certainly don't come to here to ski groomers), Hokkaido is perhaps the best place on the planet to find it.

On top of that you also get to experience charming, friendly and incredibly polite locals, a culture that is very different from that of western mountain regions, and the famous Japanese cuisine – so other than being a long way from pretty much anywhere, Hokkaido has everything going for it if the only time you like to see your ski boots is when you're sitting on a ski lift.

Turkmenistan

● Dizin

Iran

audi Arabia

Access
Nearest airport:
Tehran (70km)

Ability Level
Beginner – expert

Season
Dec – May

Other Local Activities
Mountaineering,
mountain biking,
hiking

Resort Stats
Top: 3,600m
Bottom: 2,650m
Vertical: 950m
Lifts: 16
Skiable area: 469
hectares

www.dizinskiresort.ir

DIZIN, ALBORZ MOUNTAINS, IRAN

Forget the politics and enjoy the pow

Where to start? Iran is hardly a place that most skiers would consider as a prospective ski destination – we'll get to the politics in a moment – but the country's biggest ski resort, Dizin has much to offer those with an intrepid nature (and there are around a score of other ski areas in the country if you want to explore further).

Dizin is located within easy reach of Tehran and its 15 million inhabitants, so you might expect it to be pretty busy most of the time, but skiing in Iran is generally the preserve of the privileged and well-heeled; in that respect it's changed little since the 1970s when the Shah was deposed, and whilst he is long gone much of the ski infrastructure from his time has remained, so you can expect to ascend the mountains on some decidedly ancient ski lifts.

Whilst these lifts will give you access to some decent groomers, the big attraction for most overseas visitors to Iran's main ski resort will be the terrain in between, since the off-piste areas and the backcountry further beyond are of little interest to most local skiers.

Consider employing a guide to discover the skiing beyond the resort – after all, climatically the Alborz Mountains are known for huge dumps followed by long periods of sunshine, and given the altitude (Dizin tops out at an impressive 3,600 metres and the country's highest peak, Damavand, is over 5,600 metres high) the snow conditions can be epic for days, if not weeks, at a time.

Given the west's often tempestuous relationship with Iran it would be reasonable to expect a cool welcome at best, but almost universally, western skiers who have visited the country remark upon the kindness, generosity and curiosity of the people; expect to be regularly offered food and drink and engaged in conversation when you meet locals, who, like sensible people all over the world, generally regard politics and those who practise it to be as much use as dust on crust.

There are obviously going to be certain restrictions on and adaptations to the way you may be used to behaving on a 'regular' ski trip, and women will find they have to wear mandatory headscarves in public (although it seems that ski helmets and / or hats also seem to qualify as headscarves), and you should definitely take your own gear as the stuff that's available for hire probably won't cut it, but a ski trip to Iran with its powder, sunshine, empty off-piste and friendly locals is certainly worth considering if the corporate ski experience of so many European and North American resorts is beginning to wear a bit thin.

Extensive, quiet backcountry is a feature of the Iranian ski experience
© Jakub Zdeblo / shutterstock.com

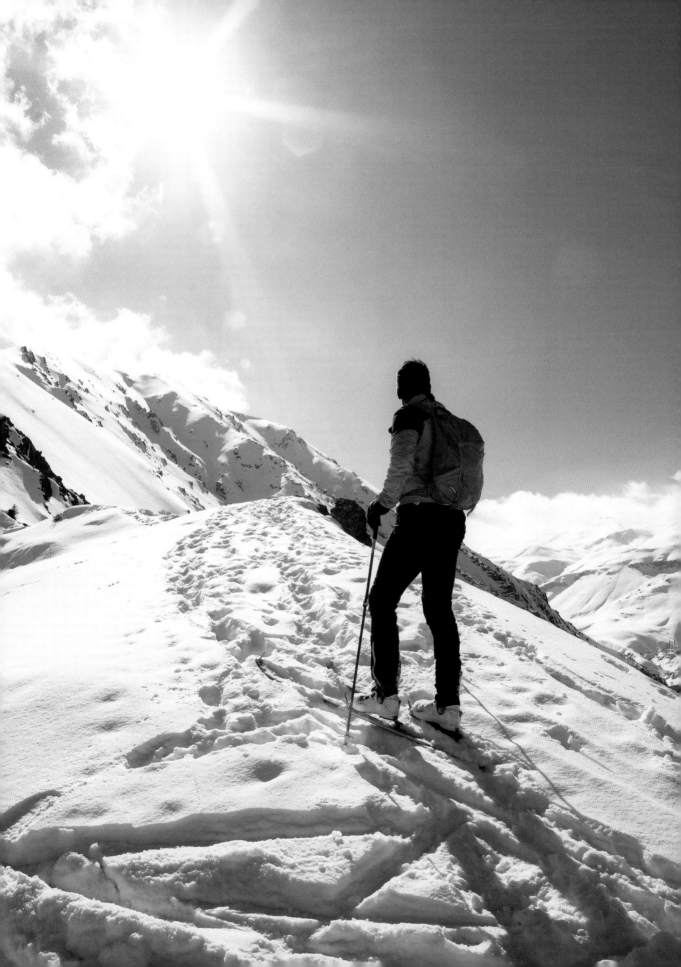

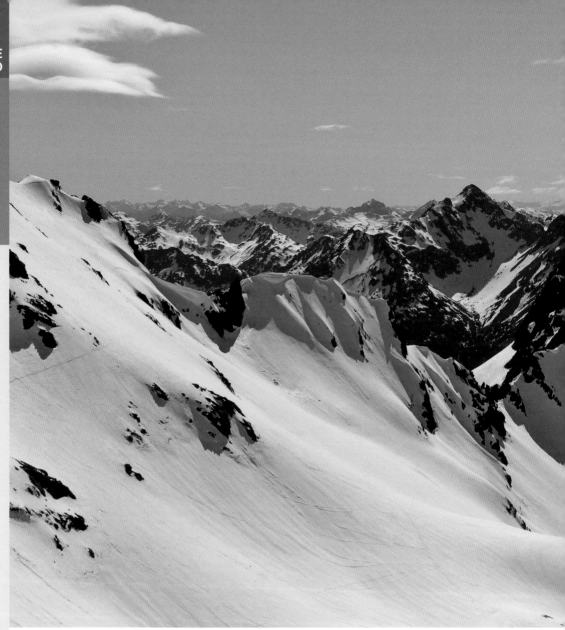

New Zealand

Craigieburn

Tasman Sea

Access
Nearest airport:
Christchurch (120km)

Ability Level
Beginner – expert

Season
Jul – Sep/Oct

Other Local Activities
Ice climbing,
mountain biking,
hiking

Resort Stats
Top: 1,922m
Bottom: 1,308m
Vertical: 614m
Lifts: 3
Skiable area: 400
hectares

www.craigieburn.
co.nz

CRAIGIEBURN, SOUTHERN ALPS, NEW ZEALAND

Not your average ski experience

Does your idea of a good time on skis involve perfectly manicured slopes, swift, modern ski lifts, upmarket hotels and fancy mountain restaurants? Then you'll hate Craigieburn.

Of groomed slopes there are none; instead of rising smoothly up the hill on a high speed chair or gondola you're be faced with New Zealand's infamous, glove-shredding 'nutcracker' lifts (and there are only three of them); and in place of chic mountain restaurants and glitzy hotels you get two cosy but basic ski in / ski out lodges.

What you also get is some of the most exciting ski terrain in NZ along with epic backcountry that really will challenge the very best – ski icon Glen Plake likes the place so much that not only is he a member of Craigieburn Valley Ski Club but he also has a run here named after him (Plake's Mistake) and those who are old enough will remember that back in the nineties Mr Plake made his reputation skiing terrain that was just a tad harder than a nice blue groomer.

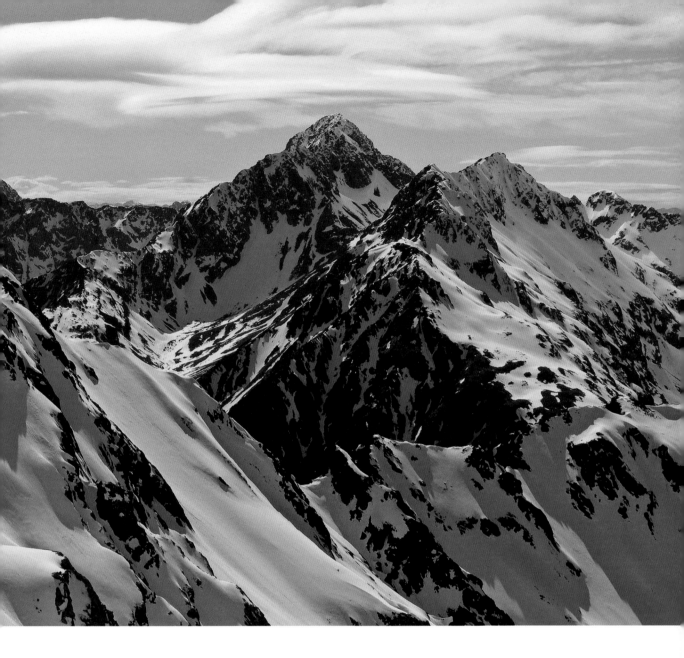

So, if Craigieburn is good enough for him, it's undoubtedly gonna be good enough for you...

In essence it comprises of two large basins which receive ample snowfall from mainly easterly but also big westerly storm systems, and whilst it tends to attract advanced to expert skiers it also has a good range of intermediate terrain too.

The layout is such that three tows take you to the top of the ski hill from where you can traverse in either direction to find the kind of skiing that best suits you; it's been described as 'poor man's heli-skiing', so expect powder and relatively quiet terrain that can vary from the very steep chutes of Remarkables to the big open powder field of neighbouring Hamilton Face, and next to this more manageable chutes of The Gut to name but a few options.

On top of this there's very easy backcountry access – short traverses or hikes will get you into a good mix of terrain – and you can also access the neighbouring club ski field of Broken River.

At day's end you'll find a friendly, ski-mad crowd in the bar at the base of the mountain, where there's the option of staying in one of two lodges that offer bunk rooms or basic private rooms, and since Craigieburn is part of New Zealand's unique club ski scene you'll be expected to help out with minor duties such as cleaning or prepping for breakfast or dinner (don't worry, it won't cut into your ski time!).

For most of us getting to Craigieburn is a bit of a mission, but if you want to ski somewhere that's noticeably different to your regular European or North American ski resort, this is perhaps the place for you.

Join the club – Craigieburn offers some epic skiing on what may be New Zealand's best club ski field
© Tobin Akehurst / shutterstock.com

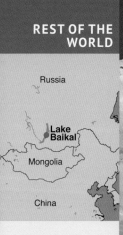

Russia

Lake Baikal

Mongolia

China

Access
Nearest airport:
Irkutsk via Moscow,
Sheremetyevo
Trans-Siberian
Express stops in
Baikalsk

Ability Level
Advanced – expert

Season
Nov – Jan

Other Local Activities
Resort skiing at
Baikalsk-Sobolinaya,
swimming in Lake
Baikal (brrr!)

Resort Stats
Top: 2,000m
Bottom: 456m
Vertical: 1,544m

www.eaheliskiing.
com

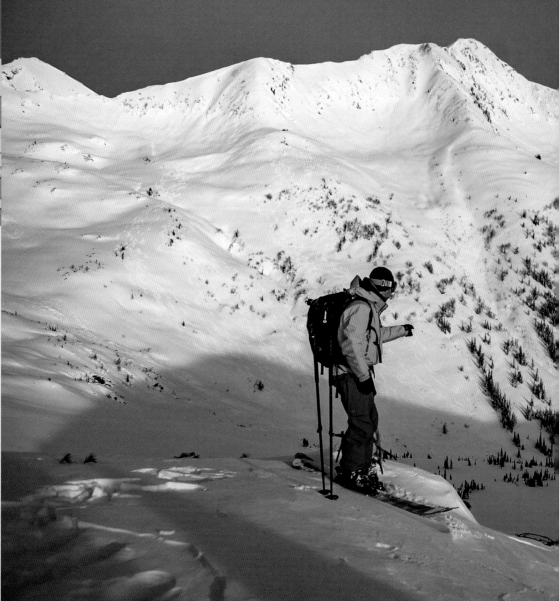

LAKE BAIKAL, SIBERIA
Siberian smoke

Clearly Lake Baikal is not a ski destination (unless you're intending to go waterskiing – difficult in winter though since it's frozen), but the southern lakeside city of Baikalsk has a small ski hill, Baikalsk-Sobolinaya, which has 15km of slopes and seven lifts between elevations of 525 and 1,004m and has even be graced by the presence of President Putin, who is undoubtedly a far superior skier to the likes of us.

This is unlikely to keep most people happy for more than a day or so, but it's a different story if you can get hold of a helicopter and ski the nearby Khamar-Dhaban mountain range close to those southern shores of Lake Baikal, which tops out at a height of 2,396 metres in the form of Utulinskaya Podkova mountain.

It doesn't seem that anyone has much interest in these mountains though, since they merit no more than a two-sentence description on Wikipedia and had remained virtually unskied until December 2018 when James Morland and a few buddies paid a visit.

James doesn't muck around – as ever his crew were using helicopters to access what he describes as

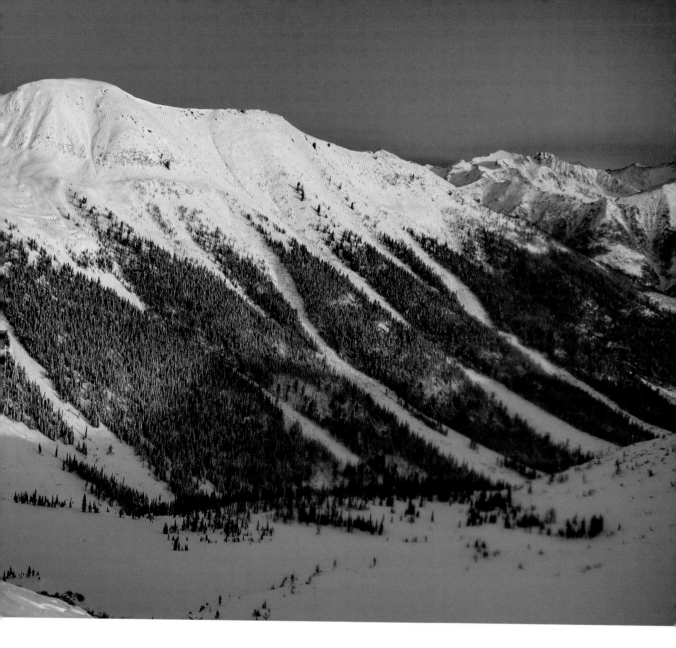

"... the most incredible powder snow on earth. After a recent cold snap of minus 30 degrees centigrade and below, the temperatures had moderated to minus 10 to minus 20 and we were greeted with some of the most spectacular snow conditions any of us had ever experienced – deep, dry, cold Siberian smoke."

In terrain not unlike that of British Columbia they skied lines that had almost certainly never seen ski tracks before (but equally certainly have seen the tracks of sable, wolverine, brown bear, reindeer, Siberian musk deer, and wild boar, all of which can be found in these wild, remote mountains).

High levels of winter precipitation result from northerly air streams that pass over Lake Baikal and pick up moisture then rise into the Khamar-Dhaban mountains to create perfect, feather-light powder, although the season is short – by mid-January the lake starts to freeze, resulting in less snowfall.

But for the eight weeks or so when the pow is falling in excitingly high amounts you can ski lovely glades which often funnel down to lower elevation chutes, pillow lines, open bowls and nice, mellow cruisey terrain all with the remarkable backdrop of Lake Baikal, where you can even go for an icy dip should the mood take you.

The remoteness, difficulty of access and cost of skiing here will ensure this mountain range never sees too many skiers, although the Trans-Siberian Express does actually stop in Baikalsk so the area is not quite as hard to reach as you might expect.

But you've still got to get into the mountains once you hop off the train...

Cold, remote and hard to access – so fresh tracks guaranteed
© eaheliskiing.com

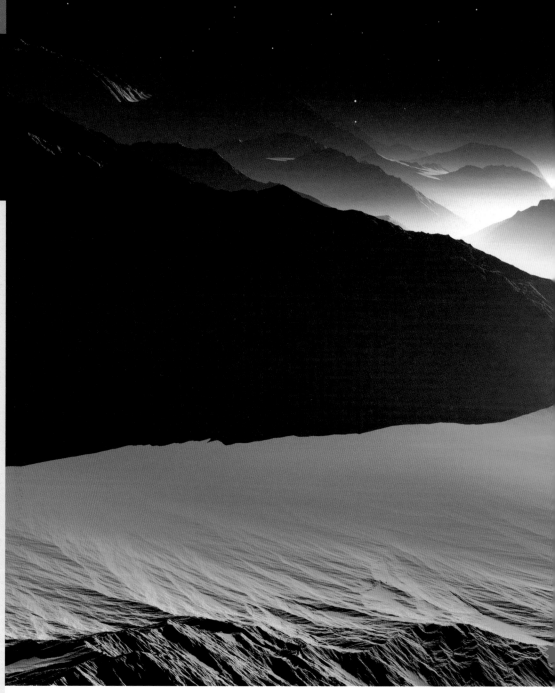

Sun

Mercury

Venus

Earth

Mars

Jupiter

Access
Nearest airport:
Kennedy Space Center
(267.77 million km)

Ability Level
Astronaut

Season
Unknown

Other Local Activities
Space walking

Resort Stats
Top: 21,230m
Bottom: 0m
Vertical: 21,230m

OLYMPUS MONS, MARS
Looking to the future

Yes, it may seem a bit mad to include a different planet in our list of 100 Epic Experiences in the snow, but let's look to the future and think positively.

Speaking to *USA Today* in 2018 NASA chief scientist Jim Green said humans will 'absolutely' be living on Mars in the future – NASA plans to send astronauts to the 'Red Planet' perhaps as early as 2040, with the long-term aim being to set up communities there (and given the way we're trashing Planet Earth that's perhaps not a bad idea).

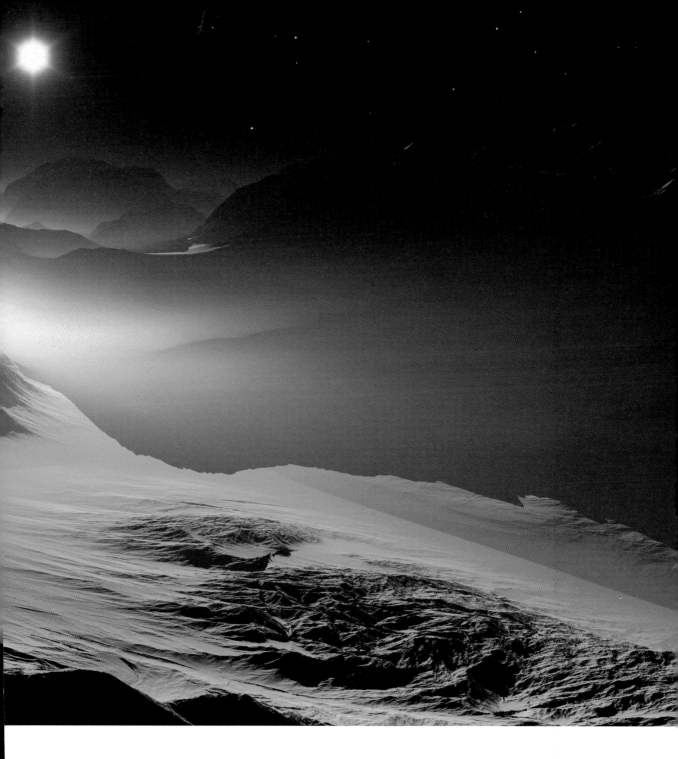

Sunset on Mars © Jurik
Peter / shutterstock.com

So, it makes sense that at some point in the future those humans who do end up becoming Martians may want to enjoy some leisure time – and they could do worse than check out the skiing on Olympus Mons, the highest mountain on the planet at a staggering 21,230 metres.

Yes, there is the little matter of snow conditions, but where we once used to think of Mars as a dry planet, water has been discovered there, so who knows, there may even be some snow on Olympus Mons.

Assuming there is, and that you could access the ridiculously lofty summit, it would be the perfect beginner slope – with an average angle of just 5 degrees if you skied from the summit to the base of Olympus Mons you'd enjoy a run so long that even novice skiers would be close to being experts by the time they arrived at the bottom station's après-ski pub, which would, of course, be called the Mars Bar.

PHOTO CREDITS

Cover: Matterhorn-im-Winter — © Pascal Gertschen

Prelim Pages
- P3 The author skiing at Les Arcs — © Hugh Rhodes
- P4 A modern-day take on the 'Arlberg technique' — © Hermann-Meier.de / Tourist Association St Anton am Arlberg
- P4 Ski jumping, Planica, Solvenia
- P5 Ylläs, Finland — © www.yllas.fi
- P5 Last Frontier Heliskiing — © Ashley Barker
- P5 Kamchatka, Russia — © Alf Alderson

Western Europe
- P7 No sign of the Sun God today — © Daniele Molineris
- P9 Modern-day take on the 'Arlberg technique' — © Hermann-Meier.de / Tourist Association St Anton am Arlberg
- P11 Last blast of the day — © Sepp Mallaun / Lech Zurs Tourismus
- P13 Cold air inversion at dawn in Kitzbuhel — © lightsandsquares / shutterstock.com
- P15 The coolest ski resort in the Alps? — © YuriKo / shutterstock.com
- P17 Getting high in Ischgl Snowpark — © Paznaun – Ischgl Snowpark
- P19 You want steep, you've got it at Mayrhofen's legendary Harakiri — © mayrhofen.at
- P21 Schladming all lit up for the night races — © Tomasz Koryl / shutterstock.com
- P23 The sight when you leave the Kuhstall Dancing Bar at 6am? — © ansharphoto / shutterstock.com
- P25 Shopping in the Powder Department — © gorillaimages / shutterstock.com
- P27 Going for a diamond run – not common in Europe — © andreas ehrensberger / shutterstock.com
- P29 Ski touring above 'Cham' — © Alf Alderson
- P31 Former FWT competitor Jérémy Prevost doing his thing in Méribel — © Sylvian Aymoz / Meribel Tourisme
- P33 'Val' looking pretty as a picture on a mid-winter evening — © Val d'Isere Tourisme
- P35 Perfect skiing at Paradiski — © Hugh Rhodes
- P37 'La Ros' on a bluebird day – who needs a helicopter? — © Julien Eustache
- P39 Les Sybelles' extensive piste map — © www.sybelles.ski
- P41 'Bonne ski' at Bonneval — © Daniel Durand / Fresh Influence
- P43 Lift off at La Grave — © Alf Alderson
- P45 Climbing on the Haute Route — © R Scott / shutterstock.com
- P47 Man and avy dog in perfect harmony in Les Deux Alpes — © Jean Michel Morlot / ANENA
- P49 Les Carroz – a traditional resort — © www.lescarroz.com
- P51 Descending from the Pic du Midi Observatory — © Luis Pantoja
- P53 More than enough at St Lary-Soulan — © Alf Alderson
- P55 Monterosa Ski – Italy's impressive answer to France's Three Valleys — © Archivio Fotografico Monterosa Ski
- P57 Sun or snow, Cortina is a magical ski destination — © bandio.it
- P59 Into the shadows, Courmayeur — © Allessandro Belluscio
- P61 Man-made blizzard above Livigno — © Alf Alderson
- P63 World-class piste skiing in Madonna di Campiglio — © A. Trovorli
- P65 Cervinia – pretty at night, spectacular during the day — © www.cervinia.it
- P67 A grand day out – part of the Sella Ronda circuit — © valgardena.it
- P69 The almost empty chair lift tells its own story — © Baqueira-Beret
- P71 Sierra Nevada: Pista Olimpica — © www.sierranevada.es
- P73 Andermatt has almost doubled in size in recent years — © Valentin Luthiger
- P75 Bumps galore at Davos — © Alf Alderson
- P77 Doing it by the book – ISTA avalanche safety course — © ISTA
- P79 As Swiss as it gets – heading into the mountains by train — © MySwitzerland.com
- P81 Racing for the train – a skier heads for Kleine Scheidegg above Grindelwald — © MySwitzerland.com
- P83 The Matterhorn never fails to impress when you ski Zermatt — © Valon's Wallis Promotions Tamara Berger
- P85 Everyone from beginners to experts like Aaron Durlester will enjoy Saas-Fee — © db.pc.keystone-sda.ch / Schweiz Saastal Tourismms AG
- P87 Champéry at its inviting mid-winter best — © jbbieuville
- P89 Scuol – at the end of the line — © Andrea Badrutt, Chur
- P91 Adi Schumann gives it a big thumbs up before heading down to Disentis — © Alf Alderson
- P93 Preparing to drop into some of Arosa Lenzerheide's great freeride terrain — © elvis.somedia.ch
- P95 Getting into the habit – Simon Murray Henwood slogging upwards in the Susten Derby — © Alf Alderson
- P97 Living in the past – vintage action on the slopes of St Moritz — © stmoritz.com
- P99 Taking it easy, for a while at least, above Val d'Anniviers — © media-photos.valais.ch Yves Garneau

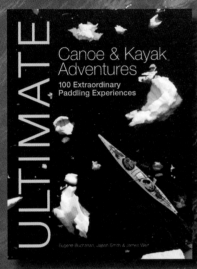
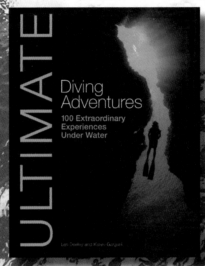
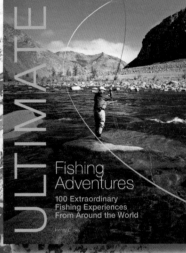
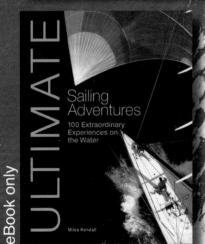
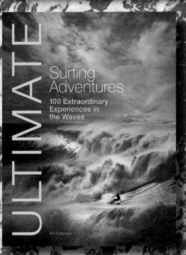
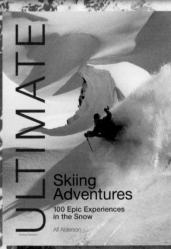